THE ENCYCLOPEDIA OF
COUNTRY MUSIC

THE ENCYCLOPEDIA OF
COUNTRY
MUSIC

RICK MARSCHALL

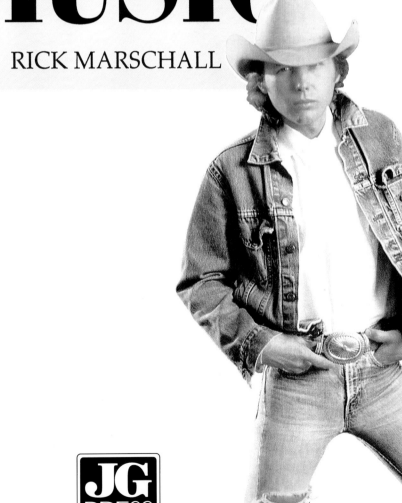

JG PRESS

Published in the USA 1995 by JG Press
Distributed by World Publications, Inc.

The JG Press imprint is a trademark of
JG Press, Inc.
455 Somerset Avenue
North Dighton, MA 02764

Produced by
Brompton Books Corporation
15 Sherwood Place
Greenwich, Connecticut 06830

ISBN 1-57215-067-X

Printed in Hong Kong

Acknowledgments

Many people have helped in the
preparation of this book, but none
more than Carl May, Dennis Wepman,
and Raymond "Rusty" Russell. Thanks
also to Patricia Hall, Stacy Harris,
Margie McGraw, and that person who
knows that without her interest and
support I couldn't achieve anything in
life, much less books like this. She
knows who she is, and this book is for
her. The publisher would like to thank
the following people: David Eldred, the
designer, Sara Dunphy, the picture
researcher and Jean Martin, the editor.

Picture Credits

**Waring Abbott/London Features
International:** page 172.
The Bettmann Archive: page 116.
Courtesy BNA: page 16.
Brompton Picture Library; pages 1
(right), 4 (top left), 5, 12 (bottom right),
17, 18-19, 20, 22-23, 26, 29, 32, 41, 46
(top left), 47 (bottom right), 48, 53, 57,
62, 69 (bottom), 72, 80 (both), 83, 86-87,
97, 104, 108, 117, 130, 135 (both), 136,
138, 139, 141, 154, 158, 166, 167, 169
(bottom), 171, 173, 176, 177, 179, 185,
190, 193, 196, 198, 199, 200, 207 (top
right).
Courtesy Roy Clark Productions: page
42.
**Country Music Foundation, Nashville,
TN:** pages 1 (left and center), 5, 6, 9,
10-11, 12 (top left), 14, 21, 25, 27 (both),
34-35, 45, 46 (bottom), 47 (top), 50, 52,
60-61, 63, 65, 77, 81, 82, 84-85, 91, 98-99,
101, 105 (bottom left), 107, 109, 118, 120
(top left), 121, 126, 127, 133, 134, 137, 142
145, 150, 151, 153, 161, 162-3, 165, 169
(top), 178, 180, 183, 189, 192, 197, 201,
202, 203, 205.
**Gregg De Guire/London Features
International:** pages 69 (top), 105 (top
right).
Donna Driesel/Retna Ltd.: page 44.
**Nick Elgar/London Features
International:** pages 30, 33.
**Simon Fowler/London Features
International:** page 146.
Gary Gershoff/Retna Ltd.: page 71, 92
(top).
**Allen Gordon/London Features
International:** page 131.
Beth Gwinn/Retna, Ltd: pages 100, 113,
129.
**Bruce Kramer/London Features
International:** page 103.
**Phil Loftus/London Features
International:** page 64, 128, 206.
London Features International: pages 4
(top right and bottom right), 36, 43, 51,
58 (bottom left), 59, 67, 73, 75, 90, 92
(bottom), 94, 110, 114, 115, 119, 143, 144,
149, 182, 186, 195, 204, 208.
**Kevin Mazur/London Features
International:** pages 13, 207 (bottom
left).
**Ilpo Musto/London Features
International:** pages 122, 123.
**Nashville Area Chamber of
Commerce, TN:** pages 8, 38, 76, 140.
**A.J. Pantsios/London Features
International:** pages 66, 157.
**John Paschal/London Features
International:** page 12 (top right).
**Tom Paton/London Features
International:** page 39.
David Redfern/Retna Ltd: page 55
(bottom).
**Ken Regan/London Features
International:** page 181.
Robert Titley; page 112.
Courtesy of Twitty City: page 187.
UPI/Bettman Newsphotos: pages 155,
175.
**Ron Wolfson/London Features
International:** pages 4 (bottom left), 15,
24, 28, 31, 49, 55 (top), 56, 58 (bottom
right), 68, 74, 79, 88, 89, 93, 95 (left),
102, 106, 120 (bottom center), 125, 168.

Page 1 (left to right): Little Jimmy
Dickens; Conway Twitty and Loretta
Lynn; Hank Williams Jr.

Page 2 (clockwise from top left): Patty
Loveless; Alan Jackson; Kathy Mattea;
Billy Ray Cyrus.

Page 3: Dwight Yoakam.

Introduction

Country music is, in its roots, folk music. Every culture has its folk music, but what we call country music is distinctively American. We have freely and enthusiastically borrowed from the folk music of other nations, peoples, cultures, and times. This mixture of influences needed certain American ingredients to make it country music as we know it.

Country music in America was first influenced by Scotch-Irish ballads; English story-songs; British dance tunes; Irish fiddle music; and a whole range of church hymns and sacred songs. African-American influences entered as blues and jazz were absorbed. When Germans immigrated to the South and brought their accordions with them, keyboards became a part of country music, and Cajuns found their squeeze-box. Hawaiian musical motifs brought steel guitars and dobros to country music as novelty shows passed through the South and rural areas in the 1920s and 1930s. When big-band jazz and swing hit the dance halls of the North, Western Swing was embraced in Texas. Some of the trappings of rock 'n' roll, which had some of its own origins in country honky-tonk, can now be found in country music. Folk music, with its tradition of storytelling singer-songwriters, has also found a contemporary home in country music.

The old Studio A in Nashville, Tennessee.

Jimmie Rodgers (left) with the Original Carter Family.

Yet in its constant evolution country music has retained a distinctive flavor – a 'sound', and a point of view, for there is a social subtext to much of country music. Patriotism and morality are assumed; tradition and convention are revered; and, despite the documented receptivity to new forms, the country music experience certainly includes a comfort with types. The difference in the 1990s is that at one time country people kept their music to themselves and found the rest of America ignoring them; now, country music still travels its own paths but finds a rush of others eager to join on the path. Country music is now heard on big-city radio stations and in dance clubs all over the country. Moreover, country music has become one of the world's most popular musical forms.

Two distinct strains of country music have developed over time. One began with the very first music in America – church music. Perhaps because of the Puritans' influence, making a joyful noise unto the Lord was not universally encouraged; it was left to rural congregations outside the formal denominations to 'line out' (chant and answer spontaneously), invent 'shape notes' for musically illiterate worshipers, and compose praise-filled gospel songs. Music became an important part of worship, and an important part of the lives of the early Americans, especially in frontier and outlying areas. It was relevant not just in country churches that dotted the landscape wherever men set foot, but also in revival crusades, week-long camp meetings, and under evangelists' tents everywhere. And when the lyrics were not strictly biblical, they told morality stories and taught lessons about living a life with or without the Lord. Few rural churches, much less camp meetings, had organs to accompany musical worship, so the instruments at hand – mostly guitars, fiddles and mandolins – entered the church, and entered the musical life of a people.

The other strain of country music aims no higher than the search for good times. This tradition started as early as the gospel tradition throughout rural America. Out of joy and companionship, or loneliness and melancholia, folks played fiddles and mandolins and sang. They played to gather people 'round; they played to get people to dance; they played to put music to stories and legends. Ancient tunes and modern tales combined in these songs. The jig grew from the same seed as the *gigue* movement in concert-hall music, and fiddler's techniques often originated in simulation of bagpipe music recalled by the Scotch-Irish who had come to the New World. American myths – white and black legends featuring Barbara Allen, John Henry, Frankie and Johnny – spread via countless troubadors singing their own versions, often with local conformations.

For centuries both of these rustic musical traditions prospered. Then in one historic week in 1927, they converged, only to go slightly different ways again, but not before significantly affecting each other – and indeed all of American music – forever.

Ralph Peer was a scout for the Victor Talking Machine Company, looking for rural white singers and musicians to match the success Victor Records had with black ('race') acts. He placed regional newspaper ads announcing that he would be in Bristol, Tennessee, the first week of August, 1927. He set up a makeshift recording studio over a store (and across the street from Bristol, Virginia). On August 2nd he recorded the Carter Family's harmonies, guitar playing, and down-home musical tales, including 'The Wandering Boy.' Two days later Jimmie Rodgers entered the studio (following his former band, which had just deserted him in the confidence they could make their own success) and recorded his yodeling-voice solo and guitar picking on 'Sleep, Baby, Sleep,' and one other song.

The songs the Carters and Rodgers recorded were different in theme – modest home-orientation versus forward love lyrics – and in many other ways: group harmony versus solo; traditional mountain sounds versus blues-tinged ballads. As they recorded further, the two acts codified the differences in their approaches to country music. The Carters, led by the superb stylist Mother Maybelle, expanded their instrumentation to include other guitars, fiddles, and autoharps. Jimmie Rodgers, whose second record contained the huge hits 'T For Texas' and 'Way Out on the Mountain,' added occasional jazz backups including trumpet and tuba, and even engaged Louis Armstrong to play in one session. All categories of country music can be traced to both the success foreshadowed that week in Bristol, Tennessee, and the types of music they played.

During the Depression there was an interesting cross-pollination occurring in American society. The rural South was being pulled from its moribund status. Economic misery and social isolation had dominated the former Confederacy since Reconstruction. The South had continued to linger over enduring traditions – linguistic, religious, musical – that stretched back for centuries while the rest of America was looking forward to future centuries. Ironically, as 'rural electrification' was designed to bring the South into the mainstream of American culture and economics, the rest of America experienced a rekindled interest in the Old South and its traditions.

Rural electrification brought phonographs to the South, making Jimmie Rodgers and the Carter Family the first superstars of American music. But the interest moved in two directions: not just the Singing Brakeman and the Carters became stars in the North and West, but also the Blue Sky Boys, the Delmore Brothers, Bradley Kincaid, and the Monroe Brothers. It was not just recordings (which were electrical by the late 1920s, bringing greater clarity) but radio as well, that spread the sound of this new music called country.

In fact, it wasn't immediately called 'country.' Ralph Peer's talent hunt was for 'race' music – usually a euphemism for black music, but also including other regional and rural forms, such as polkas and 'hillbilly' music. It was 'hillbilly' music, which encompassed such forms as Cajun music and Texas dance-bands as well, that was considered 'country music' into the 1950s.

Nashville's Grand Ole Opry was the pioneer of country music radio. The WSM ('We Shield Millions,' slogan of the station's owner, the National Life and Accident insurance company) Barn Dance was one of the first country music radio shows, and its popularity gave impetus to Nashville as a center of the music industry, not vice-versa. WSM received a 50,000-watt clear-channel signal, and reached almost half the continent with its country music; it was also a hook-up station in the NBC network. In fact its name came from host George D Hay following a network broadcast of the Metropolitan Opera of Leopold Damrosch: 'You have been listening to an hour of grand opera. Now sit back for the Grand Ole Opry!' One of its first stars was DeFord Bailey, a black harmonica player; and a longtime fixture was banjo player Uncle Dave Macon. Roy Acuff and Bill Monroe were two of the Opry's biggest enduring acts. Today, of course, Nashville and the Opry are the undisputed centers of country music activity.

In the Opry's wake, Chicago had its National Barn Dance (where comedian George Gobel got his start as a yodeling child singer) as did New York (where Tex Ritter was transformed from a folklorist and Broadway singer to a drugstore-cowboy host). There followed the WWVA Jamboree in Wheeling, West Virginia (where Grandpa Jones got his start); the Boone County Jamboree in Cincinnati (home to Merle Travis); the Ozark Jubilee of Springfield, Missouri (home base of Red Foley's radio and TV shows); the Louisiana Hayride (where Hank Williams and Elvis Presley were staff performers after the Opry rejected them); and the Hometown

Minnie Pearl trades jokes with Roy Acuff on stage at the Grand Ole Opry.

Jamboree (the Los Angeles birthplace of the career of Tennessee Ernie Ford).

To those who think that country is more than a style of music, but a state of mind, there was once a performance manifestation of that theory: as hillbilly acts toured, they offered more than concerts. Roy Acuff offered comedy as well as music; Grandpa Jones performed novelty numbers in addition to Bradley Kincaid's almost academic run-throughs of historical folk music; and the Monroe Brothers packaged day-long shows of hillbilly music, old-time tunes, gospel, recitations, comedy, and even pick-up baseball games.

On radio, there was another popular genre that is virtually lost today: the Saturday morning radio show. In these local shows, hosts would perform their popular songs and invite local singers and bands to perform, usually as cover versions of current hits. Shows invariably featured local news, ads, weather, and farm reports, as well as segments for 'shut ins' listening by radio, and gospel songs.

As hillbilly music grew in geographical scope and popularity, the designation stretched quite a bit. It was natural for such a plastic and dynamic form to develop its categories of specialization.

The two basic strains continued their convivial divergence. Jimmie Rodgers left many heirs after his death in 1933 – in the beginning most sounded, or tried to sound, exactly like him. Bill and Cliff Carlisle were Rodgers clones in theme and voice; they even harmonized their yodeling (no mean trick) after the Singing Brakeman. Elton Britt's entire career was based on his affinity with Jimmie Rodgers. Gene Autry, in his early days, was indistinguishable from Rodgers, and so was Lefty Frizzell, who eventually developed his own vocal style that inspired dozens

of stars into the 1990s. The same held true for Ernest Tubb and Hank Snow, whose later singing styles sounded not at all like Rodgers's, nor anyone else's for that matter.

But Rodgers's real legacy was thematic. He left in his wake country music's basic subjects of lost love, vicarious and forbidden relationships, drinking songs, tales of heartache and personal sorrow, and wanderlust – travel, moving on, restlessness, with trains as an actual and metaphoric element.

The other path from Bristol, following the Carter Family, was also largely thematic in addition to the legacies of instrumentation and affinities noted above. A host of singers sounded like the Carters – down to the harmonies of Sara and A P and the finger-picking of Maybelle – but the themes the Carters pioneered were as enduring: religious lessons, romantic sentiments, ironic morality tales, and aggregation – introspection, tradition, comfort zones, with home and family as metaphors.

String bands thrived primarily in the Southeast, primarily in Georgia. These were acts that featured virtuoso performances on banjos, fiddles, and guitars; lively vocals (usually solo hand-offs or unison choruses instead of harmonies); and, often, rowdy or comedic lyrics. Prominent in this group were Gid Tanner and His Skillet Lickers; the Fruit-Jar Drinkers; the Tennessee Tomcats with Merle Travis; and Clayton 'Pappy' McMichen's Georgia Wildcats.

Closely related were the brother acts of the 1920s through the 1940s, although these performers relied more on vocal virtuosity and absorbed more blues influences. They mostly hailed from the Southeast and mid-South: the Delmore Brothers; Brown's Ferry Four (the Delmores, Grandpa Jones and Merle Travis); the Carlisles; the Stanley Brothers; Sam and Kirk McGee; the Blue Sky Boys; Bill, Charlie, and Birch Monroe; the Blackwood Brothers; and others all the way to the Louvin Brothers, the Everly Brothers, and the Statler Brothers.

There was also 'mountain music,' that was perhaps the precursor of bluegrass. High harmonies; multi-part and many-voiced string instrumentation including guitars, autoharps, and dulcimers; and mournful lyrics were its hallmarks. Its practitioners included Roy Acuff; Pop Stoneman and the Stoneman Family; The Blues Chasers (later Wilma Lee and Stoney Cooper); the Dixieliners; and the Cumberland Mountain Folks with Molly O'Day.

An entirely different branch of country music – the 'Western' part of Country and Western, although some of its leaders resisted any Nashville association for a time – was Western swing. It was influenced by country musical traditions, to be sure, but also absorbed big-band swing, jazz, Louisiana dance beats and instrumentation, and black blues. It was dance music first and foremost, featuring driving instrumental licks and jazzy improvisation, and it thrived in large dance halls and on radio as well as on records. The pioneer was Milton Brown and His Musical Brownies, but the real keeper of the keys, notes and fiddle licks was Bob Wills and His Texas Playboys. Other standard-bearers of this vital music which has undergone a recent renaissance are: The Light Crust Doughboys, Spade Cooley, Tex Williams, and ensembles including the contemporary group Asleep at the Wheel, which recently organized a tribute album to Bob Wills, featuring many contemporary stars.

A related field was more artificial in origins, but thanks to talented singer/songwriters and a receptive public, became a legitimate genre with its own vital standards: cowboy music. Theoretically it was derived from tunes sung and yodeled by lonesome cowpokes on the range; in reality cowboys might have been lonely but very few sang astride their ponies and fewer yodeled. There were a handful of cowboy poets, but the cowboy song as we know it today is mostly the product of Hollywood, not Montana. However, some very talented people seized the category, writing and performing some remarkable music of lasting merit. Pioneers were Gene Autry and Roy Rogers, but the leader of the pack was Bob Nolan, who fronted Roy's group The Sons of the Pioneers; 'Cool Water' and 'Tumbling Tumbleweeds' were two of his many evocative songs. Others in this field included Patsy Montana, Rex Allen, Tex Ritter, Johnny Bond, Jimmy Wakely, T Texas Tyler, and today's *homage-a-trois*, Riders in the Sky.

Cajun music was considered country, but to many it appeared to be another country, so the French-influenced, accordion-and-fiddle hard-driven dance music remained largely regional and marginal to mainstream country, until recently. Early stars included Moon Mullican; Jimmy C Newman was Nashville's token Cajun for years; Doug Kershaw – the Ragin' Cajun who snaps countless bowstrings each performance – energized and publicized it; and now it is a national phenomenon. A new strain, Zydeco, has added black blues sounds, but a larger dose of country beat and instrumentation.

Bluegrass sounds to many modern ears like the oldest form of country. In fact, although it comes squarely from the lifelines of several older traditions, it is one of the newest, the musical invention of one man – Bill Monroe. Already a veteran performer of string band, mountain music, and brother-act harmonies, around 1945 Monroe gathered a group of musicians with special talents and fashioned a new type of music. Earl Scruggs's banjo is hugely responsible for the bluegrass sound, with his trademark three-finger, lightning-fast, syncopated counterpoint. However, Scruggs's banjo was just the final puzzle piece in Monroe's vision, for he had in place his own intense mandolin as solo and driving continuo; Mother Maybelle-style guitar sounds (and superb songwriting) from Lester Flatt; and jazzy fiddle licks from Chubby Wise and, later, Kenny Baker. Bill Monroe also contributed a high, lonesome counter-tenor as harmony, and so the bluegrass sound was born. It is now a crowded

Bob Wills – The King of Western Swing.

(Left to right) Kenny Baker, Bill Monroe, Vic Jordan, Roland White and James Monroe.

genre, with variants like Bluegrass Fusion, and has been as popular in cities and on college campuses as in the hills of Monroe's native Kentucky. Other bluegrass acts were formed by alumnae of Monroe's Bluegrass Boys: Flatt and Scruggs and the Foggy Mountain Boys; the Stanley Brothers; Reno and Smiley; Sonny and Bob; the Osborne Brothers; Jimmy Martin; and Mac Wiseman. Other acts have included Jim and

Johnny & Jack, Kitty Wells & the Tennessee Mountain Boys.

Jessie and the Virginia Boys, the Lewis Family, and The Tennessee Cut-Ups. Monroe was for a time overshadowed by his two renegades Flatt and Scruggs, and bluegrass itself seemed marginalized to folk festivals in the 1960s and 1970s, but the flame burnt bright enough to attract a new generation of performers like Alison Krauss; and, most significantly, was the very first music to appeal to contemporary superstars (and sometime bluegrass performers) Ricky Skaggs, Vince Gill, and Marty Stuart.

In the late 1940s other influences merged with country music to produce strains called honky-tonk, roadhouse, and, ultimately, rockabilly. Musically the influences included the rhythm and blues of the black circuits, as well as jazz and boogie-woogie. But just as important were new thematic preoccupations – cheating, drinking, divorce, revenge, regret, – like Jimmie Rodgers's and Riley Puckett's rowdy songs ratcheted up several notches. This was indeed music of the roadhouses and those new contraptions called jukeboxes, and because of their milieu (and having to be heard above the din of talking, drinking, and sometimes fistfights) electrification was introduced to country music. The brassy sounds of amplified instruments was a perfect symbol of the hard-edged lyrics that formed honky-tonk. Its main lights were Ernest Tubb, Webb Pierce, Floyd Tillman, Kitty Wells (the first in a long line of female stars), and, later, Faron Young and Buck Owens. But the major representative was the most important mainstream figure since Jimmie Rodgers: Hank Williams.

Hank hit the American music scene with unparalleled impact. He revived Rodgers's blue yodel; he incorporated heart-breaking blues into country songs; his writing was such that dozens of pop stars could and did record cover versions in their own styles; he caused a generation of singers to try their darndest to sound just like him; and he performed love songs, hurt songs, novelty songs, and gospel songs (under the name Luke the Drifter). And – as self-destructive as many of the lyrics suggest – he burned himself out before the age of 30, dead due to alcohol and drug abuse.

His influence was massive, and a few years after his death a crop of country singers took all of Hank's elements, added a strong dose of black rhythm and blues, mirrored his lifestyle in many cases except thumbing their noses more defiantly at the establishments they encountered – and rock 'n' roll was born. Elvis Presley, Jerry Lee Lewis, Carl Perkins, Roy Orbison, Johnny Cash, Charlie Rich and others – many of whom were from the mid-South and passed through Memphis's Sun Recording Studios – were country from the start, and many of them drifted back from prototypical rock to rocking country. Even early black rockers like Little Richard and Chuck Berry wrote and performed music that is largely country-oriented in chord structure and delivery.

In the meantime – from the 1940s to the 1960s – there was mainstream country music that was in sound and substance milder than honky-tonk and rockabilly. Sometimes called 'uptown' in its more conservative aspects, it was indeed music that was more palatable to the ears of Northern and urban audiences, that was frequently 'covered' by pop artists and received airplay on non-country stations. (In the early 1960s New York rock stations were still airing Faron Young's 'Hello Walls' and Ferlin Husky's gospel 'Wings of a Dove'.) Here were Patsy Cline, Jim Reeves, Eddie Arnold, and the 'new' Ray Price (not the old Cherokee Cowboy). Singer/songwriters like Willie Nelson and Merle Haggard maintained the best of country's heritage – gutsy, evocative lyrics, clever musical structure, tradition and innovation. George Jones, not a songwriter but a singer many consider possessing the greatest 'pipes' in the field, also displayed artistry that kept the flame burning.

At the other end of the spectrum from the 1960s to the 1980s was a dilution that almost proved the undoing of country music. The 'Nashville Sound' was a toy borne of glitzy recording-studio innovations enabling Music City's stellar talents to shine – producer Chet Atkins revealed his priorities when he jingled the coins in his pocket and said, 'That's the Nashville Sound' – but the shining was often showcasing at the expense of country traditionalism. Pop influences predominated as executives strove to make country palatable to a broader 'market,' never realizing that country's sound was appealing

enough to attract listeners on its own, and that fans of pop already had pop. So the evolution of Uptown Country (as polished country) to the Nashville Sound (as sterile country) to Pop Country (not country at all) poisoned the well.

But the traditionalist efforts of artists like Nelson, Haggard and Jones – and Loretta Lynn, Hank Snow, Emmylou Harris, Tom T Hall, Moe Bandy, Gene Watson, Conway Twitty, Don Williams, Dwight Yoakam, and with their versatility encompassing several forms, Marty Robbins and Hank Williams Jr – finally bore fruit. Starting in the mid-1980s new artists arose who eschewed the pop sounds. They wanted to sound like Haggard and Jones, not elevator-music crooners. They rejected lush string sections and took fiddles, steel guitars, mandolins, and Dobros out of Nashville's closets. They avoided Vegas and played state fairs. And they met with overwhelming critical and popular appreciation.

There were terms for them (New Traditionalists) and their music (New Country). In the beginning they were curiosities bucking the establishment, or were mere revivalists riding a fad. But soon their sound became the mainstream, and not just of country: by the 1990s country music was the most popular category of music in America, in airplay and record sales. Country stars were crossing over to rock and pop lists, and compromise wasn't in their vocabulary. Pioneers of this trend were John Anderson, Ricky Skaggs, George Strait, Keith Whitley,

The legendary Hank Williams Sr. on the air.

Randy Travis, and Clint Black. Following were Ricky Van Shelton, Alan Jackson, Travis Tritt, Marty Stuart, Holly Dunn, Mark Chesnutt, Patty Loveless, Garth Brooks, Kathy Mattea, Vince Gill, Joe Diffie, and Suzy Bogguss. The newest stars include the Mavericks, Jimmie Dale Gilmore, Faith Hill, Tim McGraw, John Michael Montgomery, Toby Keith, and Sammy Kershaw.

The sound of the new breed, if it can be categorized as one sound (and the argument for this can be made), is interesting at this juncture in country music history. There is a definite admixture of rock, folk, blues, and occasionally bluegrass in New Country. The difference from previous confluences is the self-confidence of the country component: there is no compromise, only reference and borrowing; there is no pandering.

The only downside to this plethora of popular quality talent is the grumblings heard from some older artists and fans that older artists are being neglected. Willie Nelson and Waylon Jennings have resorted occasionally to recording on small labels, as have, when they are lucky, Charlie Pride, Faron Young, and Ray Price; Merle Haggard used to fill stadiums and he now plays small clubs. Except for foreign labels (like Germany's excellent Bear Family records) you cannot buy material by, for instance, Buck Owens, who not long ago had dozens of number one hits.

Although there is a regrettable monolithic attitude among radio's program directors who limit their playlists to repetitions of top 40 country songs, basically the current situation represents another era in the long continuum of the art form called country music. In truth when Buck and Merle came up, Webb Pierce and Sonny James (who had been named Country Artist of the Decade by one source) found it hard to sing a song for anyone. And when people complain that 'everyone sounds like George (Jones) and Merle (Haggard),' they should remember that important individualists began their careers

Left: Tammy Wynette and George Jones in 1964.
Above: Clint Black, Janie Fricke and George Strait.
Below: Garth Brooks.

sounding exactly like Jimmie Rodgers, Bob Wills, Hank Williams, Bill Monroe, and Elvis Presley. The New Country artists themselves honor their predecessors: recent tribute albums to Merle Haggard (one by singers, one by songwriters), Bob Wills, and even the Eagles, have appeared to great acclaim. When Hank Williams Jr (who had never won a CMA award) won a country music video award several years ago, he remarked to the voting audience, 'Y'all should know that I do *audios* too!'

But these are cavils. A rising tide lifts all, and everybody in the business is enjoying the country music renaissance. An impressive aspect of the new scene is that it has wide appeal. Network television has recognized country's popularity by scheduling music specials – awards shows, retrospective music specials (*Women of Country*, *Salute to the Grand Ole Opry*), and artists' showcases, including specials devoted to Garth Brooks, Billy Ray Cyrus, Mary Chapin Carpenter, Trisha Yearwood, and other artists.

The Nashville Network is one of the television industry's biggest success stories, reaching millions of homes with a full complement of entertainment and features such as game shows. The centerpiece, of course, is Saturday night's peek at the Grand Ole Opry (only a half-hour long); also popular are the weekly *Statler Brothers* variety show and the Monday-through-Friday *Nashville Now!* program with Lorianne Crook and Charlie Chase which aired until mid-1995. On weekends there are fishing shows and sports. The rest of the schedule is devoted to dance and country music videos.

Videos have become an important part of promotion and entertainment in country music enjoyment; and, as in other forms of music, video production a virtual art form in itself. Country music videos are regularly aired not only on the Nashville Network, but also on the all-video channel CMT (Country Music Television) and in time-chunks on VH-1, if not yet on MTV. Their importance is reflected in awards recognition – to Hank Jr and others – and they provide fans with a graphic backdrop for the songs they like. There is no doubt that attractive and photogenic newcomers benefit from the exposure they receive via high production values. In fact, lens-friendly singers like Billy Dean and Faith Hill have had to endure criticism that, largely through country music videos, their meteoric rises have been due to good looks more than talent.

Another recent phenomenon has been the proliferation of dance clubs, dance steps, dance-instruction videos, and dance-oriented TV shows. As old as the Texas two-step and as new as the Achy Breaky (concocted for the promotion of Billy Ray Cyrus), the dance craze illustrates better than any other factor the universal appeal and impact of country music in the 1990s: line-dancing is being taught and strutted in cities as well as in country roadhouses. Country theme parks have had a

Veteran country singer Willie Nelson.

steady but tentative growth. Opryland was actually established when the Opry outgrew the Ryman Auditorium in downtown Nashville in the late 1970s; a brand-new concert hall was planned on the edge of town, but Gaylord Entertainment was nervous about drawing people to its location. More land was purchased with an eye toward supporting the Opry House. The Opry is a successful site in itself, a large, state-of-the-art performance and broadcast location, but it proved almost more difficult to build than the evolving theme park that sprouted in its long shadow. Now Opryland is one of the nation's most visited theme parks, with rides, restaurants, and a full concert schedule that allows visitors at any time of the year to see a host of name stars close up.

Branson, Missouri, evolved similarly, for it has had its dinner theaters and family attraction for years – but recently Branson has been aggressive in planning and promoting restaurants and concert theaters associated with singers. Now the hills are dotted with dozens of dinner theaters and marquees heralding such names as Mel Tillis, Glen Campbell, the Osmonds, and Yakov Smirnov. Branson is an RV magnet, attracting families and retirees in trailers, mobile homes, outfitted campers, and full recreational vehicles of all sorts.

There will be other Bransons, just as – during this New Country explosion – there seem to be not just new acts but new stars every week. Country music is not only as American as apple pie: it is also as popular and as ubiquitous.

Acuff, Roy

The King of Country Music has never been dethroned. It's been decades since he's had a hit record, but Roy Acuff is a symbol – of change when country music was in transition, of tradition when it seems to be losing its identity, and of integrity throughout his remarkable career.

Roy Claxton Acuff was born in Maynardsville, Tennessee, in 1903, to a father who was a judge and a Baptist minister. Roy's very first interests did not include country music, but rather amateur theatricals

Roy Acuff (left) with Ernest Tubb and Tex Ritter.

and athletics; he won a great number of letters at school. In 1929 it appeared that a dream would come true when the New York Yankees offered Roy a tryout. But a series of sunstrokes – from which he did not fully recover for two years – ended his hopes of a sports career.

During his long recuperation, Roy listened to his father's country music records, and was mightily attracted to the sounds; he subsequently learned to play the fiddle. A neighbor secured for Roy a position with a medicine show as singer and blackface comedian, after which he formed a band, first called the Tennessee Crackerjacks and then the Crazy Tennesseans. He began to play on local radio, and in 1936 cut his first record.

That record is ironically the one still most associated with Roy Acuff: 'The Great Speckled Bird.' For some reason, country music histories have never correctly explained its theme, which is taken from Jeremiah 12:9 ('Is my inheritance like a speckled bird of prey to me? Are the birds of prey against her on every side?') and refers to the persecuted, raptured Christian church. The song's somewhat mystical lyrics, combined with

its durable theme (a variant of 'I'm Thinking Tonight of My Blue Eyes') marked it as a country classic.

Although he had attempted to join the Grand Ole Opry, it was in February of 1938, when he was merely substituting for an absent star, that Roy sang 'Great Speckled Bird,' and the audience reaction was such that he was invited to become a regular staff member. He is credited with being the first major Opry star who was primarily a singer (not an instrumentalist) and a solo act (not part of a harmony group).

In 1938 Roy scored with his other trademark hit, 'The Wabash Cannonball.' His other hits through the years have included: 'Wreck on the Highway,' 'Fireball Mail,' 'Night Train to Memphis,' 'Low and Lonely,' 'Pins and Needles in My Heart,' 'Will the Circle Be Unbroken,' 'Weary River,' 'The Precious Jewel,' 'I Saw the Light,' 'Wait For My Call to Glory,' 'Black Mountain Rag' and 'Back in the Country.' His Smokey Mountain Boys included some of the finest mountain and country musicians of the day: Clell Summey (later comedian Cousin Jody) and Pete Kirby (known as Bashful Brother Oswald)

The members of Alabama.

on dobro, responsible for the plaintive instrumental sound on Acuff songs; Howdy Forrester on fiddle; Jimmie Riddle, harmonica and Jess Easterday, guitar.

Roy was also involved in a multitude of other activities. A successful businessman, in 1942 he formed Acuff-Rose Publications with Fred Rose; the firm became a leading American music publisher. He also owned a part of Hickory Records. He ran for governor of Tennessee in 1948 (losing, as a Republican) and he played starring roles in eight movies.

The 'King of Country Music' title was bestowed by baseball great Dizzy Dean, and Roy recalls with pride a reported epithet of Japanese soldiers in World War II – when he topped several polls as the American serviceman's favorite singer – 'To hell with Babe Ruth! To hell with President Roosevelt! To hell with Roy Acuff!'

One reason the 'King of Country Music' label stuck is that Roy Acuff for years was a practitioner of a straight-out form of country. Although his roots were in mountain and old-time music, Roy could not be pigeonholed as bluegrass, or honky tonk, or any of the newer classifications (Merle Haggard comes to mind as one of the other few artists who so defy categorization). Roy Acuff was a country music singer. Most listeners associate Roy with the limited vocal style of his later years and are unfamiliar with his prime work in

the 1930s and 1940s. Acuff's sound *was* different; it was country (a lively ensemble of fiddle, guitar and dobro), and his voice was plaintive, pure, emotional and arresting, reminiscent of the Old Harp singing styles.

Roy performed regularly on the Opry until very near his death, of congenital heart failure on November 23, 1992. In keeping with his wishes, he was buried just hours after his passing, at a service attended only by family members and the Smoky Mountain Boys. A who's who of country royalty attended the much larger public memorial service a few days later.

Alabama

Alabama, music history's largest-selling group in the country category, has its nucleus in three cousins born in Fort Payne, Alabama – Randy Owen and Jeff Cook (born in 1949) and Teddy Gentry (born in 1952). In the early 1970s they began to play locally, billing themselves as Wild Country; they secured a job at the Canyonland Park, playing backup for visiting stars. Randy plays rhythm guitar and writes many of the group's songs; Jeff plays lead guitar and fiddle and Teddy plays the bass.

In 1973 they moved to Myrtle Beach, South Carolina, where they performed and cut their own records. In 1979 they were joined by drummer Mark Herndon (born in Springfield, Massachusetts, in 1955)

and scored with their first national hit, 'My Home's in Alabama.' The next year they signed with RCA and have scored Number One with a long string of singles, including 'Tennessee River,' 'Why Lady Why,' 'Old Flame,' 'Mountain Music,' 'Take Me Down,' 'Close Enough to Perfect,' 'The Closer You Get,' 'Roll On' and 'Fire in the Night.'

Unlike many groups whose '70s and '80s pop leanings left them without listeners as more traditional sounds took the fore, Alabama has kept pace with seeming ease. Simpler arrangements and a 'down home' thematic bent (that is, in fact, the title of one of their biggest recent hits) have kept them on radio, if not at the podium when group-of-the-year awards are handed out. The group has sold more than 40 million albums worldwide.

Anderson, Bill

Born in Columbia, South Carolina, in 1937, Bill Anderson grew up in Georgia, where he formed a high school band and won talent contests. He received a BA from the University of Georgia, majoring in journalism, and thereafter took jobs for different newspapers.

But Anderson maintained an interest in country music all the while; he was a disc jockey, for instance, during college and his newspaper work. His songwriting talents served him well in 1958, when Ray Price scored with Anderson's 'City Lights,' and Anderson was later to write songs for many of country music's best interpreters, including Hank Locklin, Jim Reeves, Faron Young, Porter Wagoner, Jean Shepard and Connie Smith.

In 1959 Anderson embarked on his own career as a singer, and through the years has had more than 50 records in top chart positions, including 'Po' Folks,' 'Still,' 'I Love You Drops,' 'Quits' and others. He performed duets with Jan Howard and Mary Lou Turner and appeared in country movies and many television programs. Anderson hosted his own syndicated music show, *Backstage at the Grand Ole Opry* and secured guest spots on network quiz shows. The latter activity led to his hosting of the ABC game show, *The Better Sex*, and another, *Funzapoppin'*. He has acted on the soap opera

Anderson, John

The music of John Anderson is difficult to classify, incorporating as it does echoes of the many country music styles that have influenced him and yet remaining uniquely his own. Born and raised in Florida, he was first exposed to rock and played it with a local band. But it wasn't long before elements of traditional country music, mountain, Southern rock, and blues colored his personal style. The vocal styling and instrumentation of rock songs like 'When It Comes to You,' written for him by Mark Knopfler of Dire Straits, have a country sound. He has been described as a clone of Lefty Frizzell and has performed some of Frizzell's classic numbers. Among his other notable singles have been '1959,' 'I'm Just an Old Chunk of Coal,' 'Your Lyin' Blue Eyes,' and his million-copy sellers 'Swingin'' and 'Seminole Wind.'

John's career has fluctuated, but he remains a strong presence in the industry. He won the Horizon Award from the Country Music Association in 1983 but was without a label at the end of the 1980s. A two-year period without releasing a record was interpreted by some as evidence of a professional decline. But he has come back solidly since signing up with the new label BNA, and he is clearly back on track with recording and radio work. *Seminole Wind*, the album with which he made his comeback, was a solid entry in the traditionalist vein. He is now referred to as an inspirational type of singer – 'he's got that John Anderson sound' – and is part of the esteemed Nashville establishment, a vital member of projects like tribute albums to the Eagles and Merle Haggard with other superstars.

The country music of the 'new traditionalists' is clearly informed by the work of their predecessors, and together they have been responsible for the creation of the New Country sound. But during the 1980s, when country music was without a clear direction, a few new names appeared who worked along traditionalist lines. Along with such stalwarts as George Jones and Merle Haggard, who preserved the integrity of the medium, they helped to hold the torch and pave the way for innovators like Randy Travis and

John Anderson.

One Life to Live and has hosted the Nashville Network's *Fandango*. Anderson, who dabbled in country-disco experiments in the 1970s, also oversees a chain of restaurants, Po' Folks, named for his theme song.

Considered a 'songwriter's songwriter' among current country stars, Anderson continues to enjoy chart success – 'Which Bridge to Cross, Which Bridge to Burn,' a smash hit

for co-writer Vince Gill, is a prime example of Anderson's considerable talents and continuing popularity.

Nicknamed Whisperin' Bill, Anderson's vocal trademark is an airy, amazingly empty upper-register voice devoid of forcefulness. It has become his patented sound, however, and his individualized singing style, combined with his brilliant songwriting abilities, have ensured his placed in country music history.

Garth Brooks. John Anderson was among the singers who maintained the standards of country music. That he has remained in tune with public taste is proved by the continued, indeed revived, popular success, more than a decade later, of his traditionalist music. His latest CD, *Country Till I Die*, could be the title of a happy success-filled autobiography. In 1994 John received the Career Achievement Award (marking a comeback success) from the Academy of Country Music, presented by Randy Travis, with tributes by Billy Dean and Garth Brooks. John received a standing ovation from his peers.

Arnold, Eddy

Born near Henderson, Tennessee, in 1918, Richard Edward Arnold rose from a farmboy's life to that of a favored local performer, and he remembers riding mules to and from musical events while making that transition. By 1936 he was appearing on local radio, and then was picked up by Pee Wee King and His Golden West Cowboys.

By the mid-1940s, Eddy was signed as a solo act by RCA, and had Colonel Tom Parker, later Elvis Presley's manager, handling his career. His big hits started rolling at this time, including 'I'll Hold You in My Heart,' 'Just a Little Lovin' Will Go a Long Way' (co-written by Arnold and Zeke Clements). 'Bouquet of Roses,' 'Texarkana Baby,' 'Kentucky Waltz,' 'I Really Don't Want to Know,' 'My Everything,' 'Cattle Call,' 'Tennessee Stud' and 'Any Time.'

Eddy, who always had a smooth but upper-register voice, deepened his vocals for a surer pop appeal. Likewise his image changed. In his early performing days he had been the Tennessee Plowboy and a sometimes hick act, with blackened teeth and outlandish overalls. Now he

Eddy Arnold.

changed to tuxedos and a cocktail-lounge demeanor. Eddy thus became the first certifiable crossover star in country music, and built a massive following across the musical board with lushly arranged songs like 'Make the World Go Away' and 'What's He Doing in My World.'

Probably the most successful country singer between 1945 and 1970, Eddy Arnold has sold in excess of 70 million records. He has appeared extensively on television and radio, hosting a Mutual Broadcasting System Radio program for Purina, and three television shows – a CBS summer replacement for Perry Como (with Chet Atkins) and NBC network shows in 1953 and 1956.

Eddy Arnold, who records and performs only occasionally now, is one of the richest men in Nashville,

Asleep at the Wheel.

thanks to his investments and long-standing commercial appeal. He was inducted into the Country Music Hall of Fame in 1966, and was CMA Entertainer of the Year in 1967.

Asleep at the Wheel

An important component of the Western Swing revival, the group Asleep at the Wheel actually had its genesis in the Northeast. Ray Benson, guitarist, and Reuben Gosfield, steel guitarist, started playing together around Philadelphia in the early 1970s. Their musical tastes included shared interests in country, jazz and 1950s rock 'n' roll.

They were joined by LeRoy Preston, drums, and Danny Levin, piano – among many other musicians who were eventually to

come and go through the ensemble – and headquartered themselves in Washington, DC. They later moved to San Francisco, where they acquired an interest in Western Swing, and Texas, where in the mid-1970s the group had its first hit single, 'The Letter That Johnny Walker Read.' They added a Texas twin-fiddle sound and beefed up the group to more of an ensemble resembling old Western Swing big bands, including reeds and horns, and scored another huge hit with 'Route 66.'

Asleep at the Wheel has recorded several albums and has appeared on television. Their eclecticism has carried them beyond the Western Swing revival to blues, jazz, honky-tonk, Cajun music, 1940s rhythm and blues and pop sounds. In doing their own musical thing, and enduring so many personnel changes,

Asleep at the Wheel serves up a musical offering that too often seems like more abstract stylistic exercises than sincere renditions; perhaps more camp than affection, but splendid interpretations nonetheless.

The Wheel was seen for years as a peripheral or 'outside' act by the Nashville mainstream, no doubt due to their deep association with Texas and radio's tendency to ignore Western Swing music. Televised live appearances and video have greatly expanded the group's audience in the 1990s, however, and they have become established Music City favorites. They have garnered 16 Grammy nominations and have been named Best Touring Band by the Academy of Country Music.

In 1994 the group recorded an acclaimed tribute album, *Asleep at the Wheel Tribute to the Music of Bob Wills and the Texas Playboys*. Fully annotated by Benson, the CD contains many of the Playboys' greatest songs performed by country's finest singers – Merle Haggard, Suzy Bogguss, Willie Nelson, Vince Gill, Johnny Rodriguez, Lyle Lovett, Garth Brooks, as well as rock's Huey Newton – and musicians, including Gill, Johnny Gimble, Chet Atkins, and Marty Stuart.

The personnel of Wheel now consists of Benson; Tim Alexander on piano; Cindy Cashdollar on steel; Mike Francis on sax; Rickey Turpin on fiddle and mandolin; David Earl Miller on bass; and Tommy Beavers on drums.

Atkins, Chet

The name probably more synonymous with country instrumental musicianship than any other, Chester Burton Atkins was born in Luttrell, Tennessee, in 1924. He grew up listening to Jimmie Rodgers records and, although the guitar was to establish his musical credentials, his first instrument was the fiddle (his elder brother Jim was to play guitar with Les Paul in later years).

In the early 1940s Chet played on Knoxville radio, and through the decade he was to be featured on many country radio shows. He played with a host of entertainers, including Bill Carlisle; the Carter Family, with whom he toured; and Red Foley, with whom he guested on the Grand Ole Opry in 1946. In 1949,

Eddy Arnold (left) and Chet Atkins.

although he had been signed as a vocalist, he had an RCA hit with the instrumental 'Country Gentleman' and the next year became a member of the Opry.

Chet's RCA work also led him to perform sideman duties at recording sessions. Ultimately, through the 1950s, he moved up as an executive as well as a performer, to producer and then manager of Nashville operations for the label; in 1968 he became a division vice-president. He seldom scored hits with any single records, but through the years maintained a steady stream of popular instrumental albums. As a producer he was in demand by country artists, as well as singers from other fields of music. Among those whom Chet produced were Elvis Presley, Eddy Arnold, Al Hirt, Perry Como, Jane Morgan, Floyd Cramer, Connie Smith, Waylon Jennings, Don Gibson, Dottie West and Jerry Reed.

His guitar picking is among the most admired in country and popular music. His finger style is a pop variant of the Travis school – a smooth, rippling melodic fingerplay, counterpointed by the thumb's soft bass. It was reflective of the Nashville Sound, a production and

scoring revolution that he and Owen Bradley led, but was adopted by many segments of the industry in the 1960s and '70s. Just as with his guitar style, harder country edges were smoothed; steel guitars and fiddles were de-emphasized, while string arrangements and vocal choruses were practically mandated. It was a new evolutionary phase of country music, and it brought widespread acceptance in areas where country music had been lately derogated as hillbilly and worse.

In retrospect some may see the Nashville Sound as Atkins' Frankenstein's monster. Although its production tenets still hold, very few will claim it; pop has run amuck, smothering the last vestiges of country identity, and in other areas performers are adopting rock, or 'outlaw' or, occasionally, old-timey influences. In the meantime, Chet left RCA in the early 1980s, but has kept busy with recording and performing.

Through the years he recorded some notable duets with other outstanding talents, including albums with Merle Travis, Jerry Reed and

Les Paul. He also recorded with the Boston Pops. In the mid-1980s he revealed himself as more of a guitar devotee than a country performer, and turned his talent loose on pop standards and, increasingly, jazz. In 1985 he issued an album of jazz guitar to critical approval.

It might be that Chet Atkins's creation of and reliance on the Nashville Sound ultimately boomeranged (although, of course, he had a tremendously successful career as a guitarist and producer), because today he records with no major label. He is undergoing a sort of resurrection, as a guest on CDs like Randy Travis's *Heroes and Friends*, and as a featured player numerous times on National Public Radio's *Prairie Home Companion*. He also recorded, in 1994, a duet album with Suzy Bogguss, *Simpatico*. The project received high critical acclaim, and inspired a road tour for the pair.

Autry, Gene

A straight shooter, but always ready with a smile and a song, Gene Autry made Saturday mornings fun for a generation of American boys, and was the realest hero many of them had. Among the many trails he rode was that of cowboy star, but he began his performing career as a hillbilly singer.

Orvon Gene Autry was born on a tenant farm in Tioga, Texas, in 1907, and was raised in Ravia, Oklahoma. After high school he worked with the Fields Brothers Marvelous Medicine Show and then, more conventionally, for the St Louis and Frisco Rail Road as a telegrapher in Sapulpa, Oklahoma. One night in 1925 he was singing at his station to pass the time, and a stranger complimented his voice, advising him to turn professional. That stranger was Will Rogers, and Gene determined to make a career of music.

In 1927 he became impressed, as did the whole nation, by Jimmie Rodgers; Gene's style thereafter included yodeling and other stylings of the Singing Brakeman. Gene recorded some discs that year, with no success, but was discovered by Uncle Art Satherly, the legendary recording executive and talent-hunter who was later to sign Bob Wills and Roy Acuff to their first contracts. Billed as Oklahoma's Sing-

ing Cowboy, Gene recorded his own co-composition 'That Silver-Haired Daddy of Mine' in New York in 1929. It was a hit and has subsequently sold more than 5 million copies.

Gene thereafter became a featured star on several radio barn dances, most notably on Chicago's WLS (1931-34), where he sang his soft yodels and hillbilly songs. While in Chicago, Sears Roebuck (which owned WLS, whose call letters stand for World's Largest Store) marketed Gene Autry records, guitars and songbooks.

In 1934 Gene was signed to sing in the Ken Maynard Western film *In Old Santa Fe*. He was well received, and signed to star in a rather absurd cowboy-science fiction serial, *The*

Gene Autry, "The Singing Cowboy."

Phantom Empire. This was another hit, and the new Republic Pictures signed Gene to the first full singing Western, *Tumbling Tumble Weeds*. Over the next three decades Gene Autry was to star in more than 100 musical Westerns with Republic, Columbia, Monogram and his own companies. Between 1939 and 1956 he hosted his own radio show, *Melody Ranch* and, of course, produced his own popular television program where he continued to fight bad guys, sing some songs and win the day.

Through the years Gene's incredible list of hits has included 'Mexicali Rose,' 'You're the Only Star (In My Blue Heaven),' 'Tears on My Pillow,' 'Makes No Difference Now,' 'Tweedle O-Twill,' 'Mail Call Today,' 'Yellow Rose of Texas,' 'Deep in the Heart of Texas' and four novelty/children's songs that are among the biggest sellers in recording history – 'Rudolph the Red-Nosed Reindeer,' 'Frosty the Snowman,' 'Peter Cottontail' and 'Here Comes Santa Claus.' The songs perhaps most identified with Gene Autry are 'Riding Down the Canyon,' 'You Are My Sunshine' and 'Back in the Saddle Again.'

As a businessman, Gene has managed a financial empire that controls movie and television production companies, record firms, hotel chains and the California Angels baseball team. He even has had a town – Gene Autry, Oklahoma – named for him. One of his major legacies is the assistance he has given to other singers and actors – those who directly benefited from Autry's help and favors include Johnny Bond, Jimmy Wakely, Tex Ritter and Roy Rogers.

For all of Gene Autry's business successes and screen credits – and the symbol he was to American youth in those morality-play Western serials – the essence of his impact is still his voice and his performing manner. Gene has a friendly, nasal, warm tenor that bathes every set of lyrics he sings; it's a voice one loves to love, and bespeaks sincerity. His gentle but firm, pure vocals embodied the character that Gene Autry played in countless roles on big and small screens – he was a hero, but you knew he was also a pal.

Gene Autry was inducted into the Country Music Hall of Fame in 1969.

Bailey, DeFord

Literally the first star of the Grand Ole Opry, DeFord Bailey was a black instrumentalist known as The Harmonica Wizard. He was born in Carthage, Tennessee, in 1899 and suffered from infantile paralysis as a child; he recovered, although the four-foot, eleven-inch Bailey endured a twisted back in his adult life. His family played what he later called black hillbilly music, virtually the traditional white music of the South, and he played harmonica to their fiddles and banjo.

Bailey appeared on the *WSM Barn Dance* before the Grand Ole Opry was instituted, and was directly involved with the naming of the Opry. Early in 1926, master of ceremonies George Dewey Hay was preparing the *Barn Dance* broadcast when he listened to the NBC network hookup moments before airtime. The lead-in show was *The Music Appreciation Hour* with Dr Walter Damrosch, who closed off with some derogatory remarks about realism in classics.

Hay, the 'Solemn Old Judge,' took the cue and introduced DeFord Bailey, playing 'Pan American Blues' to open the show. After the song Hay said, 'For the past hour, we have been listening to music taken largely from the Grand Opera, but from now on we will present the Grand Ole Opry.'

Bailey was also among the first artists to record in Nashville (on September 28, 1928), although a trend was not begun until years later. Bailey did remain a member of the Opry until 1941, and in the 1940s toured with the Bill Monroe package tent show; Monroe remembers him as a superlative harmonica player.

Among Bailey's other trademark numbers were 'Lost John,' 'The Evening Prayer Blues' and 'Muscle Shoals Blues.' In his last years he was reclusive, and operated a Nashville shoeshine stand. DeFord Bailey died in Nashville on July 2, 1982.

The Harmonica Wizard DeFord Bailey.

Bandy, Moe

Born in the hometown of Jimmie Rodgers, Meridian, Mississippi, in 1944, Moe Bandy's grandfather reportedly had worked with Rodgers before the Singing Brakeman went into the music business. Moe's parents played and sang, but his real first love was rodeoing, to which he was close after his parents moved to San Antonio when Moe was six. His brother had better luck at the activity than Moe – he is a much-awarded rodeo champion – so music became his trade.

Moe joined his father's local band, The Mission City Playboys, and in 1962 formed his own ensemble, Moe and the Mavericks. For a dozen years he played clubs and TV dates in Texas, but kept various day jobs in

Moe Bandy.

more secure professions. In 1973, however, Moe pressed 500 copies of a song, 'I Just Started Hatin' Cheatin' Songs Today,' which eventually became a number five hit nationally. He followed up with other songs that attracted wide attention, 'It Was Always So Easy (To Find an Unhappy Woman)' and 'Bandy the Rodeo Clown,' co-written by Whitey Shafer and Lefty Frizzell.

A switch to the Columbia label preceded a steady stream of hit records, but was accompanied by an absurd promotional campaign that claimed that Moe's honky-tonk songs were so powerful that they resulted in broken marriages and a virtual epidemic of cheating. Nevertheless Moe's no-nonsense, no-apologies approach revived a flagging tradition of East Texas honky-tonk; thematics aside, his backup of whining steel, lonesome fiddle and elec-

tric guitars flew in the face of all the flies in the Nashville ointment at the time – pop, rock and Nashville Sound. It worked, and Moe has recorded some of the finest songs in the genre.

Other Bandy hits have included 'Hank Williams, You Wrote My Life,' 'Here I Am, Drunk Again,' 'I'm Sorry For You, My Friend,' 'Following the Feeling' and 'Let's Get Over Them Together.' In the 1970s he and Joe Stampley teamed frequently for duets like 'Just Good Old Boys,' 'Hey Joe, Hey Moe' and novelty takeoffs like a spoof on British singer Boy George; the pair won duo awards from both the Country Music Association and the Academy of Country Music in 1979.

Moe and Joe recorded a high percentage of novelty comedy songs, but the duo is best remembered as top practitioners of the honky-tonk style. Bandy is credited by many of today's top artists as one of the leaders of country's return to more traditional sounds. In 1991 Moe opened Moe Bandy's Americana Theatre in Branson, Missouri, again one of the first in what was to become a trend. The theater is one of Branson's most popular attractions. In 1994 game show host Bob Eubanks unveiled his '$25,000 Game Show Spectacular' morning show at Bandy's venue.

Black, Clint

Clint Black was born in New Jersey, the son of a contract-laborer, but acquired his country sound from growing up in the Houston, Texas area. A Texas trouper from an early age, he was playing and singing at 15 and made his professional debut at Houston's Benton Springs Club in Dallas in 1981. He was not an overnight star, holding a daytime job as an ironworker while playing local clubs until he got the call to Nashville for a recording date. But things moved fast for him after that: Hayden Nicholas signed on as collaborator and co-songwriter; ZZ Top manager Bil Ham became his manager; and Joe Galante of RCA Records Nashville heard his demo tapes, saw him perform, and gave him a multi-album contract.

Clint and his team hit the jackpot from the start. Their debut album, *Killin' Time*, was a smash on both

country music and crossover charts. Released in May 1989, it achieved double-platinum status (two million copies sold) within the next year and a half. Five of the singles it contained – the title song, 'A Better Man, 'Nobody's Home,' 'Walking Away,' and 'Nothing's News' – became number-one hits, a first in recording history. The album was number one on the charts for 32 weeks in a row. Clint's second album, *Put Yourself in My Shoes*, reached the same sales level in less than a year, and four singles from it – the title cut, 'Loving Blind,' 'One More Payment,' and 'Where Are You Now' – all appeared on the top five charts. Although he seemed to have found an easy path to success, his third album was called *The Hard Way*; his fourth album, *No Time to Kill*, produced five charted hits and went platinum-plus.

The public was not alone in acknowledging Clint's work: He racked up a Country Music Association Horizon Award in 1989 and Top Male Vocalist honors the next year; 1990 also brought him four awards from the Academy of Country Music – Album of the Year, Single of the Year, Best New Male Vocalist, and Best Male Vocalist – and The Nashville Network/Music City News awards for the Star of Tomorrow and Album of the Year. In 1992 the CMA nominated him for Vocal Event of the Year for the music video *Hold On Partner* with Roy Rogers, whose modest demeanor and youthful smile foreshadowed Clint's own personal appeal.

On the personal front, Clint's life has not gone quite so smoothly. He fired Bill Ham and brought a $5 million suit against him; and BMG, the German-based owner of RCA, successfully sued to prevent him from leaving the label. There has been a flip side, however; in 1991 Clint married TV glamor girl Lisa Hartman, star of 'Knot's Landing.'

If Randy Travis is the father of the 'new traditionalist' movement in country music, Clint Black, as the first of New Country's male sex symbols, is probably the originator of what has been called the 'hunky-tonk' movement. He and his followers are good-looking, have sensuous, emotional deliveries, and, in many cases, wear Western hats.

Clint Black.

Clint was one of the first in this genre. Like Randy Travis in the 'new traditionalist' revival, he was a prototype of the artist who seemed to come from nowhere, shoot to the top of the charts with dazzling sales records, and then share the stage with someone else. Others following this pattern have been Garth Brooks, Alan Jackson, Billy Ray Cyrus and Vince Gill.

Clint had a meteoric rise, but he is no nine-day wonder. As an original performer and a pattern for others, he is a sensitive songwriter, a riveting performer, and a versatile creative force. That versatility was shown in Clint's fifth album, *One Emotion*. Clint wrote or co-wrote all of the CD's 10 songs – including the hit single 'Untanglin' My Mind' with Merle Haggard – and provided multiple instrumentation and background vocals on many. He was also the album's co-producer, and director of the two country music videos spun off the album.

Concerts are where Clint shines, further attesting to his versatility:

BlackHawk in Concert.

1993's 'Black & Wy' tour (with Wynonna Judd) was followed by a 15-city tour, 'Up Close . . . In Concert' before audiences of no more than 3000 – intimate performances featuring his solo acoustic work.

BlackHawk

A relatively new group, centered around a veteran lead singer from the Southern rock band The Outlaws and two writers of many of Restless Heart's hits, BlackHawk has a sound that the members describe as 'very Southern.'

Henry Paul, the former Outlaw, organized the group in the early 1990s when he teamed up with Dave Robbins and Van Stephenson, who had written hits for musicians as diverse as Eddy Arnold and Eric Clapton. Many critics consider the trio musically and aesthetically to be heirs to the great traditions of the Allman Brothers Band.

The group's band consists of Dale Oliver, lead guitarist, Tere Bertke, bassist and Bobby Huff, drummer. They record on the Arista label.

Paul is from Florida, Robbins is

from Atlanta and Stephenson was born in Ohio, and also lived in Altoona, Pennsylvania, but moved to Nashville with his family when he was 10. The group, whose smash debut CD was titled *BlackHawk*, features hard electric instrumentation and hard-edged vocals. Many think it is the music of such groups – and BlackHawk seems destined to have a long life with fans – that keeps alive not only the creatively rougher aspects of country music, but also the driving force of rock 'n' roll, whose lost traditions have led former fans to country music.

Blackwood Brothers, The

In country music, four-part gospel harmony goes back to the very roots of the form. And in gospel music, quartets seem to be a way of life. But in both areas, mention of the Blackwood Brothers is tantamount to a synonym for gospel quartet music.

The original Blackwood Brothers quartet was formed in the clay hills of Mississippi in 1934, comprised of

brothers Roy, Doyle, James, and Roy's son R W. In 1954 they achieved national prominence by winning a contest on TV's *Arthur Godfrey's Talent Scouts*, but the same year R W died in a plane crash. Two years later the members regrouped and, with J D Sumner as bass singer, became the foremost gospel act in America. They recorded many albums with Porter Wagoner, won many awards, sold more than 40 million records and have toured 43 countries, including Russia and China. They have also performed with the Billy Graham Crusade.

The original members of the group have passed away, but the current Blackwoods perform with equal quality and intensity. Baritone Winston Blackwood (R W Jr) was born in 1943 and won a *Ted Mack Amateur Hour* contest at the age of 12. He and his wife Donna and a group of singers once toured with Roy Rogers and Dale Evans, Ronnie Milsap and Dolly Parton as the Blackwood Singers. RW Jr and Donna are joined these days by their children Andrea Blackwood Carter and Robbie. Ron Page sings bass (he is a former member of the Oak Ridge Boys, The Chuck Wagon Gang, and the Swanee River Boys); Everett Reece plays piano; and Cousin Char is a featured singer in the reorganized group, which today is called the Blackwood Family Show.

The Blackwoods are forever identified with a gospel style of uninhibited, lusty delivery and tight four-part harmony. For their style and their sounds (lively two-tenor/baritone/deep-bass harmonies) the Blackwood Brothers have been the standard by which a whole type of music has defined itself. As they pass their 60th anniversary in the country gospel field, the Blackwoods – via old recordings and performances they continue on the road and in their theatre – are reaching cult status with peers and fans alike. In early 1995 they received a special tribute on the Statler Brothers television show – the Statlers having acknowledged in song lyrics of their own the profound effect of the Blackwoods' original sound on ensembles like them.

The Blackwood Family Show is a nine-month-a-year attraction at the Thunderbird Theater at Branson, Missouri; the rest of the year the group tours. They have expanded their act to include country music and even standards of the '40s and '50s, but gospel remains their staple. The remarkable ensemble records these days for Choctaw Records.

Blue Sky Boys, The

One of the all-time classic brother duets, Bill (born 1917) and Earl (born 1919) Bolick both hail from Hickory, North Carolina. They were raised in the midst of the Southeastern school of country music – that of Gid Tanner, Fiddlin' Arthur Smith, Uncle Dave Macon – and were also enriched by family 'sings' of Church of God gospels. Bill, mandolinist, and Earl, guitar player, studied, collected and sang mountain and gospel music, and by 1935 were performing on radio in Asheville. The next year they recorded their first songs, and their name derived from the area around Asheville, which is called The Land of the Blue Sky. It is one of the prettiest parts of America, and was famed for its recuperative atmosphere by such varied ailing residents as humorist Bill Nye and the legendary country singer Jimmie Rodgers.

Through the 1940s the Blue Sky Boys toured widely and cut many records, including: 'Corrina, Corrina,' 'Jack O'Diamonds,' 'Midnight Special,' 'Oh, These Tombs,' 'Are

The Blue Sky Boys.

You From Dixie,' 'Kentucky,' 'There'll Come a Time' and 'I Believe It For My Mother Told Me So.' In the 1950s the Blue Sky Boys retired from music rather than compromising with the new trends. They had resisted electrified instruments and only reluctantly added a string bass in the '40s.

Recently the Blue Sky Boys have been sought out, and have performed occasionally. Bill's voice is a soft tenor, and Earl's a firmer baritone. They sing in a beautiful close harmony, almost as if their two voices are one, not in harmonics but in cadence, phrasing and purpose. Much of their material was mournful, delving back to old American and British ballads, but they could also bring light to their material with 'Sunny Side of Life' and such songs.

The Bolick brothers were youngsters when mountain music's brother harmony-duos were passing, and they were able to preserve the classic sounds until today. They are perfectly representative of the Southeastern school, devoting their music to sentiment, religion, home and simplicity itself. Their music sings also of a vanished time, one as unfortunately remote as their compelling sounds have been allowed to become.

Bogguss, Suzy

Illinois-born vocalist Suzy Bogguss was brought up on folk and country music. She began her singing career touring the Northwest in a pickup truck and camper with her dog and cat, and made her first breakthrough as a headliner at Dollywood, the Dolly Parton theme park in Tennessee. A recording contract with Capitol Nashville followed, and such hits as 'Somewhere Between,' 'Cross My Broken Heart,' 'Outbound Plane,' and 'Someday Soon' (the Judy Collins classic recast in country form), brought her a growing public. In 1992 Suzy was named the Top New Female Vocalist by the Academy of Country Music and received the Horizon Award from the Country Music Association. Her albums *Aces* and *Voices in the Wind* have both been certified gold.

A beautiful woman and an inventive songstress, Suzy stands squarely in the great tradition of New Country. She has a plaintive voice

Suzy Bogguss.

with the moving crack of the legendary female singers of the past, but employs it in the performance of thoroughly contemporary material. Her introspective love songs, many of them her own compositions or written by other women, reflect a woman's point of view which forms an important element of the New Country landscape.

The innovative stylings of Suzy Bogguss, with their classic sound and deeply felt lyrics, represent a vital contribution to New Country. In 1994 she cut an acclaimed album – and toured to acclaim – with Chet Atkins: *Simpatico*. Her recent hits have included 'Hey, Cinderella,' 'Hopeless Yours' (a duet with Lee

Greenwood), and a yodel-filled cover of the old Patsy Montana classic, 'I Want To Be a Cowboy's Sweetheart.' She played to sold out audiences with Dwight Yoakam in 1993, and Suzy's video 'Hey Cinderella' went number one on VH-1, CMT, and TNN.

Boxcar Willie

A self-anointed keeper of the hobo and train-song flames, Boxcar Willie was born Lecil Travis Martin in Sterratt, Texas, in 1931. It is a commentary on the current industry mindset in America that a perpetuator of such

Boxcar Willie.

traditional themes in country music would have to go overseas to achieve acceptance. This Willie has had to do, and although his base is now the Grand Ole Opry stage, he is still a bigger seller in Britain than in America.

Willie's early idols were Jimmie Rodgers, Hank Williams and Lefty Frizzell. His father was a railroad worker, and Willie claims that hoboes regularly camped near his house as a boy. From them, he says, was developed a fascination for their lifestyle and for railroad songs. Willie was performing on the radio at age 10, and in local clubs in his teens.

The guitar-playing singer eventually tried to score in Nashville, but found no encouragement. A visiting Scottish promoter, Drew Taylor, invited Willie to the United Kingdom, where he became a star. It was only after a television commercial offered his songs in the US – much in the same fashion as Slim Whitman's renaissance – that American audiences took note of Boxcar Willie. After massive mail-order sales of his train songs, Willie was invited to join the Grand Ole Opry in 1981.

Boxcar Willie sports hobo attire, and, although his act comes close to being as much novelty as musical, he has recorded many fine versions of genre songs, including his 1983 hit, 'The Man I Used to Be' as well as 'Daddy Was a Railroad Man,' 'Wabash Cannon Ball' and 'The Lord Made a Hobo Out of Me.'

He continues to maintain the vital country tradition trailblazed by Jimmie Rodgers, Cliff Carlisle and Goebel Reeves. Success with TV-album sales allowed Boxcar to open his own theater in Branson, Missouri, in 1987, the first Nashville entertainer to move his base of operations to the new country Mecca. He still makes an occasional appearance on the Opry.

Britt, Elton

One of country music's first superstars, Elton Britt was discovered because of his yodeling talents, and may be best remembered for his astounding yodeling versatility, but in between he had a crowded career of wide experience.

The possessor of one of the purest, prettiest voices in country music, James Britt Baker was born in 1917 in Marshall, Arkansas. The half-Cherokee youngster loved music – his father was a famed old-time fiddler in the area – and when barely a teenager he left the family farm and moved to Oklahoma, where radio singing beckoned. According to legend, the immortal Jimmie Rodgers, Britt's idol, was appearing at the nearby Pawnee Bill's Oklahoma Round-Up when he heard the youngster sing and yodel. Rodgers advised him to go to California and advance his career; Britt followed the suggestion and landed two plums: a year's contract on station KMPC in Los Angeles and a spot in the immensely popular singing group The Beverly Hill Billies, an outfit that Stuart Hamblen had just left.

Rodgers, hearing Britt sing again in California, wrote to his manager Ralph Peer, 'You'd better come out here and sign up this kid. . . . I think he's gonna make bums out of all of us. . . .' It was on his way to New York to make his first recordings that Britt heard of Rodgers's death in May 1933. It shattered him but steeled his resolve to follow in the master's footsteps.

Britt did sign with Rodgers's label, RCA, and did follow in Rodgers's style of old-time songs and mournful yodeling. Over more than 20 years, Britt recorded 672 single records and 56 albums for RCA alone; after the 1960s he recorded for several other labels as well. While still a teenager he performed for Franklin Roosevelt at the White House, and later toured extensively for US troops abroad (in Korea he contracted a fever that re-

Elton Britt.

curred throughout the rest of his life, curtailing his appearance schedule). He even starred in singing cowboy movies for Columbia and Universal.

It was Britt's smooth, warm voice alone that led to his achievements as one of the industry's most successful entertainers, however. 'There's a Star-Spangled Banner Waving Somewhere' was the first certified country gold record, ultimately selling more than 4 million copies. Other hits included 'Chime Bells,' 'Candy Kisses,' 'Born to Lose,' 'Grandfather's Clock' and 'Mockin' Bird Hill.'

The clarity and pyrotechnics of his yodels were seldom equalled in a field once crowded with such specialists, and many of his numerous hits featured his lilting falsettos. Fittingly, his last major hit was 'The Jimmie Rodgers Blues,' a seven-minute-long tribute song composed of song titles from his childhood idol's own list of hits. Elton Britt died in Pennsylvania in 1972, the Northeast having become his primary area for performing.

Brooks, Garth

Oklahoma-born Garth Brooks is a second-generation country singer who grew up in an atmosphere of show business but wasn't drawn to it himself until near the end of his high

Left and below: Garth Brooks, New Country's biggest superstar.

school years. The youngest son of Colleen Carroll, a country singer who recorded with Capitol and appeared regularly on TV's *Ozark Jamboree* during the 1950s, Garth attended Oklahoma State University on a javelin-throwing scholarship and got a degree in advertising. But music was in his blood, and while still in college he was already singing folk-rock in local clubs. In the mid-1980s, the year before he was to graduate, he tried out at Nashville's Opryland Park. His tryout was a success, and he was invited to become a part of Opryland's performance staff, but his parents talked him into finishing college first.

He was back in Nashville the next year, but the industry was not waiting with open arms for him, and a chastened Garth Brooks went home to Oklahoma to master his craft. A few years of playing honky-tonks, developing a distinctive country music style, and learning how to interact with an audience prepared him for another shot at Music City.

This time he was ready for Nashville and Nashville was ready for him. When he returned in 1989, he met ASCAP executive Bob Doyle, who formed a publishing company, and, with Pam Lewis, a management company, around him. A few months later the team received a contract from Capitol (now Liberty), which teamed Brooks with producer Allen Reynolds. It was an ideal match. Reynolds was known for the soft sound, gentle arrangements, and shuffling beat he had instilled in the performances of such popular country stars as Crystal Gayle, Don Williams, and Kathy Mattea, but he recognized that Garth's technique called for something different. He led him away from a vibrato and a manner of projection that recalled Gary Morris and toward a direct country baritone, a phrasing pattern like speech, and an emotional, throaty crack in his voice that suggests Hank Williams, Lefty Frizzell, and Merle Haggard.

The response to Garth's recordings has been nothing short of phenomenal from the beginning. His first album confidently bore the simple title *Garth Brooks* and has sold steadily since it was issued in 1989. With such singles as 'If Tomorrow Never Comes,' 'The Dance,' 'Not Counting You,' and 'Much Too

Young,' the album's sales figures now exceed five million. His next two have done even better. *No Fences*, containing such boisterous hit singles as 'Friends in Low Places,' was number one on the charts for months, and never lost that position until it was bumped by Garth's next album, *Ropin' the Wind*, which remained at the top for another four. They are the two biggest-selling albums in country-music history: *No Fences* at 11 million copies and *Ropin' the Wind* at 10 million. *Ropin' the Wind* is the only album in history to arrive on Billboard's Top 200 chart in the number one position.

Garth's videos have been no less successful. Some have been controversial: parts of *The Thunder Rolls* (starring Garth himself) were banned from some cable channels for the scenes of domestic violence they contained, but the video went on to win a CMA award. NBC aired an extremely popular television special on Garth in 1992, and PBS aired back-to-back specials featuring him in 1995. His face has become one of the best-known in country music, appearing in television news broadcasts and on the front pages of newspapers and on the covers of magazines.

Popular exposure has not been the only form Garth's success has taken; a list of his professional honors would fill pages. In 1990 the Country Music Association gave him its Horizon Award and in 1991 the Academy of Country Music conferred the first of its Country Music Entertainer of the Year prizes on him. In 1991 alone Garth received a combined total of 10 awards from the CMA and the ACM. He has also won Grammies and Nashville Network-*Music City News* awards. He was selected to sing the national anthem before the Super Bowl in 1993 – an honor conferred on only one country singer before him – and he has been made a member of the Grand Ole Opry.

Garth Brooks' popular and critical success, achieved within so short a time, has been unprecedented. One of the most popular singers not only in country music but in all entertainment history, he is a classic example of New Country. The vitality and intensity of his performance account only in part for his extraordinary impact. In personal appearances his dynamism is electric; using a microphone embedded in a headset to free him from a stationary mike, he strides and struts and storms across the stage, courting the audience with all the sensual energy of a country Mick Jagger. At the peak of his frenzy, he sometimes leaps off the stage, confident of being caught by his rapturous fans, without missing a beat of his song. These explosive performances evoke a response matched by few in country or any other kind of music.

But no less effective is the emotional authenticity of his voice; the traditionalist crack of country music that comes through as much on record as in live performance conveys a personal sincerity that the audience finds irresistible. The joy and pain in what he calls his 'heart songs' strike a responsive chord in the hearts of millions.

The video of the single 'We Shall be Free,' an anthem for world peace, was named Video of the Year by the Academy of Country Music in 1994; and Brooks was ACM's Entertainer of the Year the following year – the fifth year in a row. He has been the CMA Entertainer of the Year twice. He has been named *Billboard* magazine's Top Country Artist four times, and their Top Pop Artist twice. His 1994 World Tour played to sold-out crowds in excess of a quarter of a million people.

Brooks and Dunn

Two experienced performers who have performed as a team for a relatively short time, Brooks and Dunn met and pooled their talents only towards the end of 1990, when Tim DuBois, the head of Arista Records, brought them together. He had heard each of them and recognized the possibilities of combining their songwriting and singing talents.

Kix Brooks grew up in Louisiana, a friend and neighbor of Johnny Horton and his wife, a former wife of Hank Williams. Their example and encouragement provided the young man with his first inspiration – it was, as Kix has noted, his 'first exposure to gold records' – and while he was in college he began playing country music. His raw honky-tonk style carried him to clubs from New Orleans to Maine and even to Alaska, where he worked for a time on the oil pipeline. Finally he took a job as a staff writer with Tree

Kix Brooks and Ronnie Dunn.

Publishers in Nashville, writing for some of the leading acts in the field. His songs included 'Bobbie Sue,' written for the Oak Ridge Boys, 'I'm Only In It for the Love,' created for John Conlee, 'Modern Day Romance,' for the Nitty Gritty Dirt Band, and 'Who's Lonely Now' for Highway 101. Nashville's official theme song, 'I Still Hear the Music,' was a collaboration between Kix and Chris Waters (Holly Dunn's brother).

Ronnie Dunn is a Texan who chose music over religion when his performances in local honky-tonk joints got him kicked out of Baptist Bible College. He went to Oklahoma, where he joined Leon Russell's group in Tulsa and fronted the house band at the Duke's Country Club. Eric Clapton's drummer, Jimmy Oldecker, was impressed with Ronnie's music and registered him in the Marlboro Music Talent Roundup, a

local competition which sent him to Nashville for the nationals which he also won. This triumph brought him to the attention of DuBois.

Together, Kix and Ronnie garnered honors in several categories from the beginning of their partnership. In 1992 the team's first album, *Brand New Man*, received a nomination from the Country Music Association as Album of the Year; they won the Horizon Award given in recognition of the promise of future success; and they took the Vocal Duo Award over such competition as the Bellamy Brothers and the Judds for success already achieved. It is rare for any act to receive recognition from the CMA in three different competitions in one year. Their album was a great popular success, too, and its title cut was a big hit. Their next recording, the single 'Boot

Brooks and Dunn in concert.

Scootin' Boogie,' did even better on the charts, becoming an anthem in many dance clubs around the country.

Brooks and Dunn complement each other in a style that audiences have found very appealing. Their harmonious fusion of rock and blues, seasoned with a pinch of Mexican chili pepper, somehow remains essentially honky-tonk country music, and their stage style similarly blends unlike elements into an effective mix. Ronnie stays poised close to the mike while Kix provides the kinetic energy, interacting vigorously with the band and the audience. Together they achieve a balanced and unified presence that has found favor with a growing number of fans. They were named Top Vocal Duet by the Academy of Country Music in 1994. Their most recent CD is *Waitin' On Sundown*.

Brown's Ferry Four

Many of country's roots can be found in gospel's old-time hymns, camp-meeting songs and preoccupations with sinning and salvation. At one time virtually every country performer – even those who sang the most worldly of lyrics in their repertoire – performed a quota of gospel in their records and concerts.

This shoe fit some better than others. Keeping the country/gospel traditions, and singing with heartfelt sincerity, was the group Brown's

Ferry Four; and in evidence of their sincerity was the fact that the group never made a big push to go commercial in spite of public interest over nearly two generations. In fact the group was more a collection of friends gathering to sing gospel tunes – and a changing group of friends at that – than a formal combo.

On the *Midwestern Hayride* radio program of Cincinnati's WLW in the early '40s was a collection of some of country music's greatest contemporary talent. The Delmore Brothers, Alton and Rabon, were there, and they formed the core of Brown's Ferry Four; also at the station were guitar master Merle Travis and Grandpa Jones. These were the singers who started singing old-time gospel songs in straight four-part harmony with a minimum of guitar accompaniment. Besides the *Hayride*, the quartet sang on WLW every morning.

'Alton and Rabon lived by Brown's Ferry Road in Alabama,' Grandpa Jones remembered. 'We were trying to name the quartet and Alton said, "Why don't we call it the Brown's Ferry Four?" ' The Delmore's harmony was, as always, smooth as silk, as was Travis's guitar backup. Jones' nasal tenor was just the right touch to keep the simple gospel songs down to earth and reminiscent of local, spontaneous, homey songs.

When the King Record label started across town in 1943, Brown's Ferry Four was among the first of what was to be a long list of country and blues performers it discovered

and promoted. Through the years the group continued to sing, perform and record, usually with shifting personnel. The Delmores had Red Foley and Lewis Innis sing with them, and, in California, Rome Johnson and Roy Lanham – two voices from The Sons of the Pioneers. The group's identity was preserved long after the deaths of the Delmore Brothers, and in 1976 Grandpa Jones recorded an album side for CMH with the old straightforward gospel harmonies, sharing credit on the album cover (but not identifying the singers in this latest incarnation) with Brown's Ferry Four.

Brown's Ferry Four performed every great gospel quartet, new or old; a listing of their hymns would be a catalog itself of the earnest musical thread that underpins much of country music.

Byrd, Tracy

Another in the seemingly endless line of talented Texans in New Country music, Tracy Byrd, a native of Beaumont, is the son of hardcore country fans who took him to the Grand Ole Opry for the first time while he was still a babe in arms. His father spent 30 years as a blue-collar worker and his mother was a teacher's assistant who also drove a school bus. 'They both worked hard for a living and that's what my songs are all about,' Byrd said. His favorite music is a blend of the classic Western swing of Bob Wills and the modern melodies of George Strait.

Byrd attended college at Southwest Texas State in San Marcos and at Lamar University. He began performing as a solo act and a band singer and continued to perform while working as a law firm runner and later as a housepainter.

His musical break came when he landed a job with Mark Chesnutt who was then the headline act at Cutters nightclub in Beaumont. When Chesnutt's records hit the charts and he went on the road, Byrd succeeded him as the headliner at Cutters.

It took two trips to Nashville before he signed a contract with MCA Records. Then his single, 'Holdin' Heaven,' went to number one on the charts. His second album, *No Ordinary Man*, was produced by the veteran Jerry Crutchfield.

Campbell, Glen

Born in Delight, Arkansas, in 1936, Glen Travis Campbell was given his first Sears Roebuck guitar at the age of four, and two years later was locally famed for his picking. When he left school at 14 he joined his uncle's Western Swing band in Albuquerque. He later formed his own band that played throughout the Southwest, and then moved west to California.

Campbell's amazing guitar prowess kept him busy as a session man on recordings (a 1950s rock instrumental, 'Tequila,' was credited to The Champs, an ensemble of sidemen that included Campbell, Jimmy Seals and Dash Crofts. The group became a road act – without Campbell – for seven years). As a session player, Campbell backed up the likes of Frank Sinatra and Elvis Presley, as well as countless country singers.

Through the early 1960s various Campbell singles were released with little success, and in 1965 the eclectic musician-singer even subbed for Brian Wilson on a Beach Boys tour. But two years later his career took off when his recording of John Hartford's 'Gentle On My Mind' became a smash hit. The Academy of Country Music named Campbell Male Vocalist of the Year in 1967 and 1968; the group did not yet have an Entertainer of the Year category, which award Campbell won from the CMA in 1968. He followed 'Gentle' with the best-selling hit 'By the Time I Get to Phoenix.'

Between 1968 and 1972, Campbell hosted the *Glen Campbell Goodtime Hour*, a network program of excellent production and material; it also featured a first-rate cast of regulars including John Hartford, Larry McNeely, Jerry Reed, Mel Tillis, Pat Paulsen, Eddie Mayehoff and the Mike Curb Congregation. Campbell used his program as a showcase for important country talent.

His sudden stardom and youthful manner landed him movie roles – in *True Grit* with John Wayne, and in *Norwood*, a starring vehicle – but Campbell remained primarily a

Country-turned-gospel singer Glen Campbell.

singer, racking up more hits, including: 'Galveston,' 'Dreams of the Everyday Housewife,' 'Wichita Lineman,' 'Sweet Dream Baby' and 'Try a Little Kindness.' Just when his career seemed a little quiet he hit with enormous successes like 'Rhinestone Cowboy' (in 1975), 'Country Boy,' 'Southern Nights' and 'Any Which Way You Can,' from the Clint Eastwood movie soundtrack.

Through the years Campbell sang duets with singers in different modes – Bobbie Gentry, Tennessee Ernie Ford, Anne Murray, Rita Coolidge, Steve Wariner and Tanya Tucker, with whom he had a stormy, tabloid-splashed romance. Mac Davis's wife also moved in with Campbell at one point when he was scoring higher in the gossip columns than the music charts. But recently Campbell has experienced a religious conversion and has straightened out what he says was a troubled life.

Glen Campbell's recent conversion has been complete – not only does he have a new relationship with the Lord, but his music has been transformed into a gospel music that is more Contemporary Christian than country. He records for Word Records and tours with gospel acts, and is receiving enthusiastic airplay on Contemporary Christian music radio stations. He also owns a dinner theater in Branson, Missouri.

Carlisle, Bill and Cliff

The Carlisle Brothers, and various other Carlisle family aggregations, were some of the most versatile country music acts for years. Cliff was born near Taylorsville, Kentucky, in 1904, and first recorded around 1924. He pioneered the use of the dobro, the slide-resonant guitar first manufactured by the Dopera Brothers. Cliff had also played a slide guitar on some of Jimmie Rodgers' recordings, and kept the Singing Brakeman's style alive by performing in his mode and, later, cutting the first yodeling duets on record.

Cliff worked with Wilbur Ball in a Hawaiian-music act, the Lullaby Larkers, and later toured on the B F Keith vaudeville circuit and played the Chautauqua tents. He recorded as Cliff Carlisle and His Buckle

Mary Chapin Carpenter.

Busters, although he also cut some risque numbers as Bob Clifford. His musical specialities also included – besides Hawaiian, risque and yodeling – hobo songs and mainstream country. He retired, after a distinguished, pioneering solo career, and as half of a brother duet, in 1947.

Bill Carlisle was born in Wakefield, Kentucky, in 1908, and followed his brother Cliff into professional music. From the late 1920s to the early 1940s the brothers, often performing as a team, were very popular regional artists – in the Southern Ohio/Louisville/Lexington area specifically, and the Midwest and Southeast generally. After Cliff retired, Bill formed The Carlisles on Cincinnati radio, and specialized in novelty and comedy songs. His first big hit was 'Rainbow at Midnight,' and other popular records have included 'Rattlesnake Daddy,' 'No Help Wanted,' 'Too Old to Cut the Mustard,' and 'What Kinda Deal Is This?'

After joining the staff of the *Louisiana Hayride*, Bill was invited to join the Grand Ole Opry in 1954, where he remains today. The Carlisles today includes Sheila Carlisle; Bill Carlisle Jr and Marshall Barnes.

Besides his inevitable comedy songs and his humorous alter-ego, Hot Shot Elmer, Bill's most recognized trademark is his jumping – lustily, with a loud whoop, and with guitar in hand – at a high point or conclusion of a song.

Carpenter, Mary Chapin

Mary Chapin Carpenter brought an urban background to country music. Born in Princeton, New Jersey, and raised there, in Tokyo, and in Washington, D.C., she holds a degree in American Studies from Brown University, and began her career singing folk and protest songs to Ivy League college students in coffee houses.

Her acoustic folk singing went over well in Washington, where she won a 'Whammy' award from the Washington Area Music Association. A demo tape she made there in the basement of her guitar player caught the ear of Columbia Records and brought her a contract in 1987.

Her second album, *State of the Heart*, drew together her distinctive qualities and her personal identity. It revealed a voice with an edge to it and a New Country delivery which projects insightful lyrics with a rock beat and occasional Cajun instrumentation. From it, the single 'How Do' brought her first top 20 hit, and 'This Shirt' made the Adult Contemporary charts. Her next album, *Shooting Straight in the Dark*, was also a success: Its single 'Down at the Twist and Shout,' an up-tempo Cajun dance song, so engaged former president George Bush that he was clapping in rhythm to it on national television at the Country Music Association Awards in 1991. Mary Chapin received the Academy of Country Music's Best New Female Vocalist Award in 1989 and the CMA's Best Female Vocalist Award in 1992.

Mary Chapin describes herself as 'a singer with an acoustic guitar fronting a rock 'n' roll band.' The combination (with a pinch of Cajun spice thrown in) adds up to a solid New Country sound, combining country, rock, folk, and blues influences.

Carson, Fiddlin' John

In a strict sense John Carson was the first country music recording star. Eck Robertson ('Sally Gooden') preceded him on a record, but Robertson's disc was not heavily promoted and he did not record again for nearly a decade. Henry Whitter ('Wreck of the Old '97') recorded before Carson, but his record was not released until later. Carson was signed with a strict promotional campaign in view; it worked, and Carson became the first touted artist of a new line of American music, with his hit 'The Little Old Log Cabin in the Lane.'

He was born in Fannin County, Georgia, in 1868, three years after the end of the Civil War. By age 10 Carson was playing his grandfather's fiddle, a Stradivarius copy dated 1714. When he grew up, Carson was a jack of many trades – jockey, mill foreman, painter, moonshiner – but was decidedly a master of the fiddle. He was seven times Georgia fiddling champion, and was an attraction at

Fiddlin' John Carson.

political rallies for his friend Tom Watson, Southern Populist and vice-presidential running-mate of William Jennings Bryan. Carson was one of the first country performers to appear on radio, on Atlanta's WSB, where he became a favorite.

It was this popularity that prompted Atlanta business and local Okeh Records representative Polk Brockman to recommend Carson to recording executive Ralph Peer. On June 14, 1923, in Atlanta, Peer recorded Carson ('The Little Old Log Cabin in the Lane' and 'That Old Hen Cackled and the Old Rooster's Goin' to Crow.') Peer thought that Carson's singing was simply awful, and was even dubious about the rough-hewn fiddling. But Brockman ordered 500 copies of the record, unlabeled and uncatalogued, on the spot – and sold them out in short order.

Peer smelled success, put the record in his company's catalog and began to promote what came to be called hillbilly music. He also took off the shelf an audition recording he had also rejected a few months earlier – Henry Whitter's 'Wreck of the Old '97' – and it, too, became a hit. As the market for rural music blossomed in the 1920s, some estimates have it that Carson's premiere recording sold in excess of half a million copies.

Carson formed a band, the Virginia Reelers, that included his daughter Rosa Lee, known as Moonshine Kate. For years he toured in fiddlers' contests, accepting chal-

lenges from local players, and he continued on Atlanta radio. He was indeed a wizard on the fiddle, and mastered jigs, reels, hornpipes and breakdowns. A colorful personality as earthy and spirited as his fiddling at times was, Carson was of a region and an era that spawned other fiddlers, including Clayton McMichen, Gid Tanner and Fiddlin' Arthur Smith, who acknowledged Carson's mastery.

Carter Family, The

The First Family of country music, literally and figuratively, the Carters were focused around Alvin Pleasant Delaney 'Doc' Carter (known as A P professionally), who was born in Maces Spring, Virginia, in 1891. He had a musical father who abandoned playing for religious reasons, but Mrs Carter taught her eight children to play. A P met Sara Dougherty, a singer and autoharpist, and married her in 1915.

In 1926 A P's brother Ezra married Sara's cousin Maybelle Addington, who joined Sara and A P to form the musical Carter Family. The trio became local favorites. Although today they seem to be the essence of ancient, seminal country music, they actually stretched the boundaries of country and mountain music. They were innovative musicians who placed an emphasis on vocals and harmonies. Before the Carters there were, generally speaking, solo vocalists, and there were instrumentalists, in the various types of music that composed country – mountain, folk, old-time etc. From religious music out of the camp meetings and revivals, the shape-note hymnals and rural church quartets, came an impetus toward harmonies. The Carter's synthesis of harmony singing and prominent instrumentation – making instruments the partners of the voice, not dominant or submissive as before – was part of the revolution they wrought.

A P responded to a newspaper ad placed by Victor scout Ralph Peer, who was combing the South for local artists in an effort to score a success with rural white music (black recordings, or 'race' music, had recently proved a boon). In Peer's makeshift recording studio over a store in

AP, Maybelle (seated) and Sara Carter.

Bristol, Tennessee (across the street from Bristol, Virginia) he recorded 'The Wandering Boy,' 'Bury Me Under the Weeping Willow' and four other songs by the Carter Family. The date was August 2, 1927, according to Maybelle's later recollections. Later that week Jimmie Rodgers recorded there in the same manner.

Sara sang lead, A P sang bass and Maybelle was the alto harmony on these and subsequent recordings – for the Carters were an instant success in a nation where record players were beginning to permeate rural areas. 'Wildwood Flower' and 'Foggy Mountain Top' were two hits, and in 1931 the Carters recorded some sides with Jimmie Rodgers that included music and banter. Their other classic songs included 'Keep On the Sunny Side.' 'Room in Heaven for Me,' 'The Titanic,' 'Homestead on the Farm,' 'Meeting in the Air,' 'You Are My Flower,' 'I Shall Not Be Moved,' 'Can the Circle

June Carter and Johnny Cash.

Be Unbroken,' 'Wabash Cannonball,' 'I'm Thinking Tonight of My Blue Eyes' and 'Jimmy Brown, the Newsboy.'

Although A P and Sara separated in 1933, they continued to perform together musically (for a time with their children Joe and Janette), and in 1938 the Carter Family settled for a year in Del Rio, Texas, in order to perform on pirate station XERA in Mexico, which blanketed half of the North American continent with its broadcasts. In 1939 the ensemble dissolved, with Maybelle later forming the Original Carter Family with her daughters (Anita, Helen and June) and grandchildren. For a while in the 1950s A P performed as a soloist. A P, Sara and Mother Maybelle were elected to the Country Music Hall of Fame in 1970; A P had died in 1960, Maybelle in 1978, and Sara in 1979.

The Carter Family was influential in country music in a host of ways. A P collected and copyrighted hundreds of traditional and folk songs; while his actual authorship of many

is in question, he was not doing it to deceive but rather to earn royalties on Carter versions. Most importantly, he gathered and codified a body of rural music that might otherwise have been lost. Musically the Carters were inspirations to a generation of pickers. Maybelle's guitar licks were copied widely, and the Carters popularized the three-chord mode that still characterizes country, if not Western, music.

Jimmie Rodgers relied almost exclusively on the three-chord structure as well, which relates to the momentous week they both recorded in Bristol. Neither the Carters nor Rodgers were the first country artists on record, as is widely written. Grayson and Whitter, Eck Robertson, Carson J Robison, Vernon Dalhart, Pop Stoneman – these and many others preceded them. Riley Puckett even yodeled on record years before Rodgers sat before a microphone, and many of these artists had huge sellers among their records.

But the Carters, and Rodgers, simply caught fire. They not only recorded popular songs, as others did, but they sang a type of music that inspired people to alter their own performing styles, or to enter music professionally. The Carter Family, in subtly combining several forms of music, created a new strain.

Despite those who preceded them, it can be said that the Carters and Jimmie Rodgers founded modern country music on that sleepy August week in 1927. It is a broad but valid generalization to say (keeping in mind that there was constant cross-pollination) that all types of country music grew from the Carter Family and Jimmie Rodgers. From Rodgers sprang a line including country blues, uptown songs, honky-tonk and, with other influences, Western Swing. And while Rodgers was father to rambling and rowdy themes, the Carters were identified with home and introspection. The sound of the Carter Family was directly responsible for the various forms of mountain music, old-time, blue grass and gospel.

The latest shining light is Carlene Carter (daughter of June Carter and Carl Smith), who has charted several Country hits in the 1990s.

Carter, Mother Maybelle

Born Maybelle Addington in Nickelsville, Virginia, in 1909, Maybelle Carter was an accomplished musician from a young age, playing at dances and house parties in the Clinch Mountain area. In 1926 she married Ezra Carter, whose brother, A P Carter, was married to Maybelle's cousin Sara. 'We married brothers; that's how the Carter Family got started,' Maybelle recalled in 1973.

On records the Carter Family got started in 1927 at a pioneer recording outpost temporarily set up in Bristol, Tennessee (Jimmie Rodgers recorded his first sides the same week). The Carters became protean country 'stars,' with high record sales and a full schedule of appearances, although they maintained decidedly lower profiles than other contemporaries like Uncle Dave Macon. The Carter Family continued to play their mountain and country music around America, including a stint from powerful Mexican pirate transmitters. But in 1943 the ensemble broke up, following by several years the divorce of Sara and A P.

Maybelle played as a solo attraction on Richmond radio station WRVA between 1943 and 1947 and in 1948, in Knoxville, Tennessee, she formed The Original Carter Family ensemble with daughters who had been appearing with her in Virginia (Chet Atkins also joined the aggregation about this time). In 1949 they were featured performers on the *Ozark Jubilee* in Springfield, Missouri, moving to Nashville and the Grand Ole Opry in 1950. Maybelle remained a member until 1967.

The Original Carter Family, featuring daughters Anita, Helen and June, were original in title only, Maybelle being the only connecting link. Although the troupe retained its old-time associations and performed rural music, they also kept abreast of new trends in country music. In the 1950s they toured with Elvis Presley until his military service intervened; later, when June was married to Johnny Cash, they were part of the *Johnny Cash Show* on stage and on television. In recent years Anita's daughter Lori and Helen's son David joined the ensemble. Although the Original Carter Family recorded infrequently, in the 1970s they had a moderate single and album success with *Travellin' Minstrel Band*.

Maybelle as a soloist in recent years appeared at the Newport Folk Festival, and was a prominent component of the landmark 1972 recording project, *Will the Circle Be Unbroken*, which gathered many of country music's great talents. The following year she was the focus of a double album, *Mother Maybelle Carter*, that hinted at being a retrospective, but was really a collection of old and mostly new instrumentals with Nashville sidemen. A retrospective album would have been interesting, but this set in fact represented Maybelle's career-long modest accommodation with different trends.

She was accomplished on the autoharp (which she often picked for melody as well as strumming), an instrument that was part of country music's Virginia heritage (Pop Stoneman also played one), just as the accordion became a part of regional country sounds in Louisiana and Texas. Maybelle also played the banjo and fiddle, but the guitar was her instrument. She was one of the most influential of all country guitar pickers, possessor of probably the most copied style until the advent of Merle Travis; its hallmarks included bass licks, bass melody notes and treble chording and her patented cut-strums. Her vocals were plaintive and sincere, and, in the tradition of her mountain background, basic and unadorned.

For her amazing contributions to country music, and her love for all types of country music, Maybelle Carter well earned two honors: the nickname 'Mother of Country Music,' and election to the Country Music Hall of Fame in 1970.

Among the songs closely identified with Mother Maybelle Carter through the years are: 'Can [or Will] the Circle Be Unbroken,' 'Wildwood Flower,' 'You Are My Flower,' 'Keep on the Sunny Side,' 'I'm Thinking Tonight of My Blue Eyes,' 'The Blood that Stained the Old Rugged Cross,' 'Softly and Tenderly,' 'Walk a Little Closer,' 'Lonesome Homesick Blues' and 'I've Got a Home in Glory.' Maybelle died in 1978.

Cartwright, Lionel

Multi-talented performer Lionel Cartwright is a singer, instrumentalist, songwriter, and comedian who was born in Ohio but only, as he has noted, 'because the hospital was there.' Raised in West Virginia, he got his big break, like many country music stars, at a local equivalent of the Grand Ole Opry, West Virginia's popular Wheeling Jamboree. Already a veteran of local radio in Ohio, where he performed while still in his teens, he went on to 'Country Cavalcade' on WMNI in Columbus before returning home to Wheeling. There he worked his way through Wheeling College playing piano with the Country Roads, the house band of station WWVA's Wheeling Jamboree, where he eventually became music director of the weekly radio concert.

Nashville was the inevitable next move, and Lionel went on to work as star performer, arranger, and musical director of the sitcom 'I-40 Paradise' and its spinoff 'Pickin' at the Paradise' for the Nashville Network. He both wrote and performed the theme song of each show and performed in comedy sketches.

After establishing a solid success in Music City television, Lionel turned his full attention to singing and writing. With a contract at MCA he made it to the top 20 list with his rendition of Paul Overstreet and Don Schlitz's characteristically folksy and faith-inspired 'Like Father Like Son.' National popularity came with his 'I Watched It All (On My Radio),' a homage to nighttime radio programs which had given shape to the talented performer's burgeoning career.

Cash, Johnny

John R Cash was born in Kingsland Arkansas, in 1932, part Cherokee Indian. His dirt-poor family moved to Dyess, Arkansas, in a New Deal resettlement program and Johnny, after working long hours on poor soil, found solace in music. He started to write his own material at 12, and while in high school became a performer on local radio. He bought a guitar while stationed with the Army in Germany during the Korean War, and upon discharge moved to Memphis.

In Memphis he met Luther Perkins, guitarist, and Marshall Grant, bassist, and the trio played locally. They also auditioned for Sun Records, but were rejected for being 'too country.' However the rhythm and blues/rockabilly/rock 'n' roll label signed Johnny Cash and the Tennessee Two (as they now bill themselves) soon after Elvis Presley departed the label for RCA. 'Hey Porter' was released and became a hit. Johnny was invited to join the *Louisiana Hayride*, and he followed up with other hit singles: 'Folsom Prison Blues,' 'I Walk the Line,' and a vocal version of 'Orange Blossom Special,' among others. In 1957 Johnny joined the Grand Ole Opry.

Drummer Bill Holland joined the troupe to round out the Tennessee Three; by now Cash was recording for Columbia and scoring major country successes with records like 'I Guess Things Happen That Way' while also attracting pop and folk interest. But in spite of the sudden but steady success, Johnny's personal life was unraveling. He coped badly with the pressures, his close friend

Johnny Horton died, his marriage broke up and he became dependent on drugs and alcohol.

In public, however, Johnny's star continued to rise, propelled by a kind of obsessive creativity. During these turbulent days he recorded many classic songs, including 'Ring of Fire.' 'Understand Your Man' and 'Jackson' (a duet with June Carter who had joined his show).

Johnny married June Carter, after (and not until, as she explained) she helped him straighten out the problems in his personal life. Since then Johnny has also experienced a re-dedication to Christianity, and has

spoken of his new strength. To his road show Johnny added, in succession, the Carter Family and Mother Maybelle Carter, the Statler Brothers and Carl Perkins. He recorded 'A Boy Named Sue' – ironically it was a novelty hit that cemented this country giant's presence in all areas of the American audience – and a *Live at Folsom Prison* album. In 1969 Johnny was named Country Music Association Entertainer of the Year, and the same year he began a superb network television show that ran

Below: Johnny Cash in concert in 1983.
Right: Johnny Cash in 1994.

into 1971. Johnny has hosted several country network specials; through the years he has also starred in many movies, including a Western with Kirk Douglas: *The Gospel Road*, his own Biblical production filmed in the Holy Land; and drive-in quickies like *Door-To-Door Maniac* and *Five Minutes to Live*.

Among the large number of hit songs that are indelibly identified with Johnny Cash are 'See Ruby Fall,' 'It Ain't Me Babe,' 'Sunday Mornin' Comin' Down,' 'Daddy Sang Bass,' 'Flesh and Blood,' 'A Thing Called Love,' 'Five Feet High and Rising,' 'Ragged Old Flag,' 'One Piece at a Time,' 'I Would Like to See You Again,' 'There Ain't No Good Chain Gang,' 'Ghost Riders in the Sky,' 'I Wish I Was Crazy Again,' 'Cold, Lonesome Morning' and 'The Baron.'

As noted, Johnny through the years has appealed to listeners outside the country audience. In the late 1960s and early 1970s, for instance, he and Bob Dylan shared musical and recording influences, and Cash has recorded many speciality albums – gunfighter ballads, social-protest material on behalf of Indians, train songs, etc. It was his 'live' prison albums that fostered the myth of a dark past – actually Johnny had two extremely slight brushes with the law – but they are landmarks of genre performances as well as testaments of Johnny's enormous presence. Perhaps his own favorite was 1979's *A Believer Sings the Truth*, a double-record set of gospel songs.

In the late 1980s Cash severed his long relationship with Columbia Records and cut several albums for independent labels, notably *The Survivors* and *Class of '55*, which featured his old friends Jerry Lee Lewis, Carl Perkins and Roy Orbison. Since then his career has seen an amazing resurgence; he is again touring with The Tennessee Three, filling venues from Carnegie Hall to the most trendy pop clubs in Los Angeles. Cash received a Grammy for 1994's *American Recordings*, further evidence of his renewed popularity. He has been called 'the icon of Generation X,' a reference to his acceptance by fans who were born after he had already earned his place as a legend. Recent projects also include two best-selling books (an autobiography and a novelization of the conversion of the apostle Paul), movie and television roles and film production. Johnny Cash shows no signs of slowing down, and his "new" career promises even to eclipse the substantial accomplishments from his earlier efforts. He has even generated attention in the new field of country music videos, as a recent production showed a graphic depiction of violence in, appropriately, a return to his earliest of outlaw and outcast themes.

The voice of Johnny Cash is to many a very emblem of country music – rough, unpolished, proud and honest. As a performer Johnny is a personality to behold, full of scowls, smiles that resemble primitive sneers, a hulking, quivering body and face and an aggressive posture. He aims the guitar neck at the audience, plays it hoisted high, slings it over his back like a soldier's rifle. The patented sound of his backup band is a sure complement to his voice (sometimes it seems like Johnny Cash *talks* off-key); paper under the strings deadens the resonance of the guitar. There was never any mistaking a Johnny Cash record, or a Johnny Cash song, as straightforward and individual as the singer.

Chesnutt, Mark

The son of an aspiring performer and songwriter who played small clubs in Texas and wrote music for Cedarwood Publishing in Nashville, Mark Chestnutt served an apprenticeship in honky-tonk music; his father Bob immersed him in the sound of Ernest Tubb, Floyd Tillman, George Jones and Merle Haggard, playing him records and bringing him to clubs to hear it live. When young Mark quit high school to go on the road with his own country music performances, he did it with the whole-hearted encouragement of his father.

Mark achieved considerable success in his native Texas before making it to Music City. After a few fairly popular singles, he caught the national ear with 'Too Cold at Home,' the title cut of his first album, produced by Mark Wright for MCA. The album was the most successful debut in MCA's history, with no fewer than five number one songs. Since then he has built on his early success with such hits as 'Brother Jukebox,' 'Blame It on Texas,' and 'Broken Promise Land.' He followed his first album with *Long Necks and Short Stories*.

The affinity between Mark's native state and Tennessee has deep historical roots. Such pioneers as Tennessee's Davy Crockett joined forces with their compatriots in Texas in the ill-fated Battle of the Alamo in San Antonio, and since then the two states have shared happier occasions in the country music field. Western swing, which contributed the Western element of country-western, fuses the spirits of the two states, and Austin, Texas, has long been considered a satellite of Nashville, serving both as a refuge from Music City and a moral compass for it. East Texas and the Houston area have also served as a proving ground for many performers, providing regional talent to the country music capital. Mark Chesnutt is only one of many Texans, including such stars as Mickey Gilley, Gene Watson, and Kenny Rogers, who have repeated their regional triumphs in Nashville.

Mark Chesnutt's classic honky-tonk music owes much to the inspiration of his hero and vocal doppelganger George Jones, who has supported the younger singer with friendship and professional advice. Today Chesnutt stands solidly among the leading country stars, with records ranking among the top sellers in the genre. His most recent CD is *What a Way to Live*, and a recent hit single, 'Rainy Day Woman,' paired him with the veteran singer Waylon Jennings.

Chuck Wagon Gang, The

A unique quartet in the history of country and gospel music, The Chuck Wagon Gang has sung for half a century. Although it has had 39 members through the years, it is still largely a family group and still records and performs actively.

D P Carter founded the Carter Quartet in the mid-1930s and secured a spot on WYFO in Lubbock, Texas, for the group which consisted of himself and three of his nine children: Rose, Ernest and Anna, who was later the wife of Louisiana's singing governor, Jimmie Davis. The

Right: Mark Chesnutt.

Carter Quartet, then a Western singing ensemble, moved to WBAP in Fort Worth, where they were sponsored by Morton Salt. Soon thereafter, Bewley Flour lost their sponsored singers on the station, the Chuck Wagon Gang, and the Carters were asked to assume the role. The year was 1936, and the Carters have been singing as the Gang ever since, supported especially by the reaction of listeners and fans after they switched to gospel.

The Chuck Wagon sound is that of old-fashioned, open, country four-part harmonies. They have been virtually an *a capella* quartet, their usual backup being a lone guitar. In 1936 they began a 43-year association with Columbia Records, reportedly selling more records during that period than any other Columbia artists; today they record for Copperfield Records. Among their hit records have been 'I'll Fly Away' (they were the first to record the now-standard Brumley tune), 'The Son Hath Set Me Free,' 'Looking For a City,' 'Come Unto Me,' 'I Found a Hiding Place' and 'I'll Meet You in the Morning.' 'He Set Me Free,' a song recorded by the Chuck Wagon Gang, became the melodic basis for the Hank Williams gospel classic, 'I Saw the Light.'

The quartet has performed at Carnegie Hall and in the Hollywood Bowl, on the Grand Ole Opry, and in a motion picture, *Sing a Song for Heaven's Sake*. The Chuck Wagon Gang hosted a television series, *Gospel Round-Up*, and have recorded more than 400 songs through the years. A recent country song, 'Keep on Keepin' On,' was on music charts for 11 weeks.

Current members of the Chuck Wagon Gang – preserving the fine old sounds of four-part country and gospel harmony – include Roy Carter, Trisha Neighbors, Ruth Ellen Yates and Pat McKeehan.

Clark, Roy

The activities and talents of Roy Linwood Clark, born in Meherrin, Virginia, in 1933, seem as multifaceted and frenetic as his stage and screen personality, and indeed it seems that Clark has not rested since winning two consecutive national Country Music Banjo Championships in his mid-teens.

The young Clark grew up in Virginia, as well as in St Clairesville, Ohio; Staten Island in New York City; and Washington, DC. His father Hester was a computer programmer but – more important to Roy's development – was also an amateur musician, playing country and bluegrass music with family friends and performing at square dances.

Roy's first instrument was a cigarbox ukelele rigged by his father for a school play; at age 14 Roy received a Sears Roebuck guitar for Christmas, and by the next year he was performing with his father's square-dance band at military service clubs. In his late teens he was invited to the St Louis Browns baseball training camp, and won a string of boxing matches in Washington, DC, but his first love continued to be music.

In the early 1950s he guested on the *Jimmy Dean* TV show, and many other TV appearances followed: *Arthur Godfrey's Talent Scouts*, the *George Hamilton IV* Show, etc. He joined Wanda Jackson's band as a guitarist, and soon was a headliner himself. He played Las Vegas, and ultimately sold out Carnegie Hall and Madison Square Garden in New York. His list of TV credits lengthened – comedy appearances on the *Beverly Hillbillies* and *The Odd Couple*; singing on the *Griffin, Douglas, Sullivan* and *Dinah* shows; guest-hosting the *Tonight Show* and hosting several specials of his own.

His recording career paralleled these advancements. Clark's first number one hit was 'Tips of My

Roy Clark.

Fingers' in 1963, but his real smash – still the biggest record of his career – came in 1969 with his version of 'Yesterday, When I Was Young.' Later hits included 'Thank God and Greyhound You're Gone,' 'The Lawrence Welk-*Hee Haw* Counter-Revolutionary Polka' and 'Somewhere Between Love and Tomorrow.' Nineteen sixty-nine was also his lucky year, as he was invited to be the co-host of a network country music show, *Hee Haw*, with Buck Owens. The show was reasonably successful but countered CBS's sophisticated self-image, and was therefore cancelled. The producers decided to try its luck in syndication, and the rest, as they say, is history. The show became one of the most popular syndicated shows in history.

Probably because of his engaging personality, Clark is more popular in performance than on record. He plays nine instruments and injects a good dose of humor into his act. Indeed he has received awards as comedian as well as instrumentalist.

His voice can be described as a permanently hoarse tenor, and the emotion he brings to heart-songs sound like every drop of feeling has been wrung out for the task. His comedy includes facial grimaces during instrumental solos and throwaway lines in black dialect. It's as a picker that Clark shines, however, and the impressive talents he possesses cannot really be captured on disks. Perhaps his finest album is the *Family Album* of 1973, wherein his father, uncles and relatives gather to play bluegrass with him on *Hee Haw*.

A member of the Opry since 1987, Roy continues to host *Hee Haw* (now in syndication and on TNN). And though a long-popular showroom in Branson, Missouri, carries his name, he appears there only occasionally. Much of his time is devoted to interests outside the music business.

Cline, Patsy

Born in Winchester, Virginia, in 1932, Virginia Patterson Hensley showed an early aptitude for music and performing. At four she won a tap-dancing contest, and by eight she had sung regularly in church and had learned to play piano. When she was 16, she auditioned for a position on the Grand Ole Opry, but at that she failed, remaining in Nashville to

dance in small clubs before returning to Virginia.

In 1957 she won a prize on *Arthur Godfrey's Talent Scouts*, a network television program. Within days, her single of the song she performed, 'Walkin' After Midnight,' became an instant hit; she was signed to a Decca Records contract; she was booked on Godfrey's daily network show, and her husband, Gerald Cline, filed for divorce. Patsy took the good with the bad and within a few years – hampered temporarily by a restrictive contract with her original, local, record label – she was scoring

Patsy Cline.

country and pop hits, and was a member of the *Opry* at last.

Her hits included 'Crazy,' 'I Fall to Pieces,' 'She's Got You,' 'Faded Love' and 'Sweet Dreams.' On March 5, 1963, however, while her career was still ascending, Patsy was killed in a plane crash. She was returning with country singers Hawkshaw Hawkins and Cowboy Copas from a Kansas City benefit for an injured disc jockey. One of the few consolations to Patsy's countless fans has been the release through the

Mark Collie.

years of unreleased master recordings or re-mixed hits. These have included 'Any Time' (1969), 'Always' (1980) and 1981's 'Have You Ever Been Lonely,' a duet with the late Jim Reeves – both vocal tracks recorded at separate sessions and never originally intended as a duet.

Patsy Cline was elected to the Country Music Hall of Fame in 1973, and in 1977 Loretta Lynn – who had been befriended by Patsy when Loretta arrived in Nashville as a newcomer – recorded a tribute album, *I Remember Patsy*. Ryman Auditorium features a permanent tribute show, as does Branson's Grand Palace.

She was the first major female country singer to perform independently – not as a member of a group or duo. And in a period when female singers were finally proliferating on the country's record charts, Patsy Cline was easily the most popular of her time. Her popularity on pop radio stations reflected not only the production and arrangement on her records, but also the smoothness of her voice. But unlike others, Patsy Cline's pop smoothness was not akin to blandness; she sang almost in a personal manner, her voice full of tugs, sighs and emotion.

Collie, Mark

Mark Collie is a true son of Tennessee. Born in Waynesboro, between Nashville and Memphis, he reflects something of both of those two musical poles in his distinctive style. His career started early; his first job was playing in a band at the age of 12. ('I told them I was 14,' he recalls, 'but I'm sure they didn't believe me. I looked like I was nine.') He continued performing after he finished high school, racking up performance time throughout the South and as far west as Hawaii.

When MCA gave him a contract, his musical identity was well formed. His first two albums, *Hardin County Line* and *Raised in Black and White*, established that identity in the public ear and contained a number of hit singles. The first to make it to the top of the charts was 'Something with a Ring to It,' written with Aaron Tippin. Later 'Looks Aren't Every-thing' and 'Let Her Go' took their places in the top ten.

Mark appears widely in support of diabetes care and research. A diabetic himself, he must monitor his condition carefully in his strenuous performance schedule. Mark receives solid support from his wife Anne, whose faith in his career has sustained him through discouraging periods and who once threatened to leave him if he ever gave up music. Fortunately for him and for the public, he never has.

Mark recognizes the depth and breadth of the tradition from which he draws. 'My roots are like the roots of a tree.' he has noted. 'They go a long way in every direction.' Besides sensitive songs in the Kris Kristofferson and Willie Nelson tradition, he has fashioned a sound that fuses elements of honky-tonk, rockabilly, and country in to a style all his own.

Collins, Tommy

Born in Oklahoma City in 1930 as Leonard Raymond Sipes, Tommy Collins grew up loving country music, later singing it in local clubs while attending Oklahoma State University, and performing on several local radio stations. In the early 1950s he followed the path of many Depression-era Okies and moved to the Bakersfield area of California, which was beginning to emerge as a hotbed of country music activity.

Bakersfield in that decade spawned a host of great country talent, practically making it a Golden Age for a West Coast outpost of county purity during days of rock 'n' roll and the Nashville Sound. Besides Collins there was Buck Owens (who began as a guitar player in Collins' band), Jean Shepard, Ferlin Husky, Billy Mize, Bonnie Owens, Wynn Stewart, Red Simpson, Herb Henson, Buddy Alan and, of course, Merle Haggard, who became a close friend of Collins.

Tommy Collins.

Collins scored in records with a string of nationally popular novelty songs in the mid-1950s, and has had sporadic chart successes since then as a singer. But Collins's contributions to country music can never be any more notable than his songwriting legacy. He has composed more than 1000 songs, and many have been hits for other artists. For all of his own preoccupations with novelty songs, his output comprises an impressive collection of some of the most poetic, ironic and introspective lyrics in the field. Collins has scaled the heights and scratched the depths in his personal life; his own troubles and weaknesses have been reflected in his incredible lyrics.

Merle Haggard, for instance, has recorded a group of Collins songs that alone could stand as prime representatives of mature, significant country music at its best: 'When Did Right Become Wrong?,' 'Carolyn,'

'The Man Who Picked the Wildwood Flower,' 'The Funeral,' 'Goodbye comes Hard For Me,' 'The Roots of My Raising.'

Haggard in 1981 recorded a tribute song to Tommy Collins, 'Leonard,' chronicling not only the career of the songwriting genius, but the unique friendship and mutual support of their long relationship.

Confederate Railroad

Ten years on the road before they had their first hit record – that is the rough-and-tumble story of what may be the rowdiest country band of the 1990s. What other kind of band would think of calling their newly added trio of female vocalists The Trashettes?

A great sense of humor and a surprising sensitivity that manifests itself in change-of-pace songs are other hallmarks of the six-man band that features Chattanooga native Danny Shirley as lead vocalist. The other members of the band are Wayne Secrest, Mark Dufresne, Michael Lamb, Chris McDaniel, and Gates Nichols.

Their hit records include 'Trashy Women', (Chriss Wall/Jerry Jeff Walker anthem), 'Time Off for Bad Behavior,' and 'Jesus & Mama' (a song about a hardened criminal remembering the two people who have always continued to love him no matter what).

Vocalist Shirley came from a tough coal-mining region of East Tennessee that provided much of the inspiration for the band's songs as well as a perfect locale to film some of their videos. Their award-winning videos are clever and wild enough alone to ensure Confederate Railroads presence in country music.

For ten years the band toured with almost no changes in personnel. Finally after several labels shunned them because of their outlaw image, Rick Blackburn of Atlantic Records signed them; their first album, *Confederate Railroad* went platinum. In May 1993, the group won the Academy of Country Music award for Best New Vocal Group. Their second album, *Notorious*, contained more ballads, but at the last minute Shirley insisted on adding four songs that maintained the band's rough,

Confederate Railroad.

biker image: 'Elvis and Andy,' 'Move Over Madonna,' 'Summer in Dixie,' and what turned out to be the title tune of the album, 'Notorious'.

'She Took It Like a Man' has been one of Confederate Railroad's emblem hits, a combination of clever lyrics and hard-driving southern rock instrumentation. There is solid musicianship and vocal discipline in the group, carrying both ballads and uptempo songs, and allowing for a variety that will continue to make their albums – and their stage show, one of the liveliest and rowdiest in country music – compelling.

Cooley, Spade

Born Donnell Clyde Cooley in Pack Saddle, Oklahoma, in 1910, Spade Cooley (he earned the nickname, reportedly, for his card-playing skills) was raised on a farm. His family moved to a farm in Oregon when he was four, and there he learned to play a fiddle – actually a violin, as his training was in classical music. But finally devoting his interest to country music, Cooley played in the Modesto area when he was 20.

In 1934 Cooley moved to Los Angeles, where he worked as a stand-in for Roy Rogers in movies and played music locally with Jimmy Wakely and others. In the 1940s Spade Cooley founded his own band, a dance ensemble that was nominally Western Swing (often it

was broadened to appeal to the general public) and eventually Cooley was packing in 6000 dancers a night in his own Santa Monica ballroom. He also appeared in movies with his band, now as a musical figure, not a stand-in.

Cooley pioneered television on the West Coast when he premiered on KTLA's *Hoffman Hayride*. Some excellent musicians played for Cooley through the years – such as Tex Williams – but it was his smaller ensembles that let the country sounds shine through. Sometimes Cooley put together an enormous musical assemblage, and all too often they slavishly absorbed every latest musical or dance fad.

Spade Cooley.

In the early 1950s Cooley sustained a heart attack. He also had to deal with the decline of big-band music (he experimented widely, for a time fronting an all-girl orchestra), and coped as well with drinking and marital problems. In July of 1961, during a violent argument, Cooley killed his wife. Suffering another heart attack in jail, Cooley was a model prisoner. In 1969, while set 'free' in order to perform at a sheriff's benefit concert, Spade Cooley died backstage of a heart seizure.

Copas, Cowboy

A cowboy singer who actually came from cowboy country, Lloyd Copas was born in Muskogee, Oklahoma, in 1913. He was raised on a ranch, received the proverbial first guitar at the age of 10, and by 16 was already winning local talent contests. In 1935 he was discovered by promoter Larry Sunbrock and teamed with the Indian Natchee to appear in touring fiddle contests. 'Cowboy' Copas was a sideman to the main attraction – the 'Indian' would beat all comers, including nationally famed fiddlers. In 1940 Copas went solo; he joined the cast of the WLW *Boone County Jamboree*, and signed a recording contract with King Records, a local but important Cincinnati label.

During the War Copas recorded 'Filipino Baby,' a song that established him as a national star. In 1946 he joined Pee Wee King and the Grand Ole Opry, and rapidly had a string of hits with 'Kentucky Waltz' and 'Tennessee Waltz;' other major successes were 'Signed, Sealed and Delivered' and 'Tragic Romance.' After leaving the Golden West Cowboys he remained with the Grand Ole Opry and kept a loyal following although major record hits virtually disappeared during the 1950s.

In 1960 he scored with perhaps his biggest success, 'Alabam,' and his career seemed back on track. But he was in that doomed plane flying between concert dates in the company of Patsy Cline and Hawkshaw Hawkins. It crashed on March 5, 1963 in Camden, Tennessee, killing its legendary passengers. Eerily mirroring his own tragedy (and other events that have plagued country music like the untimely deaths of Jimmie Rodgers and Hank Williams, and the plane accidents that took the

lives of Jim Reeves and Buddy Holly) was Copas' hit record of 'Hillbilly Heaven.'

Above: Cowboy Copas (second from right).
Right: Rodney Crowell.

Crowell, Rodney

One of the most perceptive voices of modern country music, Rodney Crowell has added both shrewdness and depth to the genre. Born and brought up in the Houston, Texas, area, he was exposed to country music by his father and grandparents. He began by playing rock, but as Texas country music is hospitable to influences from such other styles as rock and folk, he was able to cross the sometimes shadowy line dividing them. The transition was complete by the time he moved to Nashville in the early 1970s.

There he found work writing songs for the popular Jerry Reed. When the celebrated singer and writer Guy Clark introduced him to Emmylou Harris, Crowell joined her Hot Band and found a perfect niche

for his talents. As a 'new traditionalist,' he was in tune with the element represented by Ricky Skaggs, who was to succeed him, while his fusion of folk, rock, and country fitted perfectly with Emmylou's style. During his time with the Hot Band, he created a number of Emmylou's biggest hits, including 'Amarillo' and 'I Ain't Livin' Long Like This.' His first album in 1977, took its title from the latter single. Songs from this album were to provide hits for other singers: Bob Seger did 'Shame on the Moon,' and Crystal Gayle had a hit with 'Till I Gain Control Again.'

Rodney's next two albums were enthusiastically received by the critics but did not sell well. It was at this point that he first joined Roseanne Cash, first as her producer and co-writer and then as her husband. The combination was stimulating and brought the duo a lot of attention in Music City. Unfortunately, though the marriage was energizing, it had a downside including bitter domestic conflict and problems with drugs.

By 1988 Rodney put his problems behind him, kicked the habit, and signed a new contract with CBS. His first album with them, *Street Language*, revealed an artist undiminished in skill, wit, and insight. His 1989 album *Diamonds and Dirt* was the one that made the breakthrough, with no fewer than five singles placing number one on the charts. Among them were 'It's Such a Small World,' 'I Couldn't Leave You If I Tried,' 'She's Crazy for Leavin',' and the Grammy-winning 'After All This Time.' *Keys to the Highway* followed with two more hits, 'Many a Long and Lonesome Highway' and 'Things I Wish I'd Said,' both moving tributes to his father. His 1992 *Life is Messy*, a poignant reflection on his divorce from Roseanne Cash, contained the hit crossover single 'What Kind of Love,' with harmony by Linda Ronstadt and Don Henley of the Eagles; two others included harmony by Steve Winwood.

An inventive and sensitive artist, Rodney had a long wait for commercial success, but the delay has done nothing to diminish his fine creative integrity.

Cyrus, Billy Ray

A combination of dynamic performing style, virile good looks, and shrewd merchandising has made Billy Ray Cyrus a superstar and has increased contemporary country music's popularity both in numbers and in range. Raised in Flatwoods, Kentucky, the son of a gospel band musician and the grandson of a preacher, he brings to the field an authentic rural background and a thorough grounding in country music.

Though he first dreamed of a career in baseball, the influence of Billy Ray's upbringing impelled him into music. He formed the band Sly Dog and toured locally, his performances leaning toward outlaw country and Southern rock rather than the gospel he had grown up with. He took the destruction of his gear by a fire as a sign, and relocated to Los Angeles, where he had a day job sell-

ing cars in Woodland Hills and formed a new band for such night work as he could pick up. Not very successful, he went back to Kentucky in 1986 and got steady weeknight work headlining at the Ragtime Lounge in nearby Huntington, West Virginia. Weekends he spent doggedly trying to sell his material in Nashville.

That was the turning point, after 10 discouraging years. A year after he began knocking on Nashville's doors, a demo tape of his caught the ear of Grand Ole Opry's Del Reeves. Impressed, Reeves recorded one of Billy Ray's songs and introduced him

Billy Ray Cyrus.

to manager Jack McFadden, whose clients had included Buck Owens and Merle Haggard. Things began to pop for Billy Ray; he got a recording contract from Mercury and was on his way to stardom. The Cyrus-Reeves connection had an unhappy ending; in 1992 Reeves brought suit against Billy Ray, whom he said he had considered 'the son I never had,' claiming the young singer had promised to cut him in on any major success he attained. And Billy Ray's first album, *Some Gave All*, was indeed a major success. Six of the album's 10 songs were his own compositions, and on a seventh he acknowledges the inspiration of, and shares credit and royalties with, his ex-wife who unintentionally inspired him when she threw the young singer out.

But the biggest hit of the album, and the song which brought Billy Ray his long-deferred stardom, was Don Von Tress's 'Achy Breaky Heart.' This became a national crazy, in part through the inspired merchandising of Mercury, which had the ingenuity to promote the song through country music dance clubs nationwide before releasing the video or radio station cuts. Mercury offered the clubs free material, including cassettes, a video of Billy Ray performing the number with a special segment instructing the viewer how to do the dance, suggestions for dance competitions with offers of invitations to Nashville for the winners, and a free appearance by Billy Ray to the winning club. After all of this, Mercury released the videos and the radio cuts to an audience which had already been worked up to a frenzy of anticipation. Certainly much of the rage for 'Achy Breaky Heart' was due to the emotional impact of the song and Billy Ray's electric performance of it, but Mercury's brilliant manipulation of the marketplace was an important factor.

The Achy Breaky was the dance of the year, sweeping the country and generating a degree of devotion to the singer who introduced it that came to be known as the 'Cyrus Virus'. The CMA unhesitatingly named 'Achy Breaky Heart' the Single of the Year in 1992, and that same year Billy Ray received the honor of singing the national anthem at the opening of the World Series. His music was everywhere on country music and rock stations. The title cut of his album, 'Some Gave All,' a tribute to veterans, was named the official song of the Vietnam observance rally on Veteran's Day in Washington, D.C. Billy Ray was the man of the hour in the media.

The explicit sensuality of Billy Ray's delivery places him in the 'hunky-tonk' tradition; he accompanies his act with suggestive bumps and grinds like a country version of Elvis, doing a partial strip-tease as he goes along, to the hysterical response of female fans who pelt him with their own undergarments. The stage presence and the emotional impact of Billy Ray Cyrus have enormously widened the audience for country music, although he has fallen short of the permanent high-grade emulation achieved by the few like Elvis Presley. The exception proved the rule about exceptional performers, and Billy Ray also encountered some resentment – personified by Marty Stuart's short-lived public criticism of Billy Ray's musicianship – from segments of the Nashville establishment. His most recent CD is *Storm in the Heartland*.

Cyrus acknowledges his many fans.

D

Dalhart, Vernon

In view of today's controversy regarding traditional country music and outside influences, it is amazing that country's first superstar was a 'crossover.' The real irony is that Vernon Dalhart crossed over from pop – and opera! – to record the first country music millionseller.

Born Marion Try Slaughter in 1883, Vernon Dalhart (who took his name from two Texas towns) was country enough, coming from a farm in Jefferson, Texas. But he had lofty musical ambitions, attending the Dallas Conservatory of Music, and seeking a career in New York. In 1912 he won a role in Puccini's opera, *Girl of the Golden West*. Within a few years he was forced to go more commercial, and he became a singer-demonstration salesman for the Edison Talking Machine Company. He began to record songs and his repertoire ranged from light opera to patriotic to the 'coon songs' then in vogue.

In 1924, however, he felt his career slipping further. He agreed – reportedly at the suggestion of Edison's son Charles – to expand his catalog of styles to include rural songs. He recorded his own version of Henry Whitter's 'Wreck of the Old "97",' and on the flip side recorded 'The Prisoner's Song,' a tragic love lament written by his cousin Guy Massey. The 'B' side proved to be a phenomenal success. It became Victor's largest-selling record of the pre-electric era, and some estimates place the total sales by the time of Dalhart's death at 75 million.

It is arguable that Dalhart viewed 'The Prisoner's Song' as just one more novelty song; certainly it was a mere assignment, and not a song from deep in his background, as other pioneer recording artists like 'Eck' Robertson and Fiddlin' John Carson were doing. However Dalhart took immediately to the genre and became the man – with the exception of Jimmie Rodgers – most responsible for establishing this new hybrid, country music, as a popular form of American music.

He teamed up with Carson Robison, the songwriter and guitar player, to produce a multitude of country songs over the next few years; many were 'saga' and 'event' songs, and most were hits. Typical among them were 'The Letter Edged in Black,' 'Golden Slippers' and 'My Blue Ridge Mountain Home.'

For all his remarkable successes, however, the singing career of Vernon Dalhart was all but finished in less than a decade after 'The Prisoner's Song.' Except for a flurry of activity in 1938, he made his last recordings in 1933; among his final musical job was singing as Singin' Sam, the Barbasol Man on radio commercials. He spent the fortune that was his, and – most ironic of all – the man who practically invented modern country music and paved the way for Jimmie Rodgers and the Carter Family died forgotten and poor, employed as a night clerk in a Bridgeport, Connecticut, hotel in 1948.

It is impossible properly to assess the full impact of Vernon Dalhart on country music, not so much because of his seminal pioneering work, but because he recorded for virtually every record label in America, using more than 100 stage names, including Wolf Ballard, Jep Fuller, Carlos B McAfee, and Val Veteran. In his day there were no exclusivity contracts, and Dalhart sometimes recorded the

Vernon Dalhart.

same song dozens of times for competing companies.

His vocal training was evident on his country records. Possessing an extremely pleasant tenor voice, Dalhart's tone and phrasing are polished, and it may well be that his professional resonance was a large part of his success on those early acoustic recordings. In recognition of his important contribution to country music, Vernon Dalhart was elected to the Country Music Hall of Fame in 1981.

Daniels, Charlie

A leader of the Southern Rock movement, Charlie Daniels was born in Wilmington, North Carolina, in 1936. He grew up listening to country music – ultimately he gained an awesome mastery of guitar, mandolin and fiddle – but got hooked on rock 'n' roll. Between 1958 and 1967 he played his music in countless small clubs, mostly through the South. He formed a band during this time and named it the Jaguars.

After this activity he moved to Nashville and became a sideman, picking up an increasing amount of work backing up recording artists; he kept at least one foot in another world by playing on Bob Dylan albums (including *Nashville Skyline*) and touring with the rock/folk-singer Leonard Cohen. He signed with Kama Sutra Records, formed the Charlie Daniels Band and, in 1973, began recording a string of hit records in his singular combination of rock and country modes.

The Southern Rock movement gathered around Daniels, and included bands like The Marshal Tucker Band and The Allman Brothers. Each year Daniels hosted the Volunteer Jam in Nashville, where such stylists gathered to play and, sometimes, record. Daniels played on the album that marked Hank Williams JR's transition to Southern Rock sounds, and produced a brilliant double-album tribute to Hank Sr, featuring Jim Owens (who tours as Hank Sr) and members of the original Drifting Cowboys Band, as well as Charlie Daniels Band personnel.

Daniels won awards as instrumentalist and band leader from the Country Music Association. The glorification of drugs in some of his

lyrics, however, as well as his liberal political identification, gave him a specialized, rather than a broad-based, audience in the field of country music.

Charlie Daniels has made some changes in the past few years, and his career has gotten a bounce. Now a born-again Christian, Charlie records for Word Records, and hosts a TNN television program every Opry night showcasing new talent. He has lost his scowl and come out from under the shadow of his trademark ten-gallon hat. Besides per-

Charlie Daniels on the fiddle.

forming and recording on his own, he has recently lent his talents to jam projects such as the Mark O'Connor fiddle all-star CD *Heroes*.

Davis, Jimmie

James Houston Davis was born in 1902 in Quitman, Louisiana, and grew up nearby in Beech Springs. He played guitar and sang in his youth, but only as a sideline; his academic pursuits led him to a professorship of

Jimmie Davis.

history at Dodd College after attaining a masters degree. The sideline, however, became a mainline as amateur singing turned professional. Davis sang in 1928 for a Shreveport radio show, and his reputation grew from local to regional and national, especially after Gene Autry recorded two of his songs, 'Nobody's Darling But Mine' and 'You Are My Sunshine.' Davis also got songwriting credit on an enormously popular Floyd Tillman song, 'It Makes No Difference Now.'

A recording star in his own right, Davis rolled up many hits, and a crowning culmination to such a career would have been starring in his own movie (1944's *Louisiana*), except that other fields beckoned. Having served in statewide public administration offices in the 1930s, Davis aspired to politics, and was elected governor of Louisiana in 1944, serving four years.

As a private citizen again he returned to music, but increasingly devoted his output to gospel songs. His big hits included in these years were 'Suppertime,' 'Honey in the Rock,' 'Take My Hand, Precious Lord,' 'Columbus Stockade Blues' and 'Someone to Care' (later the theme song of fellow Louisianan Jimmy Swaggart). He served a second term as governor from 1960-64, and then performed gospel exclusively. He still sings and records with the Jimmie Davis Trio, which includes his

wife, a former member of gospel's Chuck Wagon Gang.

'My roots in gospel are deeper than in country,' Jimmie Davis has said, and since his conversion in the 1940s he has been a strong witness. But his country career was influential, too; his early songs, ironically, are among the raunchiest in country music, with double- (and very often single-) meaning lyrics. His great songwriting talents, a pure, firm voice and his amalgamation of traditional, blues, Western Swing and early honky-tonk styles – not to mention gospel – made his contribution great.

Jimmie Davis was elected to the Country Music Hall of Fame in 1972 and is a former president of the Gospel Music Association.

Davis, Skeeter

Born Mary Frances Penick in Dry Ridge, Kentucky, in 1931, Skeeter Davis' first musical loves were Carter Family records and Saturday night Grand Ole Opry broadcasts. She formed a duo with her friend Betty Jack Davis; they called themselves the Davis Sisters and played in Lexington clubs and many radio dates (including a stint with the WWVA *Wheeling Jamboree* in West Virginia).

In the early 1950s the pair signed with RCA Records and had a hit with 'I Forgot More Than You'll Ever Know,' and then while they were driving from the *Jamboree* on August 2, 1953, an auto accident killed Betty Jack and critically injured Skeeter. After a long recovery Skeeter briefly teamed with Betty Jack's sister Georgia, but she went solo in 1955.

Skeeter toured with the RCA Caravan of Stars and with Hank Snow, Eddy Arnold, Elvis Presley and Ernest Tubbs. Later she was to tour with Buddy Holly and the Rolling Stones. In 1959 she joined the Grand Ole Opry, and her hits were among the top records in country music; through the years they have included 'Set Him Free,' 'The End of the World,' 'Am I That Easy to Forget,' 'He Says the Same Things to Me' and 'Gonna Get Along Without You Now.' She has recorded duets with Bobby Bare ('Your Husband, Your Wife'), Porter Wagoner and George Hamilton IV.

In recent years Skeeter has undergone a religious conversion, and was

once reprimanded by the Opry for evangelizing during a radio broadcast of the Saturday night show; she also got in trouble for castigating the police and the week after Opry favorite Stringbean was murdered in his home. Skeeter has sung as part of Oral Roberts' evangelistic crusades and refuses to perform in clubs where alcohol is served.

Individuality has marked the personal style as well as the musical style of Skeeter Davis. She was one of Chet Atkins' first uptown, pop-oriented experiments, and indeed her songs often charted on pop lists, just as she has found favor in the rock and folk audiences. But her basic repertoire is still country, and her unaffected soprano voice is strong with sincerity and straightforward emotions – no-nonsense, just like her opinions. Skeeter Davis has therefore trekked the familiar country roads from old-fashioned two-part harmonies to pop stylings to gospel.

Dean, Billy

The sensitive melancholy of Billy Dean has been a benchmark of the Florida-born performer since his teenage beginnings in the industry. Raised on country music and singing in his father's country band, he won the regional Wrangler Starsearch Contest and placed in the finals of the national playoffs in Nashville in the 1980s. He stayed on in Music City and formed a band of his own, opening for Mel Tillis, Ronnie Milsap, Steve Wariner, and others.

While he toured outside of Nashville, the songs he wrote were performed and recorded by many others, including Milsap, Shelly West, and Randy Travis. He received a contract as a composer from BMI at the behest of publisher/producer Jimmy Gilmer, and then signed on to perform for SBK Records. In 1991 his performances of 'Only Here for a Little While' in the New Faces Show at the Country Radio Seminar in Nashville so impressed music directors and programmers that this career took off when the single was released. That hit was to prove the turning point in his successful career.

Billy was a finalist in the Country

Billy Dean.

Music Association's Horizon Award competition in 1991 and was named New Male Vocalist of the Year (1992) by the Academy of Country Music. His moving signature tune 'Somewhere in My Broken Heart,' appearing after the issue of his breakthrough song, was number one on the charts and ACM Song of the Year (1992). Its tender, reflective mood displays the best of the singer/songwriter's personal style. 'Billy the Kid' was an introspective semi-autobiographical favorite with fans.

His recent hits have included 'Only the Wine', 'You Don't Count the Cost,' and 'I Wanna Take Care of You.' Billy is a member of the Grand Ole Opry.

Delmore Brothers, The

One of the most influential of that once common country institution, the brother duet, the Delmore Brothers had a long career with three distinct facets. And their unique tenor harmonies not only foreshadowed bluegrass, but their soft, professional vocals have made their sound extremely pleasing to modern ears.

Alton Delmore, born in 1908, and Rabon, two years his junior, both grew up singing and performing on guitar and fiddle around their birthplace of Elkmont, Alabama. Their talent – especially when they teamed – bore rapid fruit: in 1930 they won the Annual Fiddlers Contest in Athens, Georgia; the next year they were signed by Columbia Records and the following year they became members of the Grand Ole Opry. In 1938 they left the Opry and traveled across America, doing local shows and appearing on a variety of country radio programs.

The settled for a long while at one of early radio's most important country shows, the WLW *Midwestern Hayride* in Cincinnati. There they specialized in their brand of old-fashioned country duets, and created one of the memorable groups in country music history, Browns Ferry Four, named for a location near their birthplace. The group was seldom a formal aggregation, although many records were cut through the years; usually it was with whatever friends were available at the time and

felt like joining in old-time gospel harmony. Those who sat in included Grandpa Jones, Merle Travis and Red Foley.

In World War II Alton was drafted, and during the war Rabon was released as a soloist by the *Hayride*. After the war, the brothers settled in Memphis and, reflecting the local blues influences, developed a jazzy sound that was labeled Country Boogie, and is clearly a forerunner of rockabilly. During this musical stage, in 1949, the brothers recorded their biggest hit, 'Blues Stay Away From Me,' now a blues standard.

In 1952 Rabon divorced, contracted cancer and died. The deaths the same year of other family members, as well as professional reverses, kept Alton out of the spotlight, although he continued to write and perform up to the time of his death in 1964 in Nashville.

The Delmore Brothers were among country music's most innovative talents. They excelled at each of their separate 'careers.' Their straight-out old-fashioned country songs captured the rural flavor and sentiment rapidly disappearing from American music even in their time. As gospel singers they formalized the great traditions of part-singing and created a sound that ensembles have followed to this day. And their pioneering work in Country Boogie was a major link in the chain from Western Swing and mountain improvisation through rhythm and blues to rockabilly and rock 'n' roll.

Alton and Rabon's voices combined in smooth, polished, musically sound harmonies, a striking contrast to the rough-cut vocal styling of many rural performers of their day. Rabon played one of country music's few tenor guitars and the Delmore Brothers proved themselves impressive instrumentalists as well. As songwriters they also left a big mark; many of their hits were their own compositions.

Among their major records were: 'Midnight Special,' 'Beautiful Brown Eyes,' 'Brown's Ferry Blues,' 'Freight Train Blues,' 'Born to Be Blue' and 'Hillbilly Boogie.' One of their forgotten masterpieces, 'Down the Trail of Time,' was rediscovered by John Anderson, who has written some of his own songs in collaboration with a second generation Delmore, by the name of Lionel.

Diamond Rio

Their name has no geographical origin; it came from the Diamond Reo 18-wheel truck. The altered spelling was just a mistake, but the group decided to keep it, maybe because of its connotations of fluidity, or because it suggests the Southwest, or just because of its originality. Originality and fluidity are the keynotes of this eclectic and interesting combination.

The six instrumentalists and singers who make up Diamond Rio started out as the Tennessee River Boys. They caught the ear of Tim DuBois when they opened a show for George Jones in Alabama, and he signed them up with Arista Records. 'Meet in the Middle,' a cut from their first offering, was country music's first vocal-group single from a debut album to become a number-one hit. The next single they did also made the top five.

Diamond Rio received a nomination as the Vocal Group of the Year from the Country Music Association in 1991, and won the award the following year. The Academy of Country Music gave them its award in the same category in 1991.

The complex mix of rock beat, bluegrass harmony, country theme, and jazz instrumentation reflects the diverse backgrounds of Diamond Rio's members. Lead vocals are by Marty Roe, who began singing Merle Haggard's 'I'm a Lonesome Fugitive' at the age of three. Bass and vocals are handled by Dana Williams, nephew of bluegrass greats Sonny and Bob, the Osborne Brothers; he also sometimes joins the road shows of Vassar Clements and Jimmy C. Newman. The lead guitarist is the versatile Jimmy Olander, who was a banjo teacher when he was 12; he has performed with Duane Eddy and Rodney Crowell, and he uses a hybrid version of the Telecaster known as a Taxicaster.

Gene Johnson, onetime sideman with David Bromberg and J. D. Crowe and the New South, plays the mandolin and the fiddle for Diamond Rio. Dan Truman contributes a distinctive command of the piano derived from his classical training. The group's drummer is Brian Prout, married to Wild Rose drummer Nancy Given.

Diamond Rio has moved swiftly

Above: The members of Diamond Rio.
Right: Little Jimmy Dickens.

along the path to success. Its multiple influences combine to produce the sparkle and flow its name suggests. Recent smash singles have included 'In a Week or Two,' and 'Sawmill Road.' Their biggest CD to date is *Love a Little Stronger*.

Dickens, Little Jimmy

Born in Bolt, West Virginia, the youngest of 13 children, Jimmy Dickens performed locally from a young age, and played and sang country music on radio stations in Beckley and other towns. He was billed as Jimmy the Kid (it has also been a nickname of Jimmie Rodgers) with Johnny Bailes and His Happy Valley Boys.

In the mid-1940s Jimmy went solo and toured the nation. He signed with Columbia Records, and in 1948 became a member of the Grand Ole Opry. The following year he had a hit with his single, 'Take an Old Cold

Tater and Wait.' Other hits included 'Country Boy,' 'Out Behind the Barn,' 'Sea of Broken Dreams' and 'May the Bird of Paradise Fly Up Your Nose,' his biggest record and a significant crossover hit.

The emphasis on novelty songs through his career can mask the fact that Little Jimmy Dickens is a superb musician. He plays a driving, snappy guitar that was comfortable to rockabilly ears, and has always featured an excellent backup band. One of his hits, 'I'm Little But I'm Loud,' describes the singer, who was elected to the Country Music Hall of Fame in 1983; he stretches the tape at 4 feet, 11 inches, and belts out his lyrics lustily.

'Tater' has undergone a renaissance in the past few years. More than a mere survivor, he has energized his career more than his stage show (he will invariably perform his handful of old hits) although he is frequently on the road with package shows of older Opry stars. His diminutive stature and dogged loyalty to Nudie suits has made him a funky presence as Opry segment host and guest star in a popular Vince Gill music video (one that also featured a cameo with Larry 'Bud' Melman of the *David Letterman Show*). Dickens continues to write – he and Merle Haggard co-wrote 'Shopping for Dresses' that Loretta Lynn and Randy Travis sang on Travis's CD *Heroes and Friends*.

Diffie, Joe

Joe Diffie was working in a foundry and hoping to go to medical school when the music bug bit him, and when he lost his job and his marriage failed, in 1986, he took the logical step and went to Nashville. There he worked in the Gibson Guitar factory and spent his nights and weekends writing songs. In time he began singing on demo, and his solid, traditional delivery and his natural country voice earned him a contract with Epic Records.

It turned out to be a wise investment for Epic. Joe's first album, *A Thousand Winding Roads*, rose to the top of the charts, and the label had its first number one hit by a debut artist in the single 'Home.' The album also had three other number one hits: 'If You Want Me To,' 'If the Devil Danced in Empty Pockets,' and

'New Way to Light Up an Old Flame.' A second album, *Regular Joe*, did equally well.

Joe has received several professional honors for his music, including nominations as Top New Male Vocalist by the Academy of Country Music and Male Vocalist of the Year by the Country Music Association.

Diffie's music reflects the classic values of country music. His presentation is in the great tradition, combining direct, honest emotion with the free-spirited dynamism of his medium in what has been called 'a perfect country voice.' His hit

Many in Nashville say that Joe Diffie has a 'perfect country voice.'

'Home' reveals the spirit of a New Country natural, and 'Startin' Over Blues' was a new song that could have been a cover – down to the expert yodeling – of a 1920s Jimmie Rodgers song. Joe, whose charitable cause is fighting Down's Syndrome, from which his son suffers, is now a member of the Grand Ole Opry.

Recent singles have included the smash 'Honky Tonk Attitude' and 'Pickup Man;' his CD *Third Rock from the Sun*, was released in 1994.

Down Home Folks, The

See The Whites.

Duncan, Tommy

Tommy Duncan's influence – his singing voice, presence and song-writing skills – were as an important part of the seminal Western Swing flavor of the Texas Playboys as Bob Wills's fiddle licks or playful vocal interjections. Indeed, his smooth, jazzy singing style became as integral to Western Swing music as the twin-fiddle sound.

Thomas Elmer Duncan was born in 1911 in Hillsboro, Texas. It is hard to discern a connection with Jimmie Rodgers's crude, heartbreak wails and Duncan's smooth jazz-tinged vocals, but Tommy frequently and firmly claimed the Blue Yodeler as his idol.

In 1932 Duncan joined the Light Crust Doughboys, a pioneer Western Swing band whose manager, W Lee O'Daniel, had just enforced his prejudice against the group's playing at dances. Consequently there were personnel shifts – Milton Brown left to form his Musical Brownies group – and a singer was needed. Duncan was the 68th singer auditioned by the group's fiddler and front man, Bob Wills.

A year later Wills himself was fired, but a number of band members, including Duncan, left with him to form Bob Wills and the Playboys, later the Texas Playboys. When the group settled in Tulsa and added some vital sidemen, it became one of the most significant musical organizations in American history. Duncan resigned the day after Pearl Harbor to enlist in the military; toward the end of World War II he rejoined the Playboys, but big-band ensembles of all sorts were in the decline. In 1948 he resigned – reportedly after disputes over credits for songs – and took several of the Playboys with him. He formed his own band, the Western All Stars, although he returned to Wills for some classic recording sessions in the 1960s.

Tommy Duncan had an easy, confident, high baritone voice. It was smooth and had a bluesy and, appropriately, swinging lilt to it. It was constantly counterpointed by Wills's humorous asides and interjections – sometimes causing a chuckle to intrude into Duncan's lyrics – and the trademark Wills 'Aaaaah!'

Perhaps as important were Duncan's contributions as a songwriter, which must be given their due. Among his credits as writer or co-writer are classics like 'Stay a Little Longer,' 'Take Me Back to Tulsa,' 'Li'l Liza Jane,' 'Bubbles in My Beer,' 'Time Changes Everything,' 'I Knew the Moment I Lost You' and 'Misery.' Duncan died of a heart attack in 1967.

Dunn, Holly

Holly Dunn achieved success as a songwriter quite a while before her singing talents came to public notice. The Texas-born preacher's daughter sold a song to gospel singer Christy Lane while she was still in college, and when she worked in the office of a music publisher in Nashville she wrote material that was recorded by Louise Mandrell, the Whites, and Terri Gibbs.

In the mid-1980s Holly got a

Songwriter and singer Holly Dunn.

contract to sing for MTM Records. Several of her songs and albums from MTM, beginning with her breakthrough 1986 single 'Daddy's Hands,' made the charts. That moving, emotional number brought Holly the Country Music Association's Horizon Award in 1987. Following the demise of MTM, she joined Warner Brothers and received several Grammy nominations and industry awards.

Holly's family has always provided an important source of inspiration and personal support. Her father gave her the theme for her first hit, 'Daddy's Hands,' and her brother, Chris Waters, works with her as her producer and songwriting partner.

But ultimately Holly Dunn, with her powerful, independent spirit, is her own woman. A versatile performer, she commands a range of styles from sensitive self-examination sung in a tender, breathy voice, to tempestuous up-beat rockers. Especially noted for the personal integrity appropriate to the child of a preacher, she once withdrew a successful single, 'Maybe I Mean Yes,' from circulation because it was misunderstood as a justification of date rape. Holly has a message in everything she does, as a songwriter and as a singer, and those messages are among the clearest and most eloquent in New Country. A recent member of the Grand Ole Opry, Holly's newest hit CD is *Gettin' It Dunn*.

Evans, Dale

Born Frances Smith in Uvalde, Texas, in 1912, Dale Evans grew up in Osceola, Arkansas, and was briefly married (1928-30) before she began her musical career. She held vocalist positions on many stations through the Mid-South and Texas before joining Anson Weeks' band in Chicago in the late 1930s. In 1940 she was a featured performer at the Chez Paree Night Club in Chicago.

Afterwards she secured a position on the CBS radio network program, *News and Rhythm*, before becoming the vocalist on the *Edgar Bergen-Charlie McCarthy Show*. In 1943 she turned her attention to Hollywood, where she debuted in the movie *Swing Your Partner*.

Dale Evans went on to make many Westerns, most of them with Roy Rogers, whom she married in 1947. She of course shared billing on the famous *Roy Rogers* television show in the 1950s, and Roy and Dale became the First Family of Western music and screenplays. Her high-pitched vibrato complemented Roy's gentle tenor and yodeling.

Dale Evans now devotes herself to Christian causes and music. She and Roy had adopted a large family of children, and now are involved in many charitable and spiritual causes. She has recorded extensively for Word Records, and has written Christian and autobiographical books

Below left: Dale Evans in the 1950s.
Below: Dale and Roy Rogers in 1989.

including *Angel Unaware* and *Spiritual Diary*. She and Roy are frequent guests on Christian television programs like *The 700 Club* and have recorded two gospel duet albums.

Everly Brothers, The

The possessors of what was seen in rock 'n' roll as a new harmony sound, Don and Phil Everly were actually one of the last country acts in a long and distinguished tradition of brother duets. Their deep country roots included their father's reputation as one of the most influential guitar stylists in country music.

The Everly Brothers were born in Brownie, Kentucky (Don in 1937 and Phil in 1939) to Ike and Margaret Everly, who were popular country and gospel performers in the mid-South from the 1930s to the 1950s. The brothers first performed on an Iowa radio station in 1945, but when their parents retired in the mid-1950s, Don and Phil went to Nashville.

They found themselves in the midst of a rockabilly revolution, and their inclinations and style suited the new sound perfectly. Most fortunately they met the husband-and-wife songwriting team of Boudleaux and Felice Bryant, whose new songs proved tailor-made for the Brothers: 'Bye Bye Love,' 'Wake Up Little Susie,' 'All I Have To Do Is Dream' and others. The Everly Brothers became the great hope of rock 'n' roll – clean cut boys, simple instrumentation, non-suggestive lyrics – especially after Elvis went into the Army. They were possibly the biggest rock stars at that time, and they began to write their own songs ('Cathy's Clown,' 'Till I Kissed You,' 'When Will I Be Loved') with great success.

The next wave of rock, however, did not serve the Everlys as well. Psychedelic shirts and Nehru jackets weren't enough to keep their popularity from waning; and neither did Don's hitch in the Marines in the mid-1960s. They continued to perform thereafter until a stormy break-up – on stage – in 1973. They per-

The Everly Brothers: Don and Phil.

formed and recorded separately after that; Phil briefly hosted a TV rock program, but each gradually returned to the more country-tinged material of their early days.

A 1984 reunion concert marked the rebirth of the Everlys' duo career. They again maintain a Nashville band and tour steadily, though at a more relaxed pace than in their recording heyday. The brothers were among the first group of inductees to the Rock & Roll Hall of Fame in 1986.

Their unique vocals are clear and pure. They have always performed contemporary material, but the tenor-and-countertenor harmonies are as old as the hills whence came American mountain music. Their father, Ike, by the way, was taught guitar by Mose Reger, a Kentucky miner who also taught technique to Merle Travis. Both Everly and Travis practiced a style of playing that was enormously influential with a generation of guitarists.

F

Flatt, Lester

One of the prime movers and creative inspirations to a vital American musical form, bluegrass music, Lester Raymond Flatt was born in Overton County, Tennessee, in 1914. He grew up playing the guitar and loving mountain music, but was obliged to earn a living as a textile worker. His musical sideline finally won him a radio debut in Virginia in 1939, with his band, The Harmonizers. In the early 1940s he played throughout the Appalachian area with Mac Wiseman and others, performing traditional and mountain music in harmony and string-band ensembles.

He joined Charlie Monroe and the Kentucky Pardners as a mandolin player, and his wife Gladys (billed as Billie Jean) also performed with the group. But it was in 1944, when he joined Charlie's brother Bill, that the forms of a musical revolution took shape.

Bill Monroe had formed his Bluegrass Boys after the Monroe Brothers split a few years earlier, and he began refining his driving improvisational mandolin style and high, wailing tenor voice. Lester Flatt's unique guitar runs, high baritone singing and exceptional songwriting was added, and when Earl Scruggs brought his singular five-fingered banjo technique and Chubby Wise added his smooth, versatile fiddle, the bluegrass sound was born.

As important as the sound of the remarkable ensemble was the material they introduced; it was sentimental and sincere, like the traditional music in the players' backgrounds, but it was also perfectly suited in form and configuration to the new bluegrass conven-

Lester Flatt (left) with Earl Scruggs.

tions. Flatt's classic compositions included 'Sweetheart, You Done Me Wrong,' 'Little Cabin Home on the Hill,' 'When Are You Lonely' and 'Will You Be Loving Another Man.' The impact of bluegrass music was so great at that time that many musicians adopted it and formed new groups.

One of these groups was composed largely of former Monroe sidemen, including Flatt and Scruggs themselves. In 1948 they formed the Foggy Mountain Boys, with Cedric Rainwater, bass; Mac Wiseman, guitar and Jim Schumate, fiddle. The ensemble coalesced when Flatt and Scruggs were performing on Wiseman's radio show *Farm and Fun Time* in Bristol, Virginia, and the group soon all but eclipsed Bill Monroe's Bluegrass Boys as the nation's most prominent bluegrass band.

The hits of the legendary Flatt and Scruggs were to include 'Foggy Mountain Breakdown,' 'The Ballad of Jed Clampett' (from TV's Beverly Hillbillies), 'Foggy Mountain Top,' 'Earl's Breakdown,' 'I'll Never Shed Another Tear' and 'Cabin in Caroline.' In 1955 they were sponsored by the makers of Martha White Self-Rising Flour in concerts throughout the South and on the Grand Ole Opry, which they joined the same year. They were associated with the *Beverly Hillbillies* and *Petticoat Junction* TV shows as well as providing the theme music for the movie *Bonnie and Clyde*.

When bluegrass suffered lean times immediately after the advent of rock 'n' roll, Flatt and Scruggs remained relatively active, playing folk festivals. But it was the atmosphere – and influence – of these folk festivals that ultimately led to the breakup of the group in 1969. Scruggs wanted to move more in a folk and even rock direction, aided by the presence of his performing sons, and Lester Flatt was most comfortable exploring the traditional flavors of bluegrass.

Flatt formed the Nashville Grass with some outstanding sidemen, including Paul Warren on fiddle, Haskel McCormick on banjo, Roland White on mandolin and Uncle Josh Graves on dobro. With this group he performed for another decade on the road, in recordings, and on the *Opry*. In the early 1970s he recorded three outstanding albums with Mac Wiseman, performing definitive versions

of many bluegrass and traditional standards; for a time they performed together and were a celebrated Nashville act.

In the middle of the decade, Flatt endured open heart surgery, a gall bladder operation and a brain hemorrhage. He died in Nashville on 11 May 1979. Becoming a born-again Christian toward the end of his life, his last albums – among the finest he made and many recorded for CMH – reflected a return to gospel songs and a spiritual preoccupation.

Lester Flatt possessed a high baritone that blended well in the upper-register bluegrass harmonies. His personality and stylings gave impetus to the emerging bluegrass form, and the 'Flatt run' on the guitar – fancy licks at the ends of lines – was widely imitated and surpassed only, perhaps, by the influential banjo licks of his longtime partner Earl Scruggs.

Foley, Red

Clyde Julian Foley had several careers – as a singer, a television host and even a television actor. He also possessed one of the smoothest 'uptown' voices in country music, but through it all he never foresook his roots or aspired to be anything more than a country singer, and he thereby became one of the all-time greats in his chosen field.

He was born in Blue Lick, Kentucky, in 1910, and grew up playing

Red Foley.

guitar and harmonicas, most of the latter borrowed from stock in his father's general store before they were sold. At the age of 17 he won a statewide singing championship by performing the gospel standard 'Hold Thou My Hand, Dear Lord.' In 1932 he graduated from Georgetown College in Kentucky, but his musical leanings took precedence over any other activity, and he was invited to join the new WLS *National Barn Dance* in Chicago. For a while there he was a member of the Cumberland Ridge Runners with Lulu Belle (who was later to team with Scotty Wiseman), but became an audience favorite as a soloist.

In Chicago, Foley absorbed blues and jazz stylings into his traditional country and gospel sound. The result was more character and a broader appeal to his singing; Foley sang in a rich, polished baritone that distinguished him from many of his rural fellows. He could perform traditional material in ways that would attract Northern and urban ears, a fact that impressed his considerable country audience.

In 1937 Foley inaugurated his own *Renfro Valley* radio show in Cincinnati (Whitey Ford, the Duke of Paducah, was a comedian sidekick), and in 1939 co-hosted with Red Skelton a network radio show, *Avalon Time*. Five years later he became a member of the Grand Ole Opry, becoming along the way the first singer actually to record in Nashville. Among the hits in his most active period, the 1940s, were 'Old Shep,' 'Tennessee Saturday Night,' 'Blues in My Heart,' 'Candy Kisses,' 'Chattanooga Shoeshine Boy,' 'Just a Closer Walk With Thee,' 'Steal Away,' 'Alabama Jubilee,' 'Peace in the Valley' and 'Satisfied Mind.'

Between 1955 and 1961 Foley hosted the pioneer country network TV show, *Ozark Jubilee*, which featured many country acts; the program originated in Springfield, Missouri. In 1962 he co-starred with Fess Parker in the TV comedy series *Mr Smith Goes to Washington*.

Foley's daughter Betty was a country singer in the 1950s, and his daughter Shirley married Pat Boone, the country-tinged pop, rock, and gospel singer. Their own daughters have all become singers, as The Boones, a gospel group, and Debbie as a solo act.

Ford, Tennessee Ernie

The image of a suave crooner but the studied mannerisms of a 'rube' combined to serve Tennessee Ernie Ford for four decades; it reflects his appeal, which has been to a wide audience spectrum.

Ernest Jennings Ford was born in Bristol, Tennessee, in 1919; modern country music was born there eight years later when the Carter Family and Jimmie Rodgers recorded their first songs. His early jobs were as a radio announcer in towns throughout the Southeast, and, after service, in the Air Corps in World War II, he resumed the same activity in California. In Pasadena he met bandleader Cliffie Stone, whom he joined in singing gospel quartets on the latter's country radio show.

Ford's singing led to a contract with Capitol Records, and in 1949 he had a national hit with 'Mule Train.' He sang 'I'll Never Be Free' with Kay Starr, another hit, and then manifested a remarkable penchant for hillbilly boogie with such hits as 'Smokey Mountain Boogie; and 'Shotgun Boogie.' Clearly – and this is all but forgotten today – Tennessee Ernie Ford was a father to rockabilly and early rock 'n' roll.

In 1955 came his biggest hit, and one of the biggest records in country music history: 'Sixteen Tons,' written by Merle Travis. The record was eventually to sell more than four million copies, and is emblematic of a strain of hard-luck, fatalistic country

ballads. Its success led directly to Ford's move to network television, where he hosted variety programs between 1955 and 1965. Thereafter he appeared in frequent guest spots, but voluntarily maintained a scaled-down performance schedule. Devoting time to family and his ranch, he continued to record extensively, with nearly 100 albums to his credit. During the last years of his life Ford recorded gospel albums for Word Records and succeeded the late Kenny Price as bass singer in *Hee Haw's* Gospel Quartet. His album *Hymns* was the first by a country artist to sell more than one million copies. He was elected to the Country Music Hall of Fame in 1990.

Ford was rushed to a Washington, D.C. hospital after attending a White House state dinner on September 28, 1991. He died there several weeks later of complications from a long-standing liver ailment.

Of his preference for recording gospel songs, Ford once said: 'Many people get all steamed up by a new love song. Let's not forget that hymns and spirituals are the finest love songs of all.' His rich, deep voice remains a standard for bass singers in country and gospel music.

Foster, Radney

Texan Radney Foster, like so many of the younger breed of country artists, is a songwriter first, a performer second. His cerebral approach to

Below: Radney Foster.
Right: Tennessee Ernie Ford.

lyrics coupled with traditional instrumentals, is a fine, rich mixture that brought him favor, beginning with his first Arista album, *Del Rio, TX, 1959*. No fewer than three songs from that album were hits: 'Nobody Wins,' 'Just Call Me Lonesome,' and 'Easier Said Than Done.'

Foster's home town is Del Rio, famous for many years for its high-powered radio signal that boomed out across North America. From there the Carter Family and many country acts since have made their radio home. His parents' house is only a mile from the Mexican border.

'The thing about country music,' Foster has said, 'is it's all about gut level things we *all* face. No matter who you are or where you come from, we all have to deal with matters of the heart; life, death, love, remorse, regrets over past actions, those are timeless topics and they're the roots of country music.' Originally half of the musical duo Foster and Lloyd, Radney's trademark horn-rimmed glasses lend the singer an intellectual appearance.

Fricke, Janie

Jane Marie Fricke owns one of the most pliant and pleasant voices in country music, and after years of singing anonymously on commercials and behind stars, she broke through to widespread solo success. She is as well-liked as she is talented, and Nashville has applauded her overdue recognition.

Born in 1950 and raised on a 40-acre farm near South Whitley, Indiana, Janie Fricke grew up singing in her local Lutheran Church; in high school her musical tastes ran to folk and rock. While she attended Indiana University she sang commercial jingles in her spare time, and learned of the money that could be made thereby. After graduation she attempted to secure session work in Texas and California, but moved to Nashville in 1975.

With a host of commercials and radio-station jingles to her credit, Janie went to work in the recording world. First as a member of the Lea Jane Singers, and then as an independent vocalist, Janie sang on more than a thousand albums behind singers ranging from Jimmy Swaggart to Tanya Tucker. She then sang duets with Johnny Duncan on three

songs that became number one hits: 'It Couldn't Have Been Any Better,' 'Stranger' and 'Thinkin' of a Rendezvous.'

Finally Janie got the recognition she long deserved, and proved herself a formidable vocal stylist. She sings with pure surety in a voice that can slide, waver, break or soar to perfectly match any set of lyrics, and in spite of her background Janie can sound commercial without sounding too slick. Among her country hits have been 'Please Help Me, I'm Falling,' 'Pass Me By' and 'I'll Need Someone to Hold Me.' Of late her songs have become very pop-oriented.

Janie has, since going solo, recorded duets with Charlie Rich, George Jones and Merle Haggard, who released their collaborations, 'Looking For a Place to Fall,' 'Natural High' and 'Ridin' High,' in 1985. Janie has also toured with the Statler

Janie Fricke.

Brothers and is a frequent guest on television variety programs. She also introduced a line of ready-to-wear fashions.

Janie has received the Top Female Vocalist Award from the Country Music Association, the Academy of Country Music, and the *Music City News'* Readers Poll.

Frizzell, David

The younger brother of Lefty Frizzell – a fact that will both overshadow and honor his career forever – David Frizzell was born in Texas in 1941. As a teenager he toured with his legendary brother, and in the early 1960s he recorded some country music and rockabilly cuts on his brother's label, Columbia. In 1970 he had a minor hit with 'LA International Airport.'

In 1981, paired with Shelley West,

daughter of singer/songwriter Dottie West, David Frizzell had a monstrous hit with 'You're the Reason God Made Oklahoma,' a featured song from the Clint Eastwood movie *Any Which Way You Can*. It was a modern song built on old-time honky-tonk themes: loneliness, lost love and doubts. And it was a great song finally to build a career in country music upon.

The years of waiting paid off for David Frizzell. He followed with 'Texas State of Mind,' and another song that attracted a lot of notice and awards, 'I'm Gonna Hire A Wino to Decorate Our Home.'

Frizzell's voice is reminiscent of his brother's but far less disciplined; his harmonies seem to slip, but only in the rough range that has characterized fellow Texans like Floyd Tilman and others. Aware of the constant comparisons, David Frizzell entitled one of his albums *The Family's Fine, But This One's Mine*.

Frizzell, Lefty

William Orville Frizzell, the great stylist Lefty Frizzell, was born in Corsicana, Texas, in 1928. He grew up listening to Jimmie Rodgers records, then found new idols in Ernest Tubb and Roy Acuff. The Frizzell family moved frequently – the father was an itinerant oil driller – but Lefty pursued music, graduating through the years from a children's radio show to fairs to dances to clubs. During this time he was a boxer, too, giving him his nickname (from his hard left hook).

A demonstration tape made in 1950 led to a recording contract and, in short order, national acclaim and hit records. He cut a notable tribute album to Jimmie Rodgers, and his hits included 'I Love You a Thousand Ways,' 'If You've Got the Money,' 'Always Late,' 'Mom and Dad's Waltz,' 'I'm an Old, Old Man' and others. In 1952, he had four songs in the top ten simultaneously. After the early 1950s his hits came less frequently, but 1959's 'Long Black Veil' and 1964's 'Saginaw, Michigan' were big sellers and have become country standards.

Frizzell joined the Grand Ole Opry in 1952 but later moved to TV's *Country America* show in Hollywood. Drinking and personal problems kept him down, and this widely re-

spected singer was often absent from his public. In 1973 he recorded an album that is one of the finest in country history, containing new songs by himself, Whitey Shafer and others. But Frizzell died shortly after the album was released – it was ironic, but fitting, that a comeback effort was also the perfect epitaph. The album was called *The Legendary Lefty Frizzell* and contained the songs 'I Can't Get Over You to Save My Life,' 'I Never Go Around Mirrors,' 'That's the Way Love Goes' and 'Let Me Give Her the Flowers.'

Frizzell's vocal stylings live today in his obvious disciples Merle Haggard, Johnny Rodriguez, and John

Lefty Frizzell.

Anderson. His back-of-the-throat baritone was rich in both understated beauty and a vocal crack (a modern legacy of that neglected lament, the blue yodel) which captured heart-breaking feelings of sorrow and regret. Although he performed all manner of songs, he seemed the best at sad love songs and sentimental ballads.

After Frizzell's death of a stroke in Nashville on July 19, 1975, he was mourned widely. Merle Haggard recorded a tribute song, and Willie Nelson cut an album of classic Frizzell songs.

G

Gatlin, Larry

Born in Seminole, Texas, in 1948, Larry Gatlin grew up with his brothers Steve and Rudy (three and four years, respectively, his junior) singing gospel music, copying the harmonies of the Blackwood Brothers and the Statesmen. Larry, who always liked writing music as well, landed a spot on a TV show in Abilene, Texas for two years before attending the University of Houston on a football scholarship. He also continued writing – fiction and music – but in 1971 had a chance to audition for the Imperials.

Larry lost the position, but was invited to join the group during one engagement in Las Vegas while they backed up Jimmy Dean. On the same bill was Dottie West, who after hearing Larry's compositions, arranged a Nashville plane ticket for Gatlin. His earliest records met with some success and much critical respect – 'Penny Annie' (a sort of story song, reflecting, perhaps, his efforts at fiction) and 'Delta Dirt.'

Touring the promotional circuit that newcomers must travel, Gatlin was a protegé of Johnny Cash and other stars with whom he toured. He played small clubs like O'Lunney's in New York (during a date there in 1973 he backed Willie Nelson on the *Troublemaker* gospel LP) and continued to record, each song meeting with more success.

'Broken Lady' and 'I Just Wish You Were Someone I Loved' foreshadowed a modification in his ensemble's sound (he was now regularly backed by his two brothers): a reliance, almost an obsession, with vocal pyrotechnics and long, sustained harmonies. 'All the Gold in California', perhaps the Gatlins' best-known recording, represents a significantly pop-fla-

Above: Larry Gatlin.
Right: Crystal Gayle.

vored period for Larry and the brothers, one followed by an equally identifiable 'Texas' direction. It is this latter, swing-based sound with which the group is most closely associated in its post-recording days. Following a brief 'retirement' brought on by Larry's throat surgery, the brothers opened their own Myrtle Beach club in 1993.

Gayle, Crystal

Born in Paintsville, Kentucky in 1951, the youngest of eight children, Crystal Gayle was born as Brenda Gail Webb; her sister Loretta Lynn suggested the stage name as they were driving past an outlet of the Krystal Hamburger chain. Other siblings, Peggy Sue and Jay Lee Webb, also entered the country music field, but Crystal had other influences than Butcher Hollow. When she was four, her parents moved to Wabash, Indiana, and Loretta was married and gone even before Crystal was born.

She did aspire to a life in music, but in the beginning folk and pop were her dishes. After high school she toured with Loretta, had some minor hits, and appeared on Jim Ed Brown's *Country Place* TV show. She played the lower levels of country tour packages, (in 1971, in Laurel, Maryland) being billed below Jerry Lee Lewis, the Osborne Brothers,

Crash Craddock, Blake Emmons, and even a local favorite, Gordon Odell. In country music, it's the familiar routine of paying dues.

But in 1972 Crystal's dues-paying began to pay off. She was paired with producer Allen Reynolds, who was responsible for Don Williams' sound; he, in a sense, made Crystal the female counterpart to the Williams-Reynolds sound. Perfectly complementing her throaty, bluesy, restrained voice, Reynolds backed her with a gentle shuffle-beat on drums, subdued steel guitar and electric keyboards.

Her hits began coming in rapid succession and with increasing favor and airplay: 'Wrong Road Again,' 'This is My Year for Mexico,' 'Do It All Over Again' and others. By the mid-1970s she shifted to a more pop sound in backing and material, reflected by 'You'll Never Miss a Real Good Thing' and 'Don't It Make My Brown Eyes Blue.' In 1977 she was named best female country singer by the Country Music Association, the Academy of Country Music, and at the Grammy awards, and became the first female country artist to record an album selling more than one million copies.

Crystal Gayle transformed herself from the shy, giggling girl of

mid-1970s interviews to a self-assured international star. Her repertoire is now almost exclusively pop, and when she tips her bonnet to country, it's usually (as in Jimmie Rodgers's 'Miss the Mississippi') knee-deep in lush orchestration. When she varies, it's often into soft rock. But her loyal country audience has followed her hollow-timbered stylings and singular pronunciations, whether on TV variety programs or concerts.

Crystal's career has slowed down of late as she lost her chart presence, major label affiliation, and lounge dates. In 1995 she succeeded Janie Fricke as the house singer on *The Statler Brothers Show* on the Nashville Network, where she sings nostalgic

standards of country, and, appropriately, pop music, and even performs versions of the songs of her more famous and more loyally country sister Loretta Lynn.

Gill, Vince

Oklahoman Vince Gill came from a solid rural tradition of bluegrass music. His father played the banjo in a pickup band before becoming a judge in the appellate court, and Vince started his own group, the Mountain Smoke Band, while still in high school. After graduation he joined the Bluegrass Alliance, which numbered such stars of the genre as Sam Bush and Dan Crary among its members, in Kentucky. He was also, for a time, a member of Boone Creek, along with Ricky Skaggs, before

moving to California, where he joined Byron Berline's progressive bluegrass ensemble Sundance. After a couple of years with them he moved to Pure Prairie League, where he began to make his mark with his solid vocal renditions, inventive instrumental performances and ingenious songwriting. Pure Prairie League had two hits in the top ten during the days Vince was fronting for them.

A solid performer, known and admired among his colleagues, Vince was still no national name, although he had long been among those judged most likely to succeed. After a time with Pure Prairie League he married Janis Oliver, a member of the duet Sweethearts of the Rodeo, and moved on to the Cherry Bombs, Rodney Crowell's highly regarded backup band. Vince was later to collaborate with two members of the group, Emory Gordy, Jr., and Tony Brown, as producers.

His studio work in Nashville has added to the high regard in which he has been held for years. He has sung harmony and played great guitar riffs on hundreds of albums through the years. Among the most highly esteemed musicians in the business, he was known by everyone except the public until his first album with MCA, *When I Call Your Name*.

There was nothing particularly new about the album except the label; he had already done three albums for RCA with much the same material and many of the same musicians and producers. But the gradually growing reputation of this popular and respected musician had reached critical mass at last, and his slow, steady rise finally brought him the stardom everyone had been predicting. No longer only a musician's musician, he had made it to the larger public he deserved. The album included a song he had co-written with Roseanne Cash, a duet with Reba McEntire, and a title song with background vocals by Patty Loveless. He went on to record a duet album with Patty and to rack up success after success, garnering a series of gold and platinum records.

In the beginning of the 1990s he also began at last to receive the professional honors everyone had long felt were his due. 'When I Call Your Name' was voted Song of the Year by the Country Music Association in

Vince Gill displays his picking skills.

1990, and 'Look at Us' received the same honor in 1992. Vince was named Male Vocalist of the Year by CMA in 1991 and 1992 and Instrumentalist of the Year by Music City News in 1991. The CMA nominated him for Entertainer of the Year in 1992, and he received several Grammies. He was made a member of the Grand Ole Opry, and he co-hosted the CMA Awards on television with his old partner Reba McEntire in 1992.

Vince Gill's subtle mix of classical country music and bluegrass styling brings a feeling of richness to his sound as well as a feeling of continuity. His instrumentation and delivery bring together all the threads

Left: Gill holds up his ACM awards.
Below: Gill is a spellbinding singer.

of country. His compelling voice, a warm, pure mountain countertenor, conveys an emotional authenticity which never fails to move an audience. He does not evoke boisterous enthusiasm; rather he holds his hearers spellbound with the love and pain he conveys.

No one was surprised when Vince, one of the best-liked musicians in the industry, began to receive the attention he had merited for so long. Vince has been named Entertainer of the Year by CMA, ACM, and TNN/MCN for several years in a row, a remarkable testament of universal acclaim.

Gilley, Mickey

For years, when he sounded (unavoidably, he says) like Jerry Lee Lewis, Mickey Gilley had frustrating, limited success. Since he refined his own 'sound' his popularity has been ensured. His stylistic resemblance to The Killer, of course, was not coincidental; they are first cousins, and grew up playing piano together.

Born in Natchez, Louisiana, in 1937, Mickey was raised in nearby Ferriday, where his cousin – and another cousin, Jimmy Lee Swaggart, now the piano-playing evangelist – shared all the country and boogie-woogie music they could sneak off to hear. Gilley's family moved to Houston, Texas, when he was in his late teens. His cousins went their separate, notable and very different ways, and so did Mickey. He got a job in the parts department of an engineering firm. But in the mid-1950s, when Jerry Lee Lewis was becoming a national sensation, Mickey decided to sit down at the old piano.

For years he had a local following in Texas and Louisiana. He recorded on small labels with regional success (one song, 'Call Me Shorty,' got a bit of national airplay), but he remained only a Houston favorite. In the early 1970s he opened a nightclub – one of the largest in the world in terms of floor space – in nearby Pasadena, Texas. Then, in a classic 15-year overnight-success story, one of his local records became a national hit.

It was actually the 'B' side of a record, and it was a cover of a classic country standard, George Morgan's 'Room Full of Roses.' The new Playboy label picked it up, and Mickey's piano stylings combined uniquely with the mellow old song. This started a string of hits, all on the same pattern: Gilley (Lewis?)-style versions of established standards . . . although in short order his own personality was dominating: 'City Lights,' 'I Overlooked an Orchid,' 'Window Up Above,' 'Movin' On.'

In 1974 he was still an enigma: still halfway between his cousin and himself; gaining national attention for country but booked in clubs in places like Scarsdale, New York (where he met empty houses). He began recording some original songs, and they shot to the top of country charts – duets with Barbi Benton, 'Bring It On Home To Me,' 'Honky-Tonk Memories' and others.

In the late 1970s *Esquire* magazine ran an article on Gilley's Club, and the story inspired the hit movie *Urban Cowboy* (1980). Gilley acted and sang in the movie, and its success changed his career – as well as the short-term direction of country music trends and even American fashion. For several seasons, it became popular to sport cowboy hats, jeans, and boots, even in New York City. Gilley managed a line of designer Western wear, and the pop-orientated music featured in *Urban Cowboy* (which had starred John Travolta) gave him entree to showcases like the Las Vegas clubs. He also made television appearances on *The Fall Guy* and *Fantasy Island*.

A syndicated weekly radio show from Gilley's Club was popular through the early 1980s, but succumbed to disputes between Gilley and his partner Sherwood Cryer. The singer dissociated himself from the club, which he considered too rowdy, as part of a bold move to reorient his career with quality material. Today, he bases his activities at his theater in Branson, Missouri. His trademark is still the cut-time piano stylings of Ferriday times.

Gilmore, Jimmie Dale

Texan Jimmie Dale Gilmore thinks of 'real country' as the music of Webb Pierce, Hank Williams and Lefty Frizzell, and he is convinced that the public has never lost its taste for that pure, traditional sound. Indeed, it is the sound that Gilmore strives for.

One of Gilmore's classic lines from his early 1970s song, 'Dallas,' asks, 'Have you ever seen Dallas from a DC-9 at night?' If the Singing Brakeman, Jimmie Rodgers, were alive today, no doubt he would be writing about airplanes rather than trains, Gilmore believes. The emotions of the 1920s and the 1990s are not all that different, in his opinion.

Gilmore was born in Amarillo, moved to a farm near Tulla and then to Lubbock in time for first grade. He is one more example of Texas's rich musical inspiration to a new generation of singer-songwriters.

He has always loved country music and his first solo album, *Fair and Square*, was on HighTone Records in 1988. A 1991 album, on Elektra, *After Awhile*, received critical acclaim, as did his next album, *Spinning Around the Sun*.

'I've always lived in more than one world,' he says. 'Too country for city music fans, too weird for country people.' But actually this has become an asset in the 1990s, he adds. Gilmore is praised by *The New York Times* every time he plays a Manhattan club, and he has also sung tributes to Jimmie Rodgers on the Nashville Network, viscerally touching both audiences and bridging the best of both worlds.

Gimble, Johnny

In an industry blessed with outstanding musical talent, Johnny Gimble might just be the best musician of all the sidemen and instrumentalists.

Born on a farm near Tyler, Texas, in 1926, by the age of 12 Gimble's fiddle playing earned him a spot in a band; and even though it was a family band – with brothers Gene, Gerry, Jack and Bill – it was professional enough to perform at local events. When Johnny was in high school he and brothers Gene and Gerry, with James Ivie, formed the Rose City Swingsters, emulating their heroes of Western Swing like Bob Wills, Cliff Bruner and the Light Crust Doughboys.

In 1943 Johnny Gimble was in Shreveport, Louisiana, playing fiddle and banjo with Bob and Joe Shelton on KWKH, and he also served as a sideman with Jimmie Davis's band. Then in the early 1950s a childhood dream was fulfilled when he was invited to join Bob Wills and the Texas Playboys. Originally hired as a mandolin player, he graduated to one of the fiddle positions with the Old Man, and eventually wrote some of the songs the band performed.

The end of the decade – as big bands were definitely in their twilight days – saw Gimble leave music professionally; he became a barber and took other jobs back in Texas. But by 1968 he was back where he belonged, in country music, mostly in Nashville. He became a sideman at a time when the Nashville Sound was evolving from lush strings and mellow-quartet backgrounds to featuring individual, though largely anonymous, virtuosity. Other busy sidemen with Gimble (who mostly played fiddle) were Charlie McCoy on harmonica, Hargus 'Pig' Robbins on piano, Peter Drake or Lloyd Green on steel guitar, Chip Young, Harold Bradley, Ray Edenton and others on rhythm guitars.

He was busy in the recording studios, but also made concert appearances as well, touring with Tom T Hall, Johnny Rodriguez, Merle Haggard and Willie Nelson. Among the artists whose albums featured solo licks by Gimble were Connie Smith, Loretta Lynn, Nelson and Haggard. In 1976 he recorded two albums, *Fiddlin' Around* for Capitol, and *Johnny Gimble's Texas Dance Party* for Columbia, and the same year he was voted Instrumentalist of the Year by the Country Music Association. When Chet Atkins produced his tribute album to Nashville sidemen, *Superpickers*, Gimble was prominent on fiddle and mandolin.

In the 1980s Johnny Gimble was active in the revival of Western Swing. He performed with Asleep at the Wheel and was an important part of the ensemble on Merle Haggard's tribute album *The Best Damn Fiddle Player in the World* that was a catalyst in the resurgence of Western dance-band music. He played with the reformed Playboy band that recorded the significant album *Bob Wills: For the Last Time* for United Artists the very day of Bob Wills's fatal stroke, and toured with the new Playboys for a time thereafter.

He has assembled some of the best surviving members of classic Western bands and formed the Texas

Right: Jimmie Dale Gilmore.

Swing Pioneers; the group has appeared on the *Austin City Limits* TV show and recorded for CMH Records in a brilliant double album produced by Gimble. He has recorded and produced other albums for CMH, notably a double-set of Mac Wiseman singing Western Swing classics.

His fiddle and mandolin playing – as in the best traditions of Western Swing – show Gimble to be a master of country, Western, blues, jazz, swing and even bluegrass modes. A brilliant improviser whose playing is filled with energy, humor and emotion, Johnny remains in demand for Nashville sessions whenever he can be lured away from his Texas home.

Gold City

Organized in 1980, Gold City is composed of seven singers and musicians with lifelong ties to gospel music, so it was not surprising that the group quickly became one of the leading southern gospel groups in the nation.

Gold City's members are: Tim Riley, bass singer and manager; Brian Free, tenor; Ivan Parker, lead vocalist; Mike LeFevre, baritone; Gary Jones, pianist-arranger; Doug Riley, drummer; and Mark Fain, bass player. They have recorded for Dawn, Heartwarming and River-Song records.

The group has won many awards; in 1989 *Singing News* magazine's fans voted them tops in nine separate categories, including Group of the Year and they had also won the Group award in 1987 and 1988. *Cash Box* voted them Southern Gospel Group of the Year; they received two Dove nominations, and over the years they have had six number one songs on southern gospel radio.

Gosdin, Vern

Vern Gosdin, who sings with one of contemporary music's purest, down-home country voices, was born in Woodland, Alabama, in 1934. He listened to the Grand Ole Opry on a beat-up radio as a child, and particularly liked the Louvin Brothers, whose harmonies Vern and his two brothers emulated when they joined the Gosdin Family Gospel show on Birmingham radio in the early 1950s.

He liked bluegrass too, and his talent was as broad as his tastes. Vern sang in Atlanta and Chicago before moving to California in 1960 with his brother Rex to form The Golden State Boys. Later they were members of the Hillsmen before leader Chris Hillman departed to establish the Byrds. Vern, meanwhile, was becoming influential in the growing California country/rock/bluegrass movement, and, in addition, the Bakersfield scene.

But all of this activity resulted in no hit records or steady musical work, so Vern moved back to Atlanta and left music. In 1976, however, producer Gary Paxton invited Vern to sing a new version of 'Hangin' On,' one of his earlier, minor hits. Gosdin agreed, and recorded 'Yesterday's Gone' as well (with Emmylou Harris singing harmony). Hit records were now ensured as a national audience was discovering Gosdin's soulful country vocals. 'Mother Country Music,' 'Never My Love,' 'Break My Mind,' 'Too Long Gone' and 'If You're Gonna Do Me Wrong, Do It Right' were all hits. His brother Rex died in the early 1980s, but otherwise it all would have fulfilled the earlier dreams of Vern Gosdin . . . except for about 15 extremely frustrating years in between.

Vern's inspirations – country duet harmonies, gospel songs, bluegrass – have molded his style into one of the most appealing in the field today, and his credentials are impeccable. Among his bluegrass work, for instance, was an impressive traditional/progressive project in the 1960s, *Gene Clark with the Gosdin Brothers* (with Hillman and Michael Clarke from the Byrds, Leon Russell, Doug Dillard and Glen Campbell). In 1984, on the other hand, Vern

Clinton Gregory is a fifth generation fiddle player.

recorded a gospel album *If Jesus Came Today (What Then)* with a definitive version of Albert Brumley's classic 'Jesus, Hold My Hand,' and many songs written by himself. His country ballads reveal a mournful aspect to his voice, and this album displays a hopeful, joyful side.

Vern Gosdin has achieved chart success, and has a large cult following, but superstardom – which seems his due for his long service and enormous talent – has eluded him thus far. Nicknamed 'The Voice,' with a soulful reminiscence of George Jones in his vocal stylings, his more recent hits have included 'Do You Believe Me Now,' 'Way Down Deep,' 'If You're Gonna Do Me Wrong (Do It Right),' and 'I Can Tell By the Way You Dance.' He has also written songs for George Strait and for Merle Haggard-George Jones collaborations.

Gregory, Clinton

Fiddlersinger Clinton Gregory of Martinsville, Virginia, spent nearly a decade on the road performing at bluegrass festivals and dance clubs before signing a contract with Polydor Records.

Polydor knew they were getting a gem, because Gregory was one of the most successful artists ever to emerge from the ranks of independent record labels. He was the first independent artist ever to have a top-20 hit on all charts with his number 18 song, 'If It Weren't For Country Music (I'd Go Crazy).' He followed that up with several other hits before his first Polydor album, simply titled *Clinton Gregory*.

Gregory is a fifth-generation fiddle player from a region that has produced many outstanding traditional country musicians. He has backed up other musicians in Nashville, both live and in recording studios, but now is in demand as much for his star value as his fiddle pyrotechnics. He frequently appears on the Nashville Network, on shows ranging from *Nashville Now* to *The American Music Shop*, and had the honor – as a newcomer – to guest on the award-winning jam-album by master fiddler Mark O'Connor with other fiddle greats Johnny Gimble, Vassar Clements, and Charlie Daniels.

Clinton's most recent CD is *Master of Illusion*.

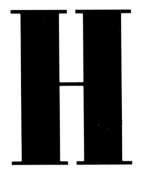

Haggard, Merle

Out of the scratchy recorded tunes that have been the common people's companions for two generations, sometimes seeming like their only companions; out of the wrenching heartache ballads and trouble-chasing dance tunes; out of the spirit-lifting gospel songs that promise a better life by and by; out of the roadhouse and tavern songs that are almost as much political as musical, speaking to shared class and social values . . . out of all the elements that have created that peculiarly American music known as Country, Merle Haggard has risen to reflect, and chronicle, his generation.

In addition to his tremendous songwriting and performing talents, his acceptance at several levels and the virtual icon he has become, Haggard symbolizes the essence of country music in one more way. Secure in his own niche, he resurrects and glorifies the great talents who have gone before, and is constantly aware of country's heritage. And, he creates a valuable heritage for future generations.

Merle Haggard was born in a converted boxcar in Bakersfield, California, to a transplanted Okie family hit hard by the Depression. His father died when Merle was nine, a fact that contributed mightily to the youngster's rebellion. At 14 he ran away from home, hoboing, drifting, working small jobs, committing petty crimes . . . and listening to country music. His favorites were Hank Williams, Bob Wills, Jimmie Rodgers and Lefty Frizzell.

In 1957 Haggard was convicted on an attempted burglary charge, and received a sentence of six months-to-15 years at San Quentin Prison. The experience sobered him; Haggard worked in the textile shop, attended educational courses and played in the warden's band. A model prisoner, he was released under parole after two years and

Singer/songwriter Merle Haggard.

Haggard has built a country legacy.

nine months (and later was granted a full pardon by Governor Ronald Reagan). Returning to Bakersfield, he played in local clubs, backed other singers (he was in Wynn Stewart's band for a time) and did session work at recording studios.

He met Bonnie Owens, former wife of Buck Owens, and they recorded a duet, 'Just Between the Two of Us,' that gained national attention. In 1965 Merle – and Bonnie, whom he was to marry – signed with Capitol Records, and formed a backup band, the Strangers, named for his first solo hit, '(All My Friends Are Gonna Be) Strangers.'

From then on, almost every single was a hit: 'Swingin' Doors,' 'The Bottle Let Me Down,' 'Sing Me Back Home,' 'Sing me a Sad Song' and 'Today I Started Lovin' You Again.'

Most were his own compositions, and many won awards.

In 1969 a quantum leap occurred in a career that was already expanding at remarkable speed. The catalyst was 'Okie From Muskogee,' a counter-counter-culture anthem that was perfect for its day and the mood of the country. The song, and Haggard's name, were on everyone's lips, and he was named Entertainer of the Year by the Country Music Association. His next single, 'The Fightin' Side of Me,' left no doubt that 'Muskogee' wasn't a novelty tune, but for the next few years Haggard resolutely avoided the pigeonhole. He recorded a double-album tribute to Jimmie Rodgers, and a double-record gospel set performed at four country churches across America.

'Irma Jackson' was a single song that sensitively dealt with interracial

love, and 'The Farmer's Daughter' – never released as a single but one of his finest songs – was a single father's soliloquy on the eve of his daughter's wedding to a city boy. His other singles of this time included 'Jesus, Take a Hold,' 'Someday We'll Look Back,' 'Grandma Harp,' 'Things Aren't Funny Any More,' 'It's All in the Movies,' 'The Root of My Raising' and 'Cherokee Maiden.'

The last song was a Bob Wills classic. Haggard had done much to initiate the Western Swing revival, recording a tribute album to Wills called *The Best Damn Fiddle Player in the World*, featuring the Strangers and some of the original Texas Playboys. Haggard was invited to sing and play on the last Playboys recording session with Bob Wills on December 3, 1973, after which Wills tragically suffered his fatal stroke.

The mid- and late-1970s were years of personal transition for Haggard. He split with Bonnie Owens, although she continued as part of the musical organization. He married Leona Williams, who was a vocalist with the troupe and has since split. In 1979 he acted in the TV mini-series *Centennial*, and sang a duet with movie star Clint Eastwood, 'Bar Room Buddies.' In the 1980s his hits included 'Think I'll Just Stay Here and Drink,' 'My Favorite Memory,' 'Rainbow Stew,' 'Poncho and Lefty,' 'Half a Man,' 'Reasons to Quit' (the last three with Willie Nelson), 'Yesterday's Wine,' 'C C Waterback' (the last two with George Jones), 'Let's Chase Each Other Around the Room.'

Having switched labels to Epic and then MCA, Merle also recorded another gospel album, *Songs for the Mama That Tried* in 1981, and a loving tip-of-the-hat song to a songwriter who helped him in the early days and shared some tough times. The song was entitled 'Leonard,' for Leonard Sipes, the real name of Tommy Collins. In the early 1980s Haggard produced an autobiography, *Sing Me Back Home*.

Also in the 1980s, Haggard recorded duet albums with Willie Nelson. And his single 'Twinkle, Twinkle, Lucky Star' was an immediate hit – as if to remind a nation and an industry that his presence was still dominant.

Merle Haggard is a master of all

musical genres he approaches, evidenced by his classics – in nostalgia 'Tearing the Labor Camps Down,' introspection, 'Mama's Hungry Eyes, Mama Tried,' fatalism, 'No Reason to Quit,' 'Tulare Dust,' nationalism, 'Dirty Old Hatbands' and 'Are The Good Times Really Over for Good,' which he performed at a televised concert for President Reagan.

With a respectful appreciation for country music's heritage, a rich output of his own, and a career that singers and songwriters will long try to emulate, Merle Haggard has built a legacy in country music that some may equal but none can top.

Hag has pulled himself back from the effects of personal demons and the obscurity that threatens to overshadow even the most talented of yesterday's active stars. He has publicly talked about his problems with alcohol, drugs, and women, and has speculated upon retiring from writing and singing (indeed, during his more active time in the 1980s he would develop fragments of lyrics and tunes and leave them to others to finish). Merle Haggard is one of a half-dozen leading lights – singer, songwriter, inspiration – in all of country music history, and it was ironic to see the current crop of stars, no matter how good they are, eclipse him. Where once he filled state fairground stadiums, in the early 1990s he was filling small clubs and sharing bills with others.

None of this says anything about his talent or performance quality; it speaks to the relatively fickle nature of otherwise loyal audiences in these crowded days of creative ferment. In 1994 he received the Hall of Fame award from the Country Music Association, and the same year saw two excellent tribute albums recorded in his honor (in a period where this laudable practice is becoming fashionable, e.g., the Eagles and Bob Wills projects) – one by prominent singers and one from the songwriters' perspective.

Not only are these tributes worthy (and long overdue: Hag should know of the deep respect, even reverence, felt for him) but they are also emblematic of the two sides of his incredible genius, singing and songwriting. Even his minor songs are major pieces of quality country music poetry.

Hall, Tom T

'The Storyteller,' Tom T Hall, gained his nickname by writing a host of story songs on the most unlikely subjects – as homey, honest, and commonplace as the country audience he wrote for – and his amazing, poetic ability to evoke moods and attitudes by single lines of lyrics. He was born in Olive Hill, Kentucky, in 1936, the son of a minister. He attended Roanoke College, majoring in journalism, before playing in a band and then hosting a country music program on the WMOR radio station in Morehead, Kentucky.

After serving eight years in the Army, Hall returned to disc-jockeying but also began writing songs that he sent to Nashville. Publisher Jimmy Key offered Hall a $50-a-week position as a staff songwriter with his firm; Hall moved to Tennessee and in 1963 he had his first hit composition: Jimmy 'C' Newman's 'DJ for a Day.' In 1968 a Hall song became one of the biggest sellers in musical history – 'Harper Valley PTA,' which to date has sold in excess of six million copies – a trademark Hall song with a message, some anecdotes, and humorous irony. His many songs recorded by a wide variety of singers include 'George and the North Woods' (Dave

'The Storyteller,' Tom T. Hall.

Dudley). 'Margie's at the Lincoln Park Inn' (Bobby Bare), 'You Can't Trust a Friend Anymore' (Lester Flatt and Mac Wiseman) and 'I'm Not Ready Yet' (George Jones).

In 1967 Hall was signed to his own recording contract with Mercury Records; his rapid and steady rise culminated only six years later when he played Carnegie Hall in New York. Two of Hall's early albums illustrate his talents and the best type of songs that were responsible for that rise.

Homecoming's title song is in the voice of a country singer, hardly as successful as he pretends, returning home for an excruciatingly brief meeting. He explains why he

Tom T. Hall in the late 1970s.

couldn't come to his mother's funeral, but would have called if he'd known they had a phone. The girl sleeping in his car is in his band, that's all; and he talks of how his next record will click. The entire song is filled with emblem-lines that represent all that is said, and all that isn't, in such a situation. Hall tells us about lives through a single vignette, and even lets us see different viewpoints.

In Search of a Song featured 'The Year that Clayton Delany Died,' an ode to a young boy's local, obscure, flawed, but admired guitar picker; 'Who's Gonna Feed Them Hogs' is a lament of a hospitalized farmer's obsession; 'Trip to Hyden' is pure musical journalism, telling the story of a recent mine disaster through the normalcy of its aftermath; 'Second

Hand Flowers' is about visiting a dying also-ran girlfriend. This is country poetry, music and lyrics of a sort that other types of music can't touch. Through the mid-1970s Tom T Hall couldn't be topped as a songwriter.

His other singles have included: 'Me and Jesus,' 'Old Dogs, Children and Watermelon Wine,' 'She Gave Her Heart to Jethro,' 'Grandma Whistled,' 'Fox on the Run,' 'Faster Horses, Younger Women, Older Whiskey, More Money,' 'What Have You Got to Lose' and 'Back When Gas Was 30 Cents a Gallon.'

In the 1980s Hall recorded children's songs (and an album) and a dose of social commentary, which is usually as leaden as his social reportage was deft; 'The Man Who Hated Freckles' is preachy, none-too-subtle and, worst, represents the type of songs that seem obligatory but jarringly out of place among other Hall songs on his albums.

Hall's voice is an unadorned nasal baritone that perfectly complements his Everyman subject matter. The Hall sound was established by Mercury producer Jerry Kennedy, who brought mostly acoustic accompaniments – guitars, dobro, harmonica, some strings at times – to the brilliant, commonplace lyrics. *Opry* member Hall has written an autobiography entitled *The Storyteller's Nashville*.

Retired from performing since the early 1990s, Hall enjoys a relaxed lifestyle on his Franklin, Tennessee, farm and sees to business interests. The stories his songs tell about people, places and events show us all to be a little spotted, perhaps, sometimes silly or boring, and occasionally noble. His were invariably true portraits.

Hamblen, Stuart

One of the select group of Western singers who really was a cowboy, Stuart Hamblen was born in Kellyville, Texas, in 1908. However, he sought to leave the ranch, attending college with the intention of becoming a teacher. After graduation his other interest, music, won out, and Hamblen sang on Dallas-Fort Worth radio as Cowboy Joe. In 1928 he recorded for Victor and moved to California.

Hamblen was very active in the

Genuine cowboy Stuart Hamblen.

Golden State in the '30s and '40s, particularly on radio and in the movies. He was a member of the famed Beverly Hill Billies, and for a while led his own group, The Lucky Stars. In the movies he often played villains, in a sense reflecting his lifestyle at that time; he admits to having been a hard-drinking rough guy. He was a very successful songwriter at this time as well, with many singers covering his records for hits in the country and even pop fields. 'My Mary' and 'Texas Plains' were two such songs, and in 1949 he scored a success with 'Remember Me (I'm the One Who Loves You),' which has since become a country standard. A later smash was 'This Ole House.'

At this time Stuart Hamblen became a born-again Christian as the result of a Billy Graham crusade, and he changed his rough and rowdy ways. In 1952 he ran for President on the Prohibition Party ticket. (In 1936 he had run for Congress, but obviously his new affiliation reflected the change in his life.)

A traditionalist in terms of Western and cowboy music, and a preserver of sweet country love ballads and sentimental songs, Hamblen has for years devoted himself to gospel music almost exclusively. Many of his compositions have become gospel classics, including 'It Is No Secret (What God Can Do),' 'Open Your Heart and Let the Sun Shine In' and 'You Must Be Born Again.'

Hamilton, George IV

Born in Matthews, North Carolina, in 1937, George Hamilton IV attended the University of North Carolina and the American University of Washington, DC. He was a fan of country music but gravitated toward rock in the mid-1950s when he entered the music business. He had a successful recording of 'A Rose and a Baby Ruth' in 1956, a soft-rock teen song that got him placed in the Alan Freed touring show with Buddy Holly, Gene Vincent and the Everly Brothers.

In 1960 Hamilton formally returned to country music, and earned a berth on the Grand Ole Opry. His considerable country successes over the next decade included 'Abilene,' 'Forth Worth, Dallas or Houston' and 'She's a Little Bit Country.' In the late '60s Hamilton was attracted by folk songs, particularly those of Canadian singers and writers like Gordon Lightfoot and Ian and Sylvia. He became identified with their music – charting such hits as 'Canadian Pacific' and 'Early Morning Rain' – although the songs were really more soft-country/pop ballads than the folk/protest music then glutting the nation.

The identification with Canadian music increased Hamilton's popularity in Canada and by extension in England. He has made many international tours, and was the first country artist to perform in several countries. His *North Country* television program, based in Canada, was syndicated around the world, and he also had a brief ABC-TV network program in 1969, *The George Hamilton IV Show*, featuring regulars Roy Clark and Elton Britt. Hamilton possesses an easy-listening, pleasant voice and he continues to tour and perform on the Opry. Part of his troupe is his son George V.

Happy Goodman Family, The

This group's name is not reflective of the front-man's nickname; it is a well-chosen description of the ensemble. One of the premier country gospel groups for years, the Happy Goodman Family infuses humor into their live act, good feelings into their recordings, and clear-as-a-bell testimonies into all their work.

The members are Howard Goodman, front; Rusty, bass; Sam, baritone; Vestal, soprano lead; Tanya Goodman Price, alto; and Johnny Cook, tenor. The group has won many awards, singly and as a group, including a 1968 Grammy for Best

Gospel Album. They were original members of the *Gospel Singing Jubilee* television show, and hosted their own *Happy Goodman Family Hour* on TV. They have appeared with Oral Roberts, on the *Dinah Shore* TV show, and with Jimmy Swaggart in North Carolina crusades.

The Goodmans have recorded almost three dozen albums and as a songwriter Rusty has penned some all-time gospel classics, including 'Had It Not Been,' 'I Wouldn't Take Nothing For My Journey Now' and 'Wait'll You See My Brand-New Home.'

Their lively singing includes alternating leads and old-fashioned country gospel harmonies; their spirited delivery of a song is as honest as their message – straightforward, no apologies, and true. The ensemble has since separated to allow individual members to record solo.

Harris, Emmylou

Born in Birmingham, Alabama, in 1949, Emmylou Harris' first love was folk music. Her youth was dissimilar to the prototypical country star's as she was a college drama major (at the University of North Carolina), and dropped out to sing folk songs in small New York City clubs. But she remembers listening to stations like clear-channel WWVA (Wheeling, West Virginia) when she would drive to visit her parents in Washington, DC.

In the late '60s she moved to Washington, and sang in local clubs like the Cellar Door, singing country-tinged folk songs. At the Door one night she was heard by members of the Flying Burrito Brothers band, who recommended her to ex-Burrito Gram Parsons. Parsons was the catalyst of the California folk/rock/bluegrass/country movement and was looking for a female harmony singer for his debut album.

Emmylou received both an offer to sing and a real education from Parsons, who introduced her to country music's heritage. She sang on Parsons' first album, *G P*, toured with him, and then sang on his brilliant last album in 1973, *Grievous Angel*. Parsons died shortly thereafter, and the loss crushed Harris. She withdrew to Washington again to write and perform locally.

But her singing had gained attention and Emmylou was offered a solo recording contract with Warner Brothers. Her first album, *Pieces of the Sky*, contained songs drawn from all her influences, but her version of the Louvin Brothers' 'If I Could Only Win Your Love' was pure country and a smash hit. She has steadily gained stature as a country singer ever since, although she assertedly records rock- and folk-tinged material as well.

Her country hits have included 'Making Believe,' 'Blue Kentucky Girl,' 'Too Far Gone,' 'Sweet

Emmylou Harris.

Dreams' and 'Together Again.' She has sung duets with, among others, Buck Owens, Roy Orbison, Don Williams, Dolly Parton and Linda Ronstadt. Her voice is folk-nasal rather than country-nasal, a natural feature of her early influences, but her stylings, arrangements and choice of material make it very comfortable indeed to country ears.

A large degree of Emmylou's popularity stems from the musical company she keeps; she is known for assembling stellar touring and recording bands. For years her various units were known as The Hot Band, and many future stars and studio kingpins passed through its ranks. Alumni include Ricky Skaggs, Mike Auldridge, Glen D. Hardin, James Burton, Albert Lee and Rodney Crowell. Subsequent lineups, groomed for the more acoustic sound she explored during the late 1980s and early 1990s, were called the Nash Ramblers. Harris and the Ramblers gave a farewell performance at the refurbished Ryman Auditorium in February 1995, and she almost immediately began sessions for her next album, said to be another musical departure.

The recipient of the Country Music Association's Female Vocalist Award, Emmylou Harris is a singer who has crossed-over *into* country music, bucking the very heavy traffic in the opposite direction. She has been widely and enthusiastically accepted not only by fans but by Nashville old-timers and traditionalists as well. Musical experimentation to Emmylou includes discovering and resurrecting the best of country music's heritage.

Without the solid support of radio usually required for elevation to major country stardom, Emmylou has undeniably reached legendary status among fans and industry insiders. She carries a reputation for artistic integrity to every project or performance, and is seen by many as *the* icon of soft-focus, folk-influenced country as well as a link to the roots of neo-traditionalism.

Hill, Faith

Many country fans compare Faith Hill's enthusiastic style to that of Reba McEntire, and her good looks to those of several beautiful movie stars, all of which seems predestined

Rising star Faith Hill.

for a girl from a town called Little Star, Mississippi.

Her first recording for Warner Brothers, 'Wild One,' jumped to number one on the charts and stayed there for four weeks, the first time that had happened since the legendary debut of the also beautiful Jeannie C. Riley with 'Harper Valley P. T. A.' 25 years earlier.

Eager to be a singer, Faith moved to Nashville when she was 19. Her first job was selling T-shirts at Country Music Fan Fair, an annual musical celebration. Later she found a job as a receptionist at Gary Morris' publishing company.

For a year and a half she kept her musical ambition a secret, but one day she was overheard singing to herself and writer David Chase asked her to do a demo of a new song of his called 'It Scares Me.' That led to other performances and finally a recording contract.

She was named Top New Female Vocalist of 1994 by the Academy of Country Music, among other honors. Her recording 'Take Me as I Am' was certified platinum. Her country music videos, high-lighting Faith's beauty as well as her impressive vocal talents, have been widely acclaimed successes.

J

Jackson, Alan

Quiet, unassuming Alan Jackson has an engaging stage presence as he bows and gallantly tips his signature white hat to the audience before he begins to sing, and it was with that same modest courtesy that he first courted success in Music City. Already in his twenties before he began to think of making a career in music, he left his home in Newnan,

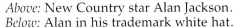

Above: New Country star Alan Jackson.
Below: Alan in his trademark white hat.

Georgia, for Nashville when his wife Denise met Glen Campbell in an airport and received the card of Campbell's publishing company there.

He did not arrive to trumpets and fanfare; his first job was working in the mailroom of the Nashville Network. But the job allowed him to do some networking of his own; he wrote songs, performed at local clubs, and got to know such fellow aspirants as Randy Travis, then singing (and cooking) at a small Nashville club. His compositions made enough of an impression to land him a job writing songs for the publishing company whose card Campbell had given Denise, and soon after that Jackson teamed up with Travis, now a rising star, as his opening act.

In 1990 his first album, *Here in the Real World,* appeared and was a smash hit from the beginning. Containing such number one hits as 'Wanted,' 'Chasin' That Neon Rainbow,' and 'I'd Love You All Over Again,' it went platinum, selling a million units in less than a year. The video 'Here in the Reel World' went gold with sales of $1 million. His second album did even better, reaching platinum in six months. It too contained several hit singles, beginning with the title cut, 'Don't Rock

Sonny James, second from right, accepts an award.

the Jukebox.' Characteristic of Alan's deferential spirit, the album contains tributes to several of his heroes in the industry, including George Jones and Hank Williams.

His high sales, along with the uniform success of his concert appearances, have brought Alan numerous honors in the trade: he was nominated for Male Vocalist of the Year and Entertainer of the Year by the Country Music Association in 1992 and was selected the Top New Male Artist of the Year by the Academy of Country Music in 1991. The CMA awarded Alan's eloquent tribute to Hank Williams, 'Midnight in Montgomery,' its Best Music Video Award in 1992.

A gentle, courtly figure, Alan Jackson projects a romantic image with straightforward love songs. A model of New Country, he draws his inspiration from the classic figures in country music, and, in keeping with one of the hallowed traditions of the genre, wears a distinctive hat as a personal trademark. It is typical of him and of the esteem in which he is held that he and his hero George Jones honor each other with bumper stickers on their pickup trucks.

Alan's smash single 'Chattahoochee' was the Academy of Country Music's Single of the Year for 1993, and his *A Lot About Livin'* CD was ACM's Album of the Year, awarded

in 1994. Other notable singles have included 'Livin' On Love,' 'Dallas,' and 'Someday.' In 1995 he was named ACM's Top Male Vocalist.

Jackson, Wanda

One of the very few genuine female rockabilly artists, Wanda Jackson has also visited many other parts of the Country in her varied career. She was born in Maud, Oklahoma, in 1937, but moved with her family to Bakersfield, California, when she was young, part of that wave of migrants chronicled in *Grapes of Wrath*. Wanda's father bought her a guitar, and she mastered it and the piano as well by the age of nine.

It was evident that Wanda was a musical prodigy. When she was 12 the family returned to Oklahoma City, and the next year she had her own radio show there (first 15 minutes, then a half-hour). As a high-school junior Wanda was heard by Hank Thompson, who offered her a solo part in a recording with his group, the Brazos Valley Boys. That record, 'You Can't Have My Love,' was a hit in 1954, and she toured with the popular Thompson. In 1955 and '56 she toured with a rising star named Elvis Presley, and evidently he did much to swing Wanda towards rockabilly.

After this switch, Wanda began to

play Las Vegas regularly and built a string of hits: 'Let's Have a Party,' 'Stupid Cupid,' 'There's a Party Goin' On' and 'Fujiyama Mama,' all rockabilly. In the '60s she moderated her style to a degree and sang in traditional honky-tonk style; 'Right or Wrong' was her major hit in this genre. She also hosted her own syndicated TV program, *Music Village*.

Wanda Jackson's early country singing was an uninhibited, rocking, earthy variety – hard-core in styles and lyrics. In the mid-1970s she was born again and since has recorded only gospel and sacred material. Needless to say, she brings as much passion and exuberance to her Christian music as she did to the secular material; she has released several gospel albums for the Word group of labels.

James, Sonny

Born Jimmie Loden in Hackleburg, Alabama, in 1929, Sonny James first performed musically with his string-band family ensemble when he was four. After the Korean War he moved to Nashville, where Chet Atkins introduced him to Ken Nelson of Capitol Records; Sonny signed a contract and soon became one of country music's biggest-selling stars through the 1970s.

In 1957 he scored with 'Young Love,' a favorite of country, rock and pop audiences alike; as 'teen music' it had the same appeal as Marty Robbins' 'White Sport Coat.' But it was in the mid-1960s that Sonny began an incredible string of 27 consecutive number one records, including: 'You're the Only World I Know,' 'Behind the Tear,' 'True Love's a Blessing,' 'A World of Our Own,' 'Only the Lonely,' 'Running Bear,' 'Since I Met You, Baby,' 'It's Just a Matter of Time' and 'Only Love Can Break a Heart.' At one point in the early 1970s *Record World* magazine named Sonny the Country Music Artist of the Previous Decade.

During the American Bicentennial in 1976, Sonny produced an album titled *200 Years of Country Music*, a fine retrospective collection, although it really collected songs of the previous half-century. Sonny's voice is a brittle, sincere balladeer's, a high baritone comfortable with heartache as well as upbeat material.

Waylon Jennings, way back when.

Jennings, Waylon

Born in Littlefield, Texas, in 1937, Waylon Jennings grew up liking music – at the age of 12 he was a pop disc-jockey on his hometown radio station. Five years later he was presenting country records on the air, and in 1958, during the first wave of rock 'n' roll, he was a rock DJ in Lubbock. During this time Jennings sometimes played backup in local bands.

Buddy Holly, then a hot star in rock, heard Jennings play and invited him to join his band as an electric bass player. But a few months later, on February 3, 1959, Holly was dead. According to legend, Jennings gave his seat in a private plane to the Big Bopper (J P Richardson, who was then hot with 'Chantilly Lace') after a concert. The plane crashed, killing Holly, the Big Bopper and Richie Valens.

Jennings returned to Lubbock, working again as a DJ and musician, and then moved to Phoenix, Arizona, where he founded his group, the Waylors. They developed a local following in rock and country music, and were heard by Bobby Bare during one of his tours; Bare recommended Jennings to his label, RCA, resulting in a recording contract in 1965. Jennings moved to Nashville (where he roomed for a time with Johnny Cash) and started building a recording career with heavy promotional assistance from RCA.

Singing with a strong tremolo baritone, Jennings covered a variety of bases in his material, almost all rock-tinged country: rockabilly ('Brown-Eyed Handsome Man'); rock (the Beatles' 'Norwegian Wood') and folk ('MacArthur Park'). Packaged and promoted as a Nashville rebel, he requested and received creative control over his own albums and indeed veered from country, opening for some rock groups in New York City, for instance.

In 1976 Jennings's career, and all of contemporary country music, received a jolt when the biggest album of the year was *Wanted: The Outlaws*, featuring Jennings, his wife Jessi Colter (former wife of rock guitarist Duane Eddy), Willie Nelson, and Tompall Glaser. The album was

actually a collection of former releases by the artists, and most of them sub-par material, but it heralded the nation's fascination with the Austin Sound, in which direction Jennings had been playing, and with the 'Outlaw' phenomenon.

Jennings later complained that the 'Outlaw' imagery was being overdone (and wrote a song to that effect), but nevertheless wrote lyrics concerning marijuana and cocaine and such, which seemed, to many listeners, to cater to the hoopla. Despite strong rock elements in his material, Jennings continues to devote most of his attention to his brand of country. Outstanding records in this vein have included 'Are You Sure Hank Done It This Way,' 'Bob Wills Is Still the King' and 'There Ain't No Good Chain Gang.'

A rock beat underpinning country instrumentation (steel guitars, etc) is one of his trademarks, as are the ringing sounds of electric guitars. Jennings' rough but in-control vocals symbolize to many listeners the whole Austin-Sound revolution.

Having roamed all over the musical lot for much of his career, Jennings has settled into his image as elder statesman in recent times and embraced a sound based on his country core. *Waymore's Blues (Part II)*, released in 1994, was critically and commercially well-received, and he has become a popular guest vocalist on recordings of young country artists. Like Merle Haggard, George Jones and Buck Owens, Waylon is a wellspring and inspiration. With Johnny Cash, Kris Kristofferson, and Willie Nelson, Jennings is a member of The Highwaymen, country's graybeard supergroup.

Jim and Jesse

The McReynolds Brothers were born in Coeburn, Virginia – Jim, guitar picker and tenor harmony, in 1927; and Jesse, mandolin player and lead singer, in 1929. Their parents played music throughout the Clinch Mountain area, and their grandfather had once recorded mountain music for Victor. Their first radio dates were in 1947 in Virginia; Jim and Jesse were among the first to pick up on the bluegrass revolution then spreading, but their progression had been through a Sons of the Pioneers sound and then gospel.

Jim and Jesse (standing, left to right) with The Virginia Boys.

In 1952 they moved to Lexington, and two years later to Knoxville as members of the *Tennessee Barn Dance*. They were also featured on CBS's *Saturday Night Country Style*. Other radio affiliations included the WWVA *Wheeling Jamboree*, where they were sponsored by Martha White. In 1962 they were signed by Epic Records, and gained national exposure with their singles, including 'Memphis,' 'Diesel on My Tail' and 'Freight Train.'

Jim and Jesse are bluegrass innovators. At first they maintained bluegrass instrumentation but played variant styles of music, the opposite of other groups that added electric and non-bluegrass instruments; they even recorded an album of Chuck Berry songs. Eventually they also experimented with diverse instruments, and among the superb musicians who have graduated from their band, the Virginia Boys, have been Bobby Thompson. Vassar Cle-

ments and Curly Seekler. In 1964 Jim and Jesse, who married sisters, joined the *Grand Ole Opry*. They have also hosted two of their own syndicated television programs: *Country-Music Carousel*, and *The Jim and Jesse Show*.

Jesse's mandolin playing is widely admired as innovative and masterful. He has developed what is called the McReynolds Crosspicking style, featuring syncopation and repeated melody patterns. He also utilizes a 'split string' style where different strings in the mandolin's pairs are fretted separately. As a mandolinist he was influenced by Earl Scruggs and cites the origin of his technique as attempting to simulate the banjo style. Jim and Jesse's clear vocals are reminiscent of the Blue Sky Boys and also show a debt to the Louvin Brothers.

Jones, George

George Glen Jones was born in Saratoga, Texas, in 1931. His mother played church piano and his father was an amateur guitarist. George got his own first guitar at nine, and his first professional jobs in the late 1940s on radio in Jasper, and playing guitar for the Eddie and Pearl duo. After a succession of other local jobs, George attracted the attention of H W 'Pappy' Daily, who signed the singer to his new Starday label in 1954. The next year George had a national hit with his own composition, 'Why Baby Why.' He was invited to join the *Louisiana Hayride*, and the next year switched over to the *Grand Ole Opry*.

George recorded some rockabilly sides as Thumper Jones and Hank Smith, but mostly he stuck to country – with a vengeance. He quickly became a prime exponent of honky-tonk lyrics, heartache ballads, and pure country interpretations. He sings more by instinct than any country singer of his time – Jones's voice breaks, whines, hushes, pleads and exults at precisely the right moments in a song; his Texas accent and clenched-teeth reserve make every song sound like it was written for him, in his style. Hardly a record released by George

Master vocal stylist George Jones.

Jones failed to be a major hit: 'Window Up Above' (also self-penned); 'White Lightnin',' 'She Thinks I Still Care,' 'Just a Girl I Used To Know,' 'The Race is On,' 'Take Me,' 'Seasons of My Heart' (another of his own songs), 'Love Bug,' 'I'm a People,' 'Tender Years,' 'Tell Me My Lyin' Eyes Are Wrong' and 'A Good Year for the Roses.'

In 1969 he married Tammy Wynette, and two years later he switched to her label and her producer, Billy Sherrill. They recorded some classic duets – 'We Go Together,' 'Let's All Go Down to the river,' 'Take Me,' 'Closing Time,' 'Something to Brag About' – but George continued his amazing string of solo singles, including 'The Grand Tour' and 'The Battle,' before his marriage, life and career broke down in 1975. He was an alcoholic and was bankrupt; not only that, but Tammy received the tour bus and the Jones Boys band in the divorce settlement.

By the late 1970s and early 1980s, like the typical figure of a George Jones song who's been stomped on and is down to his last dime, he dried out and came back. He scored the biggest hits of his career – 'He's Stopped Loving Her Today,' 'I'm Not Ready Yet,' 'I Always Get Lucky With You' – and finally received awards from the country establishment. He even rejoined Tammy for some duets and albums. 'He

Stopped Loving Her Today' – the quintessential country heartache song by Bobby Braddock and Curly Putman performed to chilling effect by Jones – was voted Song of the Year in both 1981 and 82 by the CMA.

George was one of the prime movers behind ACE, the Association of Country Entertainers, a 1970s group that fought pop influences in country music. He is no historian of country roots or a purist about the various components or schools; George Jones just wants to hear, and sing, good country songs, and no one does it better. It is probably a misnomer to label him a honky-tonk singer, since he is larger than any genre. Jimmie Rodgers, Hank Williams, Ray Price – they have all had countless imitators, but one seldom hears of a George Jones imitator in spite of the universal admiration awarded him. No one, simply, can touch him as a stylist.

He has been able to combine the wail of Roy Acuff, the intensity of Bill Monroe, the soul of Hank Williams, the vocal breaks of Lefty Frizzell and the casual phrasing of Floyd Tillman, but all the time he is distinctly George Jones.

Jones may well have recorded more duets than any other country singer. Beginning with his partnership with Tammy Wynette and his own collaboration albums (including cuts with artists as diverse as Gene Pitney and Elvis Costello), he's become a fixture as a special guest on recordings by the biggest names in New Country. The current rush to record 'tribute' albums in honor of established style-makers has contributed to all sorts of strange pairings, but most young artists, male and female, can honestly point to The Possum as a major influence. Neo-traditionalists, in fact, often imitate his phrasing and inflection as accurately as possible when trying to develop their own styles.

Jones recorded *The Bradley Barn Sessions* in 1994. Cut at the historic Nashville studio, the album features duets with Wynette, Travis Tritt, Alan Jackson, and several others. His performance on this most recent disc is as powerful and fresh as any he's ever given, putting Jones squarely in the vanguard of modern country, rather than allotting him a slot as a mere 'oldie.' Fans held their collective breath in 1992 when

George underwent open-heart surgery, but he has seemingly come back stronger than ever.

Jones, Grandpa

Louis Marshall Jones has been called a Grandpa since the age of 22; and the only thing older than his jokes are the classic old-time and mountain tunes he serves up in his colorful stage act. He was born in Niagra, Kentucky, in 1913, the youngest of 10 children of sharecropping parents who performed music locally. Jones received his first guitar when he was 11 and in the late 1920s discovered the recordings of Jimmie Rodgers. He won a talent contest in 1929 in Akron, Ohio, and bought a new guitar with the $50 prize money. In his performance, he yodeled in the Jimmie Rodgers manner.

In the next few years Jones held positions with various radio stations'

Grandpa Jones.

country shows – this was when radio was still largely live and local – billed as The Young Singer of Old Songs. In 1935, after playing in the backing band of radio's Lum and Abner, he joined the famous singer and collector of old-time songs, Bradley Kincaid, in his road act and on several top radio barn dances around America. Over the radio, Jones's voice sounded pipey-high and flinty, prompting listeners to inquire of his age. Kincaid got to calling Jones 'Grandpa' and the name stuck; Jones adopted the persona fully, dressing like an old man and establishing comedy routines as part of his act. From Kincaid, Jones learned not only performing styles but a rich repertoire of American traditional and folk music.

Grandpa joined WWVA in Wheeling, West Virginia, in 1937 with his own show of *Grandpa Jones and His Grandchildren* (it was here that he took the banjo as primary instrument), and through the years he was to appear often on that station's *Wheeling Jamboree*. In 1941 he moved to the new *Boone County Jamboree* in Cincinnati, where he formed important relationships with Merle Travis and the Delmore Brothers and recorded some classic records – among the first on Syd Nathan's King label – as a soloist and with the Brown's Ferry Four gospel quartet.

Grandpa served in World War II, and in its latter days he broadcast over Armed Forces Radio with a group he assembled as The Munich Mountaineers. In 1946 he was invited to join the Grand Ole Opry, also touring with the tent shows of Pee Wee King and, again, Bradley Kincaid. He has remained with the Opry ever since, except for a number of radio and television stints, including a featured spot on the Jimmy Dean TV show, in the Washington/Virginia area.

As an original cast member of television's *Hee Haw* since 1969, Grandpa Jones has become familiar to a new generation. His backwoods humor is appropriate for the comedy show, but many viewers have also discovered his fine musicianship. Grandpa plays the old-fashioned banjo in frailing or drop-thumb technique in the style of Uncle Dave Macon, and in his colorful performance he plays practically with his whole body, either bouncing in time

The Judds: Wynonna and Naomi.

to the music or standing ramrod-straight and letting one leg vigorously keep time. His characteristic high, nasal tenor vocals are punctuated with laughs and asides.

Grandpa's wife Ramona is an accomplished fiddler and frequently performs with him. Their three grown children have also become devotees of old-time country music, and the family band has become a superb ensemble. CMH Records has performed a great service in recording an abundance of Grandpa Jones music in recent years: records of the family band; *The Grandpa Jones Story*, with new versions of Brown's Ferry Four Classics; a tribute album to Bradley Kincaid; etc.

Grandpa Jones may preserve traditional songs and be among the last practitioners of yodeling and banjo techniques, but he has never been averse to incorporating newer sounds. Very early, for instance, the electric guitar of Merle Travis could be heard behind his hillbilly songs. Otherwise Grandpa and Ramona (who also do a novelty routine of playing bells tied to their ankles and wrists) preserve the American traditions of minstrel shows, vaudeville, old-time and mountain music.

Victorian ballads, sentimental songs, and gospel music. They have been ambassadors of an uninhibited, joyful brand of country music around the globe for nearly two generations. In 1978 Grandpa Jones was elected to the Country Music Hall of Fame.

Among his many hits through the years, many self-penned, were 'Eight More Miles to Louisville,' 'Tragic Romance,' 'Old Rattler,' 'Sweet Dreams of Kentucky,' 'Mountain Dew,' 'You'll Make Our Shack a Mansion,' 'Old Blue,' 'The Banjo Am the Instrument,' 'My Bonnie Lies Over the Ocean,' 'It's Raining Here This Morning (and They've Given Me a Number For My Name),' 'Gone Home,' 'I'm On My Way Somewhere,' 'There's a Hand That's A-Waiting' and 'I'll Meet You in the Morning.'

Judds, The

A mother-and-daughter combo, who look like sisters and sound like pop and country veterans, the Judds have only been on the charts since 1984 and are Nashville/Hollywood examplars of the 'overnight' success story. In fact, they dreamed, worked, and traveled in the course of paying the proverbial dues. Both Naomi and her daughter Wynonna (real names – respectively, Diana and Christina – were apparently considered too mundane for country audiences) were born in Ashland, Kentucky, in 1946 and 1964.

The Judds moved to Hollywood for a while to find success as singers, and worked at the inevitable odd jobs instead; then, after returning to Kentucky, they moved to Nashville. There Naomi worked as a nurse, secretary, and model (appearing on one of Conway Twitty's album covers) while Wynonna attended school.

The Judds hit their magic payoff when they were signed by RCA on the strength of a live audition in 1984. Their first release was 'Had a Dream (From the Heart),' and other hits have included 'Mama, He's Crazy,' 'Love Is Alive,' 'Grandpa,' 'I Know Where I'm Going,' and 'Maybe Your Baby's Got the Blues.'

The Judds' hard-edged harmonies have recently become more driven, mixing rock and pop stylings with their country basics. They are also notable for their extravagant hairstyles and costumes, proudly confirming country stereotypes.

The duo won Top Vocal Group honors from both the Country Music Association and the Academy of Country Music from 1985 through 1987.

In 1991, diagnosed with chronic active hepatitis, Naomi announced her retirement from touring, and mother and daughter embarked on a farewell tour that lasted nearly a year. Together, the Judds had sold over 11 million albums. Naomi, who with Wynonna and younger daughter Ashley had acted briefly in a failed TV pilot for the Fox Network, starred in the 1993 CBS-TV movie *Rio Diablo* with Kenny Rogers. The film also featured Travis Tritt. Her 1993 autobiography, *Love Can Build a Bridge*, was a best-seller. Wynonna began developing her solo career shortly after her mother's retirement. An edgier sound, a more contemporary look and a feister image were embraced immediately by Judds fans. Her solo hits include 'Is It Over Yet,' 'Rock Bottom,' 'No One Else On Earth' and 'Girl Thing,' a duet with Tammy Wynette.

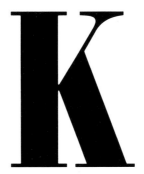

Keith, Toby

Voted the Top New Country Artist of 1993, Toby Keith had two number one and two other top five hits emerge from his first Polydor album, *Should've Been a Cowboy*.

Toby Keith was in fact a cowboy who worked for a rodeo, and was a professional football player for two seasons and an oil-rig worker in his native Oklahoma before becoming a successful singer and recording artist.

Keith began performing on the Texas-Oklahoma dance club circuit in the 1980s and by 1988 he and his band, called Easy Money, had moved up to the larger clubs. They also had recorded several songs written by Keith on an independent record label and that led to Nashville and a contract with Polydor Records (Mercury).

His first albums on the label were hits. *Boomtown* was the title of the second album. The blonde baritone's other hits have included 'He Ain't Worth Missing' and 'A Little Less Talk and a Lot More Action.'

Kentucky Colonels, The

A seminal group in the bluegrass revival of the 1960s, the Kentucky Colonels were built around brothers Roland (born 1938) and Clarence (born 1944) White, natives of Lewiston, Maine, who were raised in California. In the late 1950s the brothers formed a group called The Country Boys and performed in California on Cliffie Stone's *Hometown Jamboree*, on *Squeekin' Deacon's Show* and the *Town Hall Party*.

In 1962 they became the Kentucky Colonels, with Billy Ray Latham on banjo; Roger Bush, bass and banjo; Bobby Slone, fiddle and LeRoy Mack, dobro. Clarence played guitar and Roland played mandolin. In 1964 they recorded a landmark album for World-Pacific, *Appalachian Swing!*, that captured driving, modern versions of traditional material like 'Sally Goodin' and 'Billy in the Low Ground.' Joe Maphis wrote adulatory liner notes. The Colonels indeed brought modern exuberance to hard-driving bluegrass, and their sound was highlighted by Clarence's strong guitar leads.

In 1965 the Colonels split up. Clarence became a sideman for rock and country recordings; he joined the Byrds in 1968 and later played with other groups including the marvelous but short-lived progressive bluegrass group Muleskinner (other members included David Grisman, Peter Rowan, Richard Greene and Bill Keith). Roland White stayed traditional, and played with both Bill Monroe's Bluegrass Boys and Lester Flatt's Nashville Grass.

Latham and Bush joined the Dillard and Clark Expedition, and Bush later was a member of Byrone Berline's Country Gazette.

In 1970 there was a short reunion of the group, and a get-together for a Swedish tour in 1973 led to the for-

New Country artist Toby Keith.

mation of the New Kentucky Colonels. It was just as they were re-aligning in the bluegrass mode that Clarence was killed on July 14, 1973. A drunk driver struck him while he was carrying his guitar to his car. In the opinion of many of his contemporaries during his lifetime, Clarence was the finest flatpicking guitar player who ever played. After Clarence's death no attempt was made firmly to re-establish this influential bluegrass group. Several other albums – live recordings – remain as documents of their classic sounds.

Kershaw, Doug

Born in a houseboat near Tiel Ridge, Louisiana, in 1936, Douglas James Kershaw was a Cajun who grew up speaking the local dialect of French, playing Cajun music, and living the back-country Cajun lifestyle of fishing and hunting. Cajuns are Louisiana descendants of French Canadians who had been dispossessed of the land that they call Acadia; 'Cajun' is a corruption of Acadian.

Doug learned fiddle and guitar and appeared in performances with his mother on local stages when he was young. In 1953 his brother Rusty (born 1940) teamed with Doug on local radio, and within a few years they were featured performers on the *Louisiana Hayride*. They cut records that became regional hits, and joined the Grand Ole Opry in 1957. The following year each enlisted in the Army, so that their discharges would coincide.

In 1961, billed as Rusty and Doug, they recorded 'Louisiana Man,' a major hit full of bright and brooding chords and cadences; it became their theme and cemented the rest of the country's perception of Cajun music and stylings. 'Diggy Liggy Lo,' like its predecessor, was full of exotic terms and sounds, and was also a major success. Pop listeners as well as country audiences were intrigued by this 'new' music, although the Kershaw sounds reflected generations-old traditions in the Louisiana bayous. In the mid-1960s Doug and Rusty split to pursue solo careers.

Doug, certainly the more prominent of the brothers, is known as the 'Ragin' Cajun' in reference to his outlandish stage style – bizarre Victorian-style costumes, Mephistophelean grimaces, aggressive fiddle playing (strings will routinely snap during his concerts, and several bows stand ready for inevitable replacement) and a perfervid approximation of St Vitus' dance. Such an extraordinary theatrical presence (never captured on disc) makes for a fine concert but can obscure the authentic Cajun origins of Doug's music, and even more so as he has incorporated rock flavorings into his musical gumbo.

Kershaw has a considerable audience in rock, rockabilly and folk areas too. He was a favorite, for instance, at Al Aronowitz's landmark country concerts in New York City in the 1970s. Now that Cajun and Zydeco music have become national sensations, Kershaw is busy, more with appearances than record sales – but better to showcase his legendary stage presence.

Kershaw, Sammy

Cajun music, with its robust, lilting quality, has always been a distinctive, popular variety of country music and new stars such as Sammy Kershaw continue to emerge from the Bayou Country to the delight of traditionalists. Kershaw, a man of the 1990s, says 'the hardest thing in the world to do is keep something simple, but simplicity works.'

Kershaw's first two Mercury albums were certified gold and barely missed platinum. The first, in 1991, was *Don't Go Near the Water* followed in 1993 by *Haunted Heart*. His followup in 1994 was *Feelin' Good Train*, a mixture of songs as varied and tasty as the down-home dishes Kershaw grew up on. Hit singles have included 'National Working Woman's Holiday,' 'Third Rate Romance,' and 'Southbound.'

Kershaw, who is frequently compared to George Jones, his hero, is one of the important contributors to the 1990s new wave of country stars. Born deep in Louisiana Cajun country in Abbeville and reared in nearby Kaplan, Kershaw recalls hearing his mother sing Hank Williams song as lullabies. The old-

Below: Sammy Kershaw.
Right: Doug Kershaw.

est of four children, Kershaw was first jolted by tragedy when, at age 11, his father, a construction worker, died of lung cancer. Encouraged by his mother, Kershaw at age 12 went to work for a local country entertainer, J. B. Perry, 'who sounded a lot like George Jones,' and who became a second father to young Kershaw. Soon Sammy found himself singing and opening for some of the industry's biggest names, including Jones and the late Mel Street.

'I grew up a lot quicker than I should have,' Kershaw admits, and the results were honky-tonk life, substance abuse and failed marriages. At one time things became so tenuous that Kershaw quit music and worked as a carpenter fulltime for two years, supervising remodeling in Wal-Mart stores.

The interlude taught Kershaw responsibility, and he picked up on Sam Walton's famous philosophy of service to his customers. 'That's what the fans are, customers,' Kershaw said. 'I try to take care of the fans.'

Hal Ketchum with Gene Autry.

Ketchum, Hal

When Hal Ketchum entered the world of country music in 1981, he came out of a background unlike that of most others in the field. Born and brought up in a small town in upstate New York, he was over 40 and had worked most of his life as a carpenter when he moved south. Gruene (pronounced Green), Texas, his new home, is a center of folk-country-rock music, and Hal responded to the Austin sound he heard there. Frequenting Gruene Hall, he absorbed the styles of its music as he evolved his own. An avowed liberal in politics, he is decidedly a maverick in New Country.

In time he graduated from fan to performer in Gruene, and by 1990, now a full-time country singer and songwriter, he moved on to Nashville. There his expertly wrought songs about the daily lives of small-town America brought him a contract with Forerunner Music. With co-producer Allen Reynolds, who has helped guide the music and the careers of such country music notables as Crystal Gayle, Garth

Brooks, and Kathy Mattea, he did a first album, *Past the Point of Rescue*, for Curb; Kathy Mattea sang harmony on some of the cuts. One more element of Hal's unorthodox profile was the fact that the album was first released in Germany.

Hal's single 'Small Town Saturday Night' typifies his subject matter and his personal identification with the heartaches of the common man. According to one trade publication, it was the biggest country music radio song of 1991. His voice has a stylistic range from smooth purr to emotional roar, from sultry to passionate. His second big success was the contemplative ballad 'I Know Where Love Lives.' Another powerful song, written by his producer Allen Reynolds, was 'Five O'Clock World,' a cover of the 1960s hit by Jay and the Americans.

Now a member of the Grand Ole Opry, the shaggy-headed, gray-haired Ketchum has had hits with 'Tonight We Might Just Fall in Love Again,' 'That's What I Get For Losin' You,' and 'Heads Are Gonna Roll'; and top-ten CDs with *Every Little Word* and *Sure Love*.

Kincaid, Bradley

Called 'The Kentucky Mountain Boy with his Hound-Dog Guitar,' Bradley Kincaid was born in Point Leavell, Kentucky, in 1895. He learned the banjo at five, and loved the music of the hills, beginning a life-long obsession with gathering the country tunes and folk songs of rural America.

He first performed for Chicago radio station WLS in 1925 while in college, and the following year joined the staff of that station's famed *National Barn Dance*, remaining until 1931. He graduated college in 1928 and, between radio performances, toured as a singer and collector of old songs and traditional melodies. Kincaid cut many records – under many names – through the 1940s. In the 1930s he appeared on many stations' country radio programs, including those of WLW, Cincinnati, and WWVA, Wheeling, West Virginia. He was a member of the Grand Ole Opry between 1944 and 1949.

Bradley Kincaid discovered Grandpa Jones, and toured with him for a time. On the road he marketed his

Bradley Kincaid.

personalized 'Hound-dog' guitar, and was the first to publish a song-book of exclusively country scores. For his material, Kincaid specialized in traditional songs, holdovers from the thematic preoccupations of the Victorians – death, tragedy, senti-ment, love and irony. He sung in a soft, smooth, high tenor, not as rough-edged as many of his rural contemporaries. His great contribu-tion, besides influencing many of his generation like the young Grandpa Jones, was collecting, preserving and popularizing hundreds of other-wise-forgotten old-time songs from rural America.

King, Pee Wee

Born Frank Anthony Kuczynski in Abrams, Wisconsin, in 1914, Pee Wee King grew up in Milwaukee and was encouraged to learn music by his father, a polka-band ocarina and fid-dle player. In high school Pee Wee played the fiddle and accordion in polka bands, and in 1933 joined the *Badger State Barn Dance* on WRJN. As he leaned increasingly toward country music, his idol was Fiddling Pappy McMichen, and Pee Wee specialized in playing square dances. Soon he was adapting the modern sounds of cowboy and Western sounds into his music, and that is when Gene Autry discovered him.

Autry took Pee Wee to Louisville, Kentucky, where he had a radio show. King formed a backup band, the Golden West Cowboys, and the aggregation remained when Autry went to Hollywood. For a while Pee Wee played the *Mid-Day Round-Up* on Knoxville, Tennessee station WNOX, but in the mid-1930s he and the band joined the Grand Ole Opry, remaining until 1947. On the *Opry* Pee Wee King's outfit was among the first Western bands, and among the first to play electrified instruments on stage.

From the 1930s to the 1950s Pee Wee also starred in many Western movies, with Gene Autry, Johnny Mack Brown and Charles Starrett. Later he was a regular member of several television shows, and once was on four at one time. In 1968 he re-tired his band as well as his own schedule of performing and record-ing. In 1974 he was elected to the Country Music Hall of Fame.

Among Pee Wee's major records are: 'Tennessee Waltz,' 'Bonaparte's Retreat' and 'Slow Poke.' 'You Belong to Me' was covered in the pop market by Jo Stafford, and 'Tennes-see Waltz' was a major pop hit for Patti Page. It was also designated a state song of Tennessee.

It might be said the Pee Wee King and His Golden West Cowboys are the original, legitimate recipients of the label 'Country-Western.' Cer-tainly their music wasn't as Western as the Texas and Oklahoma swing bands of the era; they retained too many country conventions. Also there was a pop-ish, smooth, sometimes schmaltzy aspect to their music that sometimes manifested itself. They had neither the rough edges of much of country music nor the driving jazz elements of Western Swing. However, this was obviously their key to success and broad acceptance, and why so much of their extremely engaging music was covered by other stars.

Among the many alumni from Pee Wee's superb band were Eddy Arnold, Ernest Tubb, Cowboy Copas, Minnie Pearl, and Redd Stewart, the guitar, fiddle, and piano player who co-wrote 'Tennessee Waltz,' which became a virtual anthem of country music.

Kingsmen, The

One of the most popular and honored gospel groups, the Kingsmen was founded in 1957 and is based in Asheville, North Carolina.

The Kingsmen present gospel music and witness, and are famed for their humor on stage. Favorites in concert situations, they have also hosted their own syndicated television program, *Music City Special*, and

Right: Alison Krauss.
Below: The Kingsmen in concert.

co-hosted a syndicated television show with Archie Campbell.

Eldridge Fox, who once sang with the Statesmen Quartet, sings baritone while other members of the popular Kingsmen include: Ray Dean Reese, bass; one-time Oak Ridge Boy Big Jim Hamil, lead and MC; Ed Crawford, baritone; Garry Sheppard, tenor and songwriter; Anthony Burger, pianist; Gary Dillard, steel guitarist; Arthur Rice, vocals and bass guitar and Greg Fox, drummer.

The Kingsmen have won more than a dozen Dove awards and perform about 250 concerts a year. As gospel music expands in all directions, they are exemplars of the traditional Southern Gospel Sound.

Krauss, Alison

In 1988, when she was only 16 years old, prodigy Alison Krauss had won seven fiddle championships in five states and was receiving high praise for her traditional country vocals.

Alison skipped her last two years of high school to perform and to enroll at the university in her home town of Champaign, Illinois. There she became one of the youngest voice majors at the University of Illinois. Her voice teacher was the renowned opera singer William Warfield.

Success was nothing new to Alison, who began taking violin lessons at age 5 and entering contests at age 8. She joined her first band at age 10 and won her first state fiddle championship at age 12. Rounder Records signed her as an artist when she was 14, and at 15 she appeared at the Newport Folk Festival.

She was only 13 when she joined the band Union station, led by John Pennell, who was 21 years her senior. A year later Union Station was named best new bluegrass band in America at the Kentucky Fried Chicken Festival in Louisville. Since going solo, Alison has led a regeneration of bluegrass, imbuing it with folk and blues flavors.

The youngest member of the Grand Ole Opry, Alison is always in demand by other performers to back them up on their performances. Several times she has had wild jams – driving country and soulful gospel – with the likes of Vince Gill and Marty Stuart on the Opry stage. She also routinely receives standing ovations, something rare since the days of Hank Williams Sr.

Her two newest CDs, confirming her immense talent for bluegrass fusion to a growing number of admirers across the spectrum, are *Now That I've Found You* and *I've Got That Old Feeling*. Smooth fiddle licks find their counterpoint in Alison's warbly soprano voice.

Kristofferson, Kris

Born in Brownsville, Texas, in 1936, Kristoffer Kristofferson is the son of a retired Air Force major general who became manager of air operations for Aramco in Saudi Arabia. As a youth, Kris endured the typical pattern in military families of living in many locations, but his family finally settled in California. He liked country music (buying Hank Williams records marked him as a

Singer/songwriter Kris Kristofferson.

'square' in his community, he recalls), but it was literature and athletics he pursued at Pomona College. He sent entries to an *Atlantic Monthly* short story contest and won first and third places as well as two honorable mentions. Awarded a Rhodes Scholarship, he went to Oxford after graduating from Pomona in 1958.

While at Oxford he attempted novel writing and songwriting. Signed by Tommy Steele's manager, he became Kris Carson, with lackluster results as a performer. After receiving a degree, the literary life also produced little encouragement, so Kris enlisted in the Army and served

in Germany; he continued to write songs and perform in base clubs. After five years of service, and just before he was to assume a teaching post at West Point, he vacationed in Nashville, following up on an earlier contact with songwriter Marijohn Wilkin. He never did go to West Point to teach.

The sacrifice was not immediately fruitful. He struggled, as most young songwriters do, and got jobs as a janitor at Columbia Studios and as a bartender at the Tally Ho Tavern, where many aspiring singers and songwriters congregated. He also called

upon his army helicopter training to transport men and equipment to oil rigs in the Gulf of Mexico. A few of his songs got recorded – Mercury artists Roy Drusky cut 'Jody and the Kid' and Dave Dudley did 'Vietnam Blues.' Then Mercury star Roger Miller deviated from his pattern of recording his own compositions and cut three of Kris's songs, 'Darby's Castle,' 'The Best of All Possible Worlds' and the legendary 'Me and Bobby McGee,' reportedly written on the basis of the title suggested by Fred Foster of Monument Records (which was to be Kris's label as a singer).

After 'McGee' Kristofferson hit his stride as a songwriter, and the stars waited in line for his songs. Janis Joplin covered 'McGee' in the rock field; Mark Lindsay (soft-rock/pop) and Johnny Cash recorded 'Sunday Morning Comin' Down,' Ray Price did 'For the Good Times,' 'I Won't Mention It Again' and 'I'd Rather Be Sorry'; Sammi Smith sang 'Help Me Make It Through the Night.'

Kris began recording his own material, and scored hits with 'Lovin'

Kristofferson – one of the Highwaymen.

Her Was Easier,' 'Josie' and 'The Pilgrim: Chapter 33.' For his success as a singer, Kristofferson has a rather unconventional voice, even in country music where polish is seldom applied; he growls at the bottom and roughly slides up the scale to a scraping baritone. His cadence is imprecise and he sometimes talks the melody as well as the lyrics. But the style is honest, a perfect reflection (in his performing context) of remarkably sincere writing.

When he became established as a singer in the early 1970s his written material tended more toward rock and folk; this was especially true after he teamed with Rita Coolidge, his recording/touring partner and for a time, his wife. Kris then became one of his generation's most popular movie stars, appearing in a wide variety of roles to critical acclaim and box-office success. He returned to country in the 1990s as a member of the Highwaymen with Willie Nelson, Johnny Cash and Waylon Jennings. They cut two albums and toured the U.S. and Europe.

So much has been written on Kristofferson as a poet that it has become a cliche; but, like most cliches, there is elemental truth in it. His country lyrics were impressively sensitive, and the phrases suggested common emotions in the singers and listeners, touching well-springs of feelings. He almost single-handedly saved Nashville from the Nashville Sound, which was turning on itself, sacrificing meaningful lyrics for clever studio instrumentation. It is forgotten now that his T-shirt and beard even challenged the Nashville lifestyle at the time. The changes wrought by 'outlaws' seem cosmetic when compared to Kristofferson's quiet revolution. And, for all the new roads he has traveled since leaving a strict country application, it should be remembered that it was Kristofferson, not a product of a country upbringing, who sought out Nashville as the place to tell his story in song.

Among the many other stars who have recorded his songs: Jerry Lee Lewis ('Once More With Feeling'); Ronnie Milsap ('Please Don't Tell Me How the Story Ends') and Christy Lane ('One Day at a Time'). Among his many distinctions are numerous Grammy awards and election to the Songwriters Hall of Fame.

Lawrence, Tracy

Tracy Lawrence admits that he divided his time in college between study, fun, and music. When he decided on music as his first priority, he took the logical step and moved to Nashville. The event remains clearly etched in his memory: It was September 2, 1990, a Monday night,' he recalls, 'and it was nine o'clock. I hit that I-295 bypass and saw that Nashville skyline . . . and felt like I was at home.' The city welcomed him in the same spirit. He had a recording contract within a year and two hits at the end of another: 'Sticks and Stones,' the title cut from his first album, and 'Today's Lonely Fool' both made it to the number one spot.

It wasn't all clear sailing for Tracy. Just after making his album he was attacked on the streets of Nashville, suffering gunshot wounds to the hip, arm, and knee. But he remained undaunted after three months of convalescence and therapy and returned to touring. Neither mugging nor marriage is going to interrupt Tracy's career: 'Performing is all I think about right now,' he assures his fans. 'I'm a long way from settling down.'

An engaging style, consistently high standards of material, and a strong new traditionalist voice assure Tracy a long future in the field. His recent hits include 'Hillbilly with a Heartache' (a duet with Alan Jackson), 'God Made a Good Woman on a Good Day,' and 'Texas Tornado.' His CDs have included *Alibi* and *I See It Now*.

Lee, Brenda

Brenda Mae Tarpley was born in Conyers, Georgia, in 1942 and was the proverbial child prodigy. At a young age she could repeat songs

Tracy Lawrence (left) and Brenda Lee (above).

that would be played for her, and as a youth she was soon appearing on local radio, and then local television. In 1956 she signed with Red Foley's manager who arranged for her to appear regularly on Foley's network TV program, the *Ozark Jubilee*, which led to other appearances.

At the height of rockabilly she recorded 'Rockin' Round the Christmas Tree' and other genuine rockabilly songs, but followed with her biggest record, 'I'm Sorry,' a more pop-oriented ballad. She settled into that groove – finding enormous popular acceptance – and at one point her manager vehemently denied any country music association in her repertoire or focus.

Fortunately Brenda's recording did not precisely match the disclaimer. A portion of her work continued to be country – 'Johnny One-Time,' 'Too Many Rivers' and some superb country singles in a spurt during the mid-1970s, including 'Wrong Ideas,' 'Big Four-Poster Bed,' Cowboy and the Dandy' and 'Broken Trust.' Brenda's loyal fans are legion, and responsible for continued high album sales, as well as forming the core of her consistent Las Vegas- and concert-appeal. Her voice – probably the most obvious element of her country identification – sounds perpetually hoarse, but contains that dry crack that can manifest both exuberance and sorrow, depending upon the material. Brenda, who is under five feet tall, is indeed a bundle of exuberance, and performs a lively stage show.

Brenda's current status reflects the bizarre situation that faces many giants in contemporary country music. She has made more than 250 records during her career, recently performed regularly before sold-out rooms in Las Vegas, and has fans around the world. Yet her records are not programmed by the 'Contemporary Country' radio stations that form a defacto network in big American cities. Consequently, despite her popularity, Brenda Lee does not have a label on which to record at this writing. In the summer of 1988, she cut back on her road schedules of 200 appearances a year and made a decided effort to reidentify with Nashville, appearing in a daily presentation at Opryland Park called *Music! Music! Music! Starring Brenda Lee*. She has also recorded background vocals with Loretta Lynn and Kitty Wells on an album by K. T. Oslin.

Lewis, Jerry Lee

One of the rawest natural talents to touch country music, Jerry Lee Lewis was born in Ferriday, Louisiana, in 1935. He showed an early interest in the piano, and his father borrowed against the little property he owned to buy a Stark upright piano for Jerry Lee. The youngster listened to country and gospel, boogie woogie and race music, and would sneak away – with his cousins Jimmy Swaggart and Mickey Gilley – to black clubs to eavesdrop on juke music.

His first performance came in 1949 when a car dealership sponsored his playing, and later a group of local supermarkets ran a 20-minute radio show featuring Jerry Lee. Coming from a close-knit group of relatives who had recently turned Pentecostal, Jerry Lee enrolled in the Assemblies of God Southwestern Bible Institute in Waxahachie, Texas; he

remained three months, however, and that time was largely spent sneaking to juke joints in Dallas at night.

In 1956, enthralled by the sounds of rock 'n' roll and enticed by the success of country boys like Elvis Presley, Jerry Lee made a pilgrimage to Sun Records in Memphis. After his original auditions he was judged too country by owner Sam Phillips and engineer Jack Clement, but he played some session work for Carl Perkins and others. Soon two Lewis recordings took off faster than any in Sun's history: 'Crazy Arms,' a hard-beat cover of the Ray Price song, and 'End of the Road,' a rocker that Jerry Lee wrote to order.

'Jerry Lee Lewis and His Pumping Piano,' read the credit, and Jerry did indeed bring the piano to prominence in rock 'n' roll. His left hand was reminiscent of Moon Mullican's, with a driving, boogie beat, sometimes played with knuckles instead of fingers. The right hand picked at notes and played arpeggios and glissandos. As with Sun's other artists, the backup was sparse (only drums on 'Crazy Arms'), but echo-chamber effects were heavy. Mostly, it was Jerry Lee and his piano.

In 1957, the musical world became his when 'Great Balls of Fire' and 'Whole Lotta Shakin' Goin' On' achieved massive hit status (the latter song was at the top of country, R&B, and rock charts simultaneously, and has sold more than six million copies to date). He was a guest on the Steve Allen television show (and was called back the following week due to public demand) and followed with other hits like 'Breathless.'

But the following year, while on tour in England, it was revealed that his new bride was only 13 years old. She was also Jerry Lee's cousin, a fact that did not strike the British (or Americans either) as seemly. It further developed that Jerry Lee's second marriage – this was the 23-year-old singer's third – was bigamous. Jerry Lee was driven from England and was virtually blacklisted from American stations. He became the focal point of fulminations against evil rock 'n' roll; where he was once poised to assume Elvis' mantle when the latter was drafted, Elvis was now a squeaky-clean obedient boy to the Establishment, vs.

Jerry Lee as the trashy, dangerous rebel.

His career in a shambles, Jerry Lee was reduced to playing small clubs and low-paying dates. He switched labels to Smash (a division of Mercury), where they tried every music category but Society-dance-band: rock, soul, rockabilly, country and several (superb) live albums. Finally – and logically, as Jerry Lee had always been country-oriented – an exclusively country music emphasis was charted by producers Eddie Kilroy and Jerry Kennedy. The response was instantaneous, and overwhelming, Jerry Lee Lewis had returned. Country stations gave him airplay, either forgiving or forgetting his wild past, and he responded by recording some outstanding country classics. His first hits included 'Another Place, Another Time,' 'What's Made Milwaukee Famous (Has Made a Loser Out of Me)' and 'To Make Love Sweeter For You.'

To cement his return to country, Jerry Lee recorded two *Country Music Hall of Fame Hits* albums, full of splendid interpretations, and from which 'One Has My Name (The Other Has My Heart)' was a single. His follow-up album was *Together* with his sister Linda Gail Lewis; the LP also collected a group of classic country songs.

The single hits continued, with masterful versions of 'She Even Woke Me Up to Say Goodbye' and 'One More Time With Feelin'.' Others included 'There Must Be More to Love Than This,' 'Touching Home,' 'When He Walks On You (Like You Have Walked On Me),' 'Would You Take Another Chance On Me,' 'Me and Bobby McGee,' 'Who's Gonna Play This Old Piano,' 'Think About It, Darlin','' 'Chantilly Lace,' 'Sometimes A Memory Ain't Enough,' 'Don't Boogie Woogie,' 'My Life Would Make a Damn Good Country Song,' 'Middle Age Crazy,' 'Over the Rainbow,' and 'Thirty-Nine and Holding.' There were also concept albums – more live recordings, a gospel album, a Muscle Shoals album (*Southern Roots*) and *The Session*, a double album recorded in London with a host of tribute-paying British rockers. In 1989 the film *Great Balls of Fire*, starring Dennis

Jerry Lee Lewis's talent was sometimes obscured by his scandals.

Quaid as Lewis, revived interest in Lewis's life and music.

Jerry Lee's rough and rowdy ways are legendary. He has been hospitalized frequently for chronic alcohol and drug problems; he is perpetually in debt to the government and countless creditors; he is the most notorious no-show since Hank Williams; he has passed through several more marriages, including one where his wife died under suspicious circumstances; his two sons have died in

The Light Crust Doughboys.

tragic accidents; he was sued for shooting his drummer twice in the chest; and he was arrested waving a pistol outside Elvis Presley's mansion while Presley slept one night.

If his life would make a damn good country song (as the song title goes), then he opens his life to concert audiences. Often on stage he will stop a performance and debate, with himself, the state of his soul. He believes his music is sending people to Hell, and has referred to the Devil on stage and in interviews. He knows, he says, that man cannot

serve two masters, and he is too weak to serve the Lord.

So, in the words of yet another Lewis hit, he's rocking his life away. He attacks his piano as he plays out his conscience's battle. He's the most charismatic performer of his age – possessing an enormous stage presence, he shouts and sobs, swaggers and smiles. He indeed attacks the keyboard, kicking the piano stool away, resting his boot on the keys, sometimes jumping atop the piano itself in a rocking frenzy – and audiences invariably go wild. His

concerts offer an astonishing medley, not only of rock and country, but of moods; Jerry Lee slips from sleazy lyrics to gospel; he will shed tears for his mother and the next minute direct filthy language at his fans.

Lewis continues to perform regularly, though in recent years health problems have forced a lighter schedule. An anthology of his work was released in 1992, and he recorded an album in Nashville in 1994 (release date unavailable at this writing).

Jerry Lee Lewis has tried to kill himself several times over, and seems to keep trying. The tragic immortality that early deaths have brought other geniuses – like Jimmie Rodgers and Hank Williams – has only partially eluded Jerry Lee, who calls himself The Killer. Nevertheless his electrifying performances, his personality, and his massive enigmas, are already notable monuments in country music history.

Lewis Family, The

Called the First Family of Bluegrass Gospel, the Lewis Family is indeed a superb bluegrass ensemble and a large, close-knit family unit representing three generations.

Roy (Pop) Lewis of Lincolnton, Georgia, began the singing clan in the 1950s in the Georgia-South Carolina region; a television program begun in 1954 in Augusta, Georgia, led to a syndicated gospel music show in the South and Southeast. The Lewis Family preserves the flavor of their region, from which sprang old-time string-band music and reverent gospel harmonies. They perform many traditional gospel songs along with bluegrass and contemporary tunes.

Among the other members of the group are Little Roy Lewis, banjo and guitar; Wallace Lewis, guitar; Travis Lewis, bass; Miggie, Polly, and Janis, female vocals; and young Lewis Phillips, a banjo virtuoso. The Lewis Family is known especially for its concert appearances that mix humor, enthusiastic playing, and gospel messages in down-home fashion.

Light Crust Doughboys, The

Just as there was traditional and mountain music before Bill Monroe synthesized those elements and his gifts into bluegrass, so was there Western and cowboy music before a talented aggregation fused them with jazz, swing and their own stylings to form Western Swing. Before the Light Crust Doughboys, the elements of Western Swing had not been put into place.

Bob Wills was the centerpiece in this musical revolution, although there are other important players in the Doughboy story. Fiddler Wills and guitarist Herman Arnspiger had formed the Wills Fiddle Band – later adding vocalist Milton Brown and his brother Durwood, guitarist, and Clifton Johnson on banjo – playing radio and dances to regional favor in Texas. The group picked up radio sponsorship and became The Aladdin Laddies when they were invited to greener pastures, a regional radio network showcase sponsored by Burrus Mills, manufacturers of Light Crust Flour. They debuted in January of 1931.

Their show became immensely popular through the Southwest and Midwest, and the group cut records that sold well. A sales executive of Burrus Mills, Wilbert Lee 'Pappy Pass the Biscuits' O'Daniel, became the announcer and front-man for the group. It was O'Daniel's decision that the group stop playing dances that caused the Brown Brothers to leave (they formed their own group, Milton Brown and His Musical Brownies). Wills's own devotion to dance rhythms and a dance band's function, as well as personal problems, led to his being fired in August of 1933. Most of the personnel followed him, leading to the creation of Bob Wills and the Texas Playboys.

O'Daniel himself was fired in 1935 and established the Hillbilly Flour Company, organizing another band. His musical reputation, and some performing former Doughboys, aided O'Daniel's political aspirations. A Democrat, he served as governor of Texas from 1939 to 1941, and United States senator from 1941 to 1949. But after O'Daniel's departure the Doughboys continued, with Eddie Dunn, and later Cecil Brower, as front. In 1942 Burrus withdrew its sponsorship for a while (the group was then underwritten by the Duncan Coffee Company as The Coffee Grinders), but later resumed its role. In fact the Light Crust Doughboys continue to this day, recently under Jack Derry, recording for the Burrus Mills label.

The Light Crust Doughboys band is notable for its seminal role in defining a new, and vitally distinctive, form of American popular music. Besides those listed, other influential musicians played for the band through the years, including Leon MacAuliffe, John W 'Knocky' Parker, and Leon Huff.

Little Texas

Four of the six Little Texas band members are actually from the Lone Star State, but their catchy name, surprisingly was inspired by a neighborhood in historic Franklin, Tennessee, that was once so rough that it was nicknamed 'Little Texas.'

For a year or so the band didn't even have a name, but the members had a dream and a strong sense of what they wanted to do. They have written almost all of their songs. They don't use outside players or backup vocalists in the studio, and in concert each song sounds just as it does on their records, a faithfulness to the musical arrangement that all the big dance bands once practiced with great success and which is a relative rarity in Nashville.

It all began when two natives of Longview, Texas, Porter Howell and Duane Propes, moved to Nashville to attend Belmont University, a school known for its technical training in music. There they met Tim Rushlow and Dwayne O'Brien, who had enjoyed some success performing in the Dallas-Fort Worth area. The four joined forces and hit the road.

It was in Springfield, Massachusetts, that they met Del Gray and keyboardist Brady Seals, who had grown up near Cincinnati. The addition of the two solidified the Little

Texas sound; and the selection of a name for the group completed the formula for success that led one trade publication to brand them 'the hottest band in country music.'

Organized in the late 1980s, Little Texas began recording for Warner Brothers in 1990. Their hits include 'Some Guys Have All the Love,' and 'God Blessed Texas,' a number-one record that prompted former Texas governor Ann Richards to name them 'Honorary World Ambassadors of the Great State of Texas.'

Among their many honors, they were named the top vocal group of 1994 by the Academy of Country Music and Group of the Year by Country Music Television, and they scored CMT's Number One Video of the Year for 'My Love.' They had more CMA nominations that year than any other group.

Their *First Time for Everything* album reached gold status and *Big Time* went platinum. They also had three of the top 24 country singles in 1994, including the smash 'What Might Have Been.' Their most recent CD is *Kick a Little*.

Locklin, Hank

Lawrence Hankins Locklin was born in McLellan, Florida, in 1918, and as a boy acquired his first guitar from a pawn-shop. In the 1930s he performed on several Florida radio

Above: Little Texas on stage.
Right: The Louvin Brothers: Ira (left) and Charlie.

stations before touring the South. After World War II Hank secured a position on the KWKH *Louisiana Hayride* and in 1949 recorded his first song. 'The Same Sweet Girl.' His next record, 'Let Me Be the One,' was his first national hit, leading to an invitation from the Grand Ole Opry in 1953.

His later hits included 'Geisha Girl,' but it was his own 'Send Me the Pillow You Dream On' and 'Please Help Me, I'm Falling' that assured his stature as a songwriter and singer. In fact his stature was, and still is, international in scope, for Hank is a popular artist in England and Ireland and was a member of the pioneer European tour in 1957, 'Concert in Country Music.'

Locklin followed with more hits sung in his high, ringing Irish tenor vocal style. He still performs to fans at the Opry, and still lives in McLellan, where he is now honorary mayor. Hank established a large ranch, The Singin' L, incorporating land where he once chopped cotton.

Louvin Brothers

The Louvin Brothers were born Ira and Charlie Loudermilk in Rainesville, Alabama , in 1924 and 1927 re-

spectively. They were raised in Henegar, Alabama, by a poor farming family. They picked and sang together, winning a local talent contest, and finally won a modest spot on a Tennessee radio station.

In the mid-1940s Ira and Charlie secured spots on the *Mid-Day Merry-Go-Round* radio show in Knoxville, and in 1951 Fred Rose – publisher, songwriter, talent hunter and manager of Hank Williams – arranged a contract for the Louvins with Capitol Records. They began touring widely and inaugurated a string of hits: 'Hoping That You're Hoping,' 'You're Running Wild,' 'My Baby's Gone,' 'When I Stop Dreaming,' 'If I Could Only Win Your Love,' 'The Weapon of Prayer' and 'I Take the Chance.' Fully one-half of their material was gospel oriented. The Brothers team won many duet awards and were invited to join the Grand Ole Opry in 1955.

But in 1963 the Louvin Brothers split. Charlie charted with singles of 'I Don't Love You Any More,' 'See the Big Man Cry' and 'Something to Brag About,' a duet with Melba Montgomery. Ira performed with his wife Florence (she used the name Anne Young) and concentrated on gospel material, releasing the albums *Nearer My God to Thee*, *The Family Who Prays*, *Satan is Real* and *Keep Your Eyes on Jesus*. He died in a car crash near Jefferson City, Missouri, on June 20, 1965.

As time passes, the Louvin Brothers are increasingly honored and revered for their stewardship of the magnificent traditions of old-time mountain harmonies and brother duets. Ricky Skaggs and Emmylou Harris are two who have adapted Louvin Brothers standards to the progressive bluegrass mode. Ira's high, tense tenor and Charlie's baritone recalled the Blue Sky Boys and Monroe Brothers tradition; the Louvins also recorded a tribute album to the Delmore Brothers. Their mandolin and guitar picking underpinned their flawless performances and choice of material – the mountain-music preoccupations of gospel, tragedy, sentiment and Victorian story-type songs dealing in death and irony. Ira and Charlie (who still performs today on the Opry) both preserved and bequeathed a splendid body of country music memories.

Loveless, Patty

Patty Loveless.

Born Patty Ramey in Pikeville, Kentucky, versatile New Country singer Patty Loveless has had a diverse career spanning several music styles. Growing up around mountain and bluegrass music, she began performing at the age of 12, and two years later met Porter Wagoner in Nashville and received the help and encouragement of his partner Dolly Parton. Patty also came to know her cousin Loretta Lynn, the great country music star who was in the process of leaving her job as opening act for the Wilburn Brothers. Patty accepted the Wilburns' offer to sing, travel, and write for their publishing company Sure Fire, interrupting that work only to finish high school in Louisville.

When she married the Wilburns' drummer Terry Lovelace, she began a 10-year period of singing in North Carolina clubs and honky-tonks, incorporating a characteristic energy of performance style and adding a hard edge to her voice from the rock songs in which she then specialized. After divorcing Lovelace, whose name she has retained in an altered form, she went back to Nashville in 1985 and signed a contract with MCA Records. A career including a wide and challenging range of styles had provided Patty with a confident mastery of rock, ballads, honky-tonk, and blues, and each had left some trace in the eclectic style that emerged. Her career, under the management of her second husband, producer Emory Gordy, Jr., has advanced steadily. A popular and much sought-after duet partner, she has had great success singing with such performers as Vince Gill and Marty Stuart. She has won the American Music Award for Best New Country Artist, has become a member of the Grand Ole Opry, and toured with some of the leading performers in New Country, including Clint Black, George Strait, and Hank Williams, Jr. From her first album, *Patty Loveless*, with its hit single 'After All,' she has had many hits, appearing often at the top of the charts.

A leading exemplar of the 'new traditionalist' sound, but also an adept haudler of rocking country and folksy styles, Patty Loveless has drawn her sound from the many diverse strands of her career. She is an animated performer with a tone of great emotional depth and has achieved a devoted following with such moving songs as her popular 'Can't Stop Myself from Loving You,' which dips into minor chords, reminding her listeners of the blues elements that also underpin much of her music.

Her recent hits have included 'How Can I Help You Say Good Bye,' and 'Blame It On Your Heart.' CDs include *When Fallen Angels Fly*.

Lovett, Lyle

Maybe it's the wild hair, or what his former wife Julia Roberts described as his 'Abraham Lincoln' looks, but Lyle Lovett seems to stand apart from the other young country singers who returned country music to its roots when it seemed in danger of merging with popular music.

Although Lovett incorporates elements of several different styles of music in the songs he writes and sings, he is undeniably country. And he has what *Rolling Stone* magazine called a 'wicked intelligence' and 'absurdity and wit.' Lovett says he merely tries to write songs that 'express a feeling or an emotion or an idea in a way that someone else hasn't done before.'

Lovett's early recordings were all Nashville products, but more recently he has recorded on the West Coast, which began even before he married Hollywood actress Julia Roberts (with whom he split up in 1995). He appeared in Robert Altman's film *The Player*, after Altman attended a Lovett concert and then called the singer to offer him the role.

Lovett is a fourth-generation Texan who grew up 25 miles north of Houston in the Klein community, a German farming community named for his great-great grandfather Adam Klein, one of the original settlers of the area in the late 1840s. Young Lyle spent his summers working in the dairy barn and hay field. But as he grew up, nearby Houston too was growing and it soon destroyed much of Klein's rural ambience.

Following high school, Lovett attended Texas A&M University where he received a degree in journalism in 1980 and a degree in German in 1981. As a college student he began writing songs and performing them in songwriter-showcase clubs in major Texas cities.

In 1984 he drove from Houston to Nashville with a four-song demo tape. There he signed a songwriting deal with Criterion Music and later a recording contract with MCA/Curb Records. Frequent appearances on the *Tonight* show and European tours enhanced his fame. And when he married Julia Roberts his photograph suddenly began appearing on magazine covers everywhere.

Through it all Lovett says he continues to 'have fun' with his music and he hopes he always will. His plaintive baritone carries his wide-ranging music styles from old-time, honky-tonk, '40s-style country music to a blues-jazz fusion. His tag-sale suits paired with his wild hair style only add to his mystique – intriguing to readers of *The New York Times* as well as *Music City News*. His newest CD, *I Love Everybody*, speaks to all his musical inspirations.

Lyle Lovett.

Lynn, Loretta

Born in Butcher's Hollow, Kentucky, in 1943, Loretta Webb has had a life that could be the stuff of a country song, literally and figuratively. Born to a coal-mining father who worked the Van Lear Mines, Loretta was named for the movie star Loretta Young, and grew up liking country music, especially the songs of Molly O'Day. When she was 13 she met O V Lynn (Mooney or Doolittle, as he was called) and married him.

The next year the Lynns (with Loretta's brother Jay Lee) moved to Washington State where their impoverishment was relieved by baking and canning contests Loretta

Loretta Lynn.

entered at fairs, and her cathartic singing around the house, the latter activity prompting Mooney to buy his wife a guitar. He dreamed of a career in country music for her, and surprising perhaps everyone but herself, the housewife was a success.

Loretta played dates on local radio and formed a band with Jay Lee. She became a regional Northwest favorite and Mooney mailed copies of her self-financed record 'Honky-Tonk Girl' to radio stations even when record stores didn't have copies. But in 1962 she arrived in Nashville where she garnered more hit records, a growing reputation, and friendly encouragement from established performers Patsy Cline and the Wilburn Brothers.

Her hits included: 'Blue Kentucky Girl,' 'You Ain't Woman Enough To Tame My Man,' 'Don't Come Home A-drinkin',' 'Fist City,' 'Your Squaw's on the Warpath Tonight,' 'Wings upon Your Horns,' 'Coal Miner's Daughter,' 'Lead Me On,' 'They Don't Make 'Em Like My Daddy Any More,' 'Mississippi Woman, Louisiana Man,' 'After the Fire Is Gone,' 'When the Tingle Becomes a Chill,' 'Somebody, Somewhere,' 'Out of My Head, Back in My Bed,' 'We've Come a Long Way, Baby' and 'Alone With You.'

Loretta recorded some classic honky-tonk duets with Ernest Tubb, and has practically had a separate career as half of a duet act with Conway Twitty. Their many records attest to a unique match-up of styles and voices, and their songs are so sincere that many fans have assumed the pair was married.

Loretta owns a town in Tennessee, Hurricane Mills, about 60 miles from Nashville. Located there is the Loretta Lynn Museum and her commercial Dude Ranch.

In spite of personal tragedies (the deaths of her son and duet partner Conway Twitty), Loretta still makes many public appearances. While her recordings are seldom played on radio any more, her fans remain loyal, and she performs frequently.

Her autobiography, co-written by George Vecsey, a sportswriter for *The New York Times*, is a remarkably candid and warm account of her struggles, dreams, heartbreak and happiness. *Coal Miner's Daughter* sold more than a million copies and inspired an Academy Award-winning movie with Sissy Spacek in the title role.

Loretta's voice is a throaty, airy alto that delivers lyrics frankly and can be either sarcastic (as she threatens women who flirt with her man) or sentimental (as in love ballads with Conway Twitty). If Kitty Wells and Patsy Cline opened country music to independent women, Loretta pioneered the role of the assertive woman; wronged, but feisty.

Her music has undergone a bit of a pop trend – although hardly as much as that of younger sister Crystal Gayle. But when Loretta sings one of her hits, 'You're Lookin' at Country,' she still sings the truth. In 1994 she cut a trio album with Tammy Wynette and Dolly Parton.

M

McAuliffe, Leon

William Leon McAuliffe, was born in Houston in 1917, and mastered the guitar soon after receiving his first on his 14th Christmas; soon afterwards he discovered the steel guitar. In 1932 he joined Houston station KPRC and soon was a member of its Swift Jewel Cowboys. He was then hired by Pappy O'Daniel for the Light Crust Doughboys, but after Bob Wills was fired, McAuliffe followed him to Tulsa in 1935.

McAuliffe's appeal was his mastery of the steel guitar, an instrument that he electrified and played with great virtuosity. Bob Wills let it share a prominent position in the Western Swing sound, and he made 'Take it away, Leon!' a catchword of country jazz kickoffs. McAuliffe adapted an old race tune, 'The Guitar Rag,' to his now-standard 'Steel

Leon McAuliffe.

Martina McBride.

Guitar Rag,' and he co-authored the instrumental version of 'San Antonio Rose.'

With Bob Wills, McAuliffe made many concert and movie appearances, and when World War II came, his service included playing in the Glenn Miller Band under Tex Beneke. He later fronted his own ensemble, The Western Swing Band, in Tulsa, afterwards organizing The Cimarron Boys. He ultimately owned and operated a ballroom in Tulsa, and became a local TV favorite with later hits like 'Panhandle Rag.'

McAuliffe came out of retirement to participate in the 1973 reunion album, *Bob Wills and the Texas Playboys for the Last Time*. The fun of working with the old Playboys, and the warm reception afforded the album, led McAuliffe and Leon Rausch to reorganize the Playboys for records and concerts. McAuliffe is still active on the instrument he revolutionized and continues to play it to its improvisational limits.

McBride, Martina

Intense delivery of songs with serious themes – that is the formula that propelled Martina McBride to the forefront of the gifted pack of young 1990s country music stars, at once respectful of tradition but also independent.

'Independence Day' is the cry of liberation of a woman who has been trapped in an abusive relationship. 'That Wasn't Me' is the plea of a young woman who does not want her love interest to confuse her with other former loves who have hurt him. 'Goin' To Work' is the story of a woman who uses her work to escape the pain of a broken relationship.

Born and reared in the small town of Sharon, Kansas, Martina grew up listening to traditional country music, but like so many of her contemporaries she has added a modern twist to her own style. A folk element

– themes, instrumentation, lyrics – informs her music and buttresses the profile of New Country in the 1990s as an attractive amalgam of musical traditions.

Her first album for RCA was *The Time Has Come*, followed by *The Way I Am*. Not a songwriter, she expresses herself in other ways as co-producer of her albums. Martina is known in Nashville as one of the most particular reviewers of material she chooses to record and with which to identify. Her albums have been compared to Willie Nelson's theme-album examinations of relationships recorded in the early 1970s, and are much admired as creative landmarks.

McClinton, Delbert

His songs are country but there is plenty of jazz, blues, rock 'n' roll and roadhouse in the music he writes and sings. In short, Delbert McClinton treads a fine country line and is pretty much at home anywhere in the musical spectrum.

Born in Lubbock, Texas, McClinton is the son of a railroad switchman and a beautician. He says he can't remember a time when he wasn't singing. He liked to listen to country music but he liked to play rhythm and blues, so he combined the two, which he still does. His first public appearance was in 1957, and his first group was called the Straightjackets; his earliest recordings were on the Le Cam and United Artists labels. In the early 1960s he formed a group called the Rondels and for a time he teamed up with fellow Texan Glen Clark. In the 1970s he had several successful records on the ABC and Mercury labels, and in 1978 Emmylou Harris had a Number One hit with McClinton's song, 'Two More Bottles of Wine.' In 1980 Dan Ackroyd and John Belushi included his song 'B Movie Boxcar Blues' on their *Blues Brothers* LP.

In 1992 McClinton and Bonnie Raitt won the Best Rock Vocal Duo Grammy Award for 'Good Man, Good Woman.' He has also paired with Tanya Tucker on the award-winning 'Tell Me About It.' Currently on Curb Records, McClinton's most recent album is *Never Been Rocked Enough*. Frequently seen on the Nashville Network and hyped by

the likes of Don Imus, McClinton is an award-winning harmonica player and froths his Muscle Shoals-sounding band with coarse-voiced country/blues lyrics.

McEntire, Reba

Born into a rodeo family in Chockie, Oklahoma, in 1954, Reba McEntire recalls learning country songs that her mother would sing at home while her father was out on the rodeo circuit. In fact, Reba believes, her mother possessed talent enough to make her a country music star, and it seems that the steady encouragement Reba received to succeed in Nashville served as a vicarious experience for her mother.

In high school, Reba formed a country band, but she maintained the family tradition of being involved with rodeos as well. The two in-

terests coincided in 1974 when she sang the National Anthem at the National Rodeo Finals, and was heard by Red Steagall. He arranged an audition for Reba that led to a record contract. Her first hit was 'I Don't Want To Be a One-Night Stand,' others followed, including 'Runaway Heart,' 'Sweet Dreams' and '(You Lift Me) Up to Heaven.'

She also recorded duets with Jacky Ward, and was named 1984's Female Artist of the Year by the Country Music Association. Since then Reba McEntire has become one of the most dominant female personalities, and voices, in country music. She was named Female Vocalist of the Year from 1985 through 1987 by both the Country Music Association and the Academy of Country Music, has won accolades from the fan-sup-

Reba McEntire.

ported *Music City News* balloting, and won a Grammy awarded in 1987 for her single 'Whoever's in New England.' Other major hits have included 'One Promise Too Late,' 'I Can't Even Get the Blues,' 'You're the First Time I've Thought About Leaving,' and 'The Last One to Know.'

Divorced from her first husband in 1987, Reba is married to her personal manager, Narvel Blackstock. Reba is an actress as well and she has starred in several movies and miniseries, including *The Gambler* with Kenny Rogers, *Tremors, North* (with Dan Ackroyd) and *The Little Rascals*. Tragedy struck in 1991 when a plane carrying members of her touring entourage crashed on a California hillside. Seven of her band members were killed, as was her tour manager. Reba's decision to get right back to work after the accident (in only two weeks) was, she has said, the best way to deal with the loss.

McEntire's string of hits continued as she further explored the torch style hinted at in earlier recordings.

'Does He Love You,' a duet with backup singer Linda Davis, earned the pair 1994's Grammy for Best Performance by a Duo and launched Davis's solo career. Reba has incorporated her acting interest into her musical life, shooting videos that are among the most elaborately produced in country. She has six platinum and three double-platinum albums to her credit. In 1995 Reba was named ACM's Top Female Entertainer.

McGee, Sam and Kirk

The major members of the Fruit Jar Drinkers, an excellent pioneer string-band and early Opry stars, Sam and Kirk McGee were born in Franklin, Tennessee, in 1894 and 1899, respectively. Their father was a fiddler, and the brothers picked banjos, playing local dances in their teens. In 1923 they heard the legendary Uncle Dave Macon and the next year they joined his troupe; when he joined the

The McGees, Sam (left) and Kirk (center).

Grand Ole Opry they were there as members of his Fruit Jar Drinkers. Sam picked the guitar and Kirk played the fiddle.

The McGee Brothers also performed as soloists and toured with Opry packages via the RKO vaudeville circuit, starring Dr Humphrey Bate and the Possum Hunters. Sam accompanied Uncle Dave in New York in April of 1926 on one of the pioneer country recordings, 'Down the Old Plank Road,' and both brothers were recorded with Macon and fiddler Mazy Todd on further recordings.

Sam and Kirk teamed through the 1930s with other traditional country talents specializing in old-time and mountain music with little jazz infusions. With Arthur Smith they formed the Dixieliners (and had a reunion in the 1960s at the Newport Folk Festival); they played the Opry and toured the South. They worked in early and later years with the

Crook Brothers, an act that still has Opry billing. The McGees also performed with the comedy team of Sara and Sally in the late 1930s, and then joined Bill Monroe as group members and soloists in his troupe.

In 1975 they picked up their instruments to play at the Nashville

Fan Fair, and shortly thereafter Sam was killed when a tractor fell on him while he was working – still, at 81! – on his farm. Kirk died in 1988.

The McGee Brothers were superb instrumentalists in the days of country music's very birth, and they mightily influenced a whole generation that followed. Sam was especially proficient with his flat-top

guitar; he pioneered the instrument as a lead (not chord or rhythm functions) with finger-picking that was influenced by blues and rag-time.

McGraw, Tim

You might expect the son of former New York Mets pitcher Tug McGraw to be a baseball player, but Tim McGraw isn't. He was reared by his mother and a stepfather who loved country music, so young Tim grew up loving country music too.

He didn't know his birth father was actually a famous athlete until he was 11 and his mother Betty and stepfather Horace Smith divorced.

Tim grew up in tiny Start, Louisiana, a farming community, and his favorite singer was the late Keith Whitley. He even sneaked backstage at a concert to meet his hero.

Tim and Tug began seeing each other with some regularity after the boy turned 18 and enrolled in Northeast Louisiana University. Both parents were concerned when he dropped out in 1989 to move to Nashville to try his luck at music. He sold his car and almost everything else he owned to finance the trip, and made the journey by bus.

He got his first chance to sing at Skull's Rainbow Room in famous Printer's Alley and performed there most nights for a year and a half. Curb Records signed him in 1990 and a string of successful records followed.

His hits have included 'Indian Outlaw,' 'Don't Take the Girl,' and 'Down on the Farm,' the first two of which were gold. His album, *Not a Moment Too Soon*, was double platinum. Success seemed long in coming, but Tim followed Tug's famous dictum, 'Ya Gotta Believe!' His impressive hits have caused people to compare his meteoric rise to the success of Garth Brooks and Billy Ray Cyrus.

McMichen, Clayton

Born in Allatoona, Georgia, in 1900, 'Pappy' McMichen grew up in rural Georgia and loved the fiddle, playing at local dances. He was destined to become the first great fiddle player on records, and he influenced a generation of fiddlers.

Tim McGraw.

Uncle Dave Macon and his son Dorris.

As a young man, McMichen got a job as stoker on the Nashville, Chattanooga, and St Louis Rail Road. In the 1920s he joined station WSB in Atlanta and performed on its country radio programs. He formed a group called the Melody Men, and then joined Gid Tanner's Skillet Lickers in 1926. The remarkable band was an influential and popular ensemble performing (and recording) old-time music and comedy. And as Tanner was primarily a front man and comedian, McMichen's fiddle led the group.

In 1931 he left the Skillet Lickers to tour the country playing in fiddle contests; he was paired against the legendary Fiddlin' John Carson (whose influence and support McMichen gratefully acknowledged) and Natchee the Indian (who was rumored actually to be Italian). He continued these old-time events, where audience members could also challenge the stars, until 1952. McMichen formed a band, the Georgia Wildcats, and played at WLW for a time in the 1930s, and then toured with the band; the great guitar player Merle Travis was once a Wildcat member.

McMichen's flashy style inspired a host of fiddling disciples. He bridged the old-time era with the modern, working into the 1950s. He was with Jimmie Rodgers in his last troubled days, and played with some of the most influential musicians of his time. And 'Pappy' McMichen was a comedian as well, starring in the Skillet Lickers' 'Corn Likker Still in Georgia' routines as well as his own stage acts. Among his most famous songs are: 'Down Yonder,' 'Sally Gooden' and 'Wreck of the Old '97.' His controlled, intelligent fiddle could at times show the influence of jazz and other forms to enrich the country basics.

Macon, Uncle Dave

Born in Smart Station, Tennessee, in 1870, David Harrison Macon was one of the founders of modern country music. His career lasted more than 35 years, yet he only became a professional a few years short of his 50th birthday. The story of 'The Dixie Dewdrop,' as he was known, is a true country success story.

Macon played the banjo growing up on the family farm, but when the family bought a hotel in Nashville, Dave was able to absorb the music and material of all the singers and vaudeville comedians who passed through. He acquired a vast mental file of old-time and country songs, and frequently played his banjo for local events. Legend has it that he was asked to play a dance he was disinclined to play. To make the refusal easier, he asked for a $15 fee, expecting the offer to be withdrawn. Instead the man paid the fee, and at the dance a scout for the Loews chain heard Macon. He offered a tour, and the first bookings in Birmingham, Alabama, were huge successes. Uncle David Macon was never out of the spotlight after that.

In 1924 he recorded country music in New York City, including 'Hillbilly Blues' with Sid Harkreader on fiddle, and later included guitarist Sam McGee in pioneer recordings. In 1926 he joined the fledgling Grand Ole Opry, and became its first major star. He worked as a soloist with the Fruit Jar Drinkers, and also formed a side group, the Dixie Sacred Singers; very religious, Macon was a some-time-preacher and would freely mix Christian homilies with his old-time songs and humor. In the late 1940s, when he was almost 80 years old, Uncle David joined the travelling Bill Monroe Tent Show, which also included exhibition baseball games. Macon performed up to the time of

The Maddox Brothers and Rose.

his death; after an Opry set in March of 1952, Macon went to a hospital and died soon after.

Uncle Dave Macon's contributions to country music are enormous. He was a pioneer recording artist; he preserved countless obscure country tunes; he became the first 'name' star on a country radio program; and his exuberant performances gave the nascent business its first theatrical glow. Macon played the banjo sitting down, rearing back, and wildly kicking a foot. He would punctuate his songs or others' solos with asides and approving shouts, much as Gid Tanner did with the Skillet Lickers, and Bob Wills was to do in Western Swing. Macon, having been raised on vaudeville and music, incorporated humor into his act, thereby serving as godfather to a long line of country comedians.

His unique style of playing the banjo was influential among his contemporaries as well as next-generation players like Grandpa Jones and Dave 'Stringbean' Akeman. It featured a flailing or drop-thumb technique that produced a driving, plunking sound. It was the banjo's major role – along with rapid chord-

strums for basic rhythm effect – until the advent of Earl Scruggs. In addition to all this, the image of Uncle Dave Macon, his chair leaning back, a smiling mouth full of gold false teeth, seems the very personification of seminal, old-time country music . . . for that is just what he was. Macon was elected to the Country Music Hall of Fame years after his death in 1966.

Maddox Brothers and Rose

The Maddox family contributed one of the most diversified and colorful country ensembles to American music, and in fact, with their gaudy Western costumes, they billed themselves as The Most Colorful Hillbilly Band in America. The most prominent member was Rose, born in Boaz, Alabama, in 1926. She and her brothers (Cal, guitar; Henry, mandolin; Fred, bass; and Don, fiddle and comedy) grew up in Alabama and Bakersfield, California, where the family picked crops and played music locally. They gradually built a statewide reputation, which, in the

early 1950s, propelled them to the *Louisiana Hayride* and national popularity.

Their hit records included: 'Philadelphia Lawyer,' 'Tramp on the Street,' 'Gathering Flowers for the Master's Bouquet' and 'Will There Be Any Stars In My Crown?' In the 1950s the group returned to California as members of the *Town Hall Party* show in Compton, and around 1960 Rose went solo. She had a hit with 'Sing a Little Song of Heartaches' and then she teamed with Buck Owens to record some classic duets, including 'We're the Talk of the Town,' 'Loose Talk' and 'Mental Cruelty.' Rose Maddox won many awards as a highly popular female vocalist.

Maddox Brothers and Rose were one of the most interesting of country's groups. They sparkled with a driving, raucous energy featuring bold vocals and flashy electric instruments. As stylists they took on all modes of country music – gospel, honky-tonk, hillbilly boogie, rockabilly and sentimental; there was even a bluegrass album with Bill Monroe and Reno & Smiley – and they performed it all masterfully.

Mandrell, Barbara

Born in Houston in 1948, Barbara Mandrell was raised in a musical environment and supposedly could read music before English, playing the accordion as her first instrument. When she was young her family moved to Oceanside, California, where her father Irby bought a music store. Among the customers was Norm Hamlet, later of Merle Haggard's Strangers, who taught the youngster steel guitar.

Proficiency on the steel guitar was a good investment, because country guitar legend Joe Maphis once heard Barbara play and invited the 11-year-old to be part of a Las Vegas engagement he was to play. In the show, she played steel guitar and saxophone. Maphis arranged for her to appear on the California country TV show *Town Hall Party*, and she proceeded from there to the *Five-Star Jubilee* on the ABC-TV network. In 1961 she also appeared with Johnny Cash in concerts.

In 1967 Barbara married and retired from the music business. As she tells the story, her father went into the construction business in

Barbara Mandrell.

Nashville, and Barbara decided to move there while her husband was in military service; when they were in the Opry audience one night she vowed to become a performer again and, presumably, a star. She quickly signed a contract with Billy Sherrill, Nashville's hottest producer at the time, and Irby formed a Family Band with other siblings.

Barbara's early hits were country covers of rhythm and blues songs (her sales have always been good in that market). She sang some duets with David Houston, and became a member of that Opry she wistfully visited a few short years earlier.

Every record of Barbara's seemed to become a bigger hit than the last, and she became one of the country's leading female singers. She garnered many awards (including the CMA Entertainer of the Year honor an unprecedented two years running) and hosted a slickly produced network television variety show from 1980-82 with her sisters Irlene and Louise. Adding to her broad-based popularity in the 1980s (or maybe because of it) she had adjusted her material to pop almost exclusively.

Among her country hits have been 'After Closing Time' and 'Treat Him Right' and a slew of cheating songs, perhaps her foremost thematic preoccupation: 'Married But Not To

Each Other,' 'Sleeping Single in a Double Bed,' 'I Don't Wanna Be Right' and 'You Can Eat Crackers In My Bed Any Time.'

One of the most likeable personalities in Nashville, she is widely respected and held in affection; the industry's heart went out to her after a serious auto accident and a long recuperation that lasted into late 1984. But she was back the following year with a rousing TV special. Country fans got their quota with a few minutes of Roy Acuff as a guest, and the program affirmed Barbara's versatility as she played dobro with Roy but later sang an elaborate punk rock number.

Martin, Jimmy

A double-threat bluegrass man – fine singer and influential guitar picker – James Henry Martin was born in Sneedeville, Tennessee, in 1927. In 1949 he joined Bill Monroe's Bluegrass Boys, which had recently been affected by the loss of Flatt and Scruggs and other personnel; Martin immediately replaced Mac Wiseman, who had been a member for less than a year. The 22-year-old Martin fit in well with Monroe's style, and recorded several classic sides in the Bluegrass Boys' discography.

In the early 1950s Martin himself left Monroe, and formed a duet with mandolinist Bobby Osborne; the group later became a trio when banjo player Sonny Osborne joined. In 1954 Jimmy Martin and the Osborne Brothers were a regular act on Detroit radio. Martin finally formed his own ensemble, the Sunny Mountain Boys, and plays with that group to this day.

Some of Martin's biggest hits through the years have been novelty songs, and he has had to temper the commercial satisfaction with the fact that this catalog has kept him from the full and serious attention he deserves as a bluegrass singer. He has a high, crackling country voice, and his duets with Bobby Osborne, the higher of their two tenor voices, were among the finest ever recorded. Martin has been blessed with talented sidemen; his own guitar picking – in the Charlie Monroe and Lester Flatt tradition – is widely admired.

Among the songs most identified with Jimmy Martin are 'Ocean of Diamonds,' 'Free Born Man,' 'Mr Engineer' and 'Widow Maker.' He was fortunate to receive justified recognition by being a featured artist on the landmark album set, *Will the Circle Be Unbroken*, fronted by the Nitty Gritty Dirt Band. He performed his own compositions 'Losin' You (Might Be the Best Thing Yet); and 'My Walkin' Shoes' as well as several other standards.

Mattea, Kathy

One of the most distinctive performers in contemporary country music, Kathy Mattea has been, from the beginning of her career, open to new material and new styles of presenting it. A native of Cross Lanes, West Virginia, she has built on a solid foundation of country music a com-

Kathy Mattea.

plex and flexible technique that incorporates elements of an ever-widening range of styles. Kathy began with folk music, which attracted her while she was a student at West Virginia University, and she joined a group devoted to folk. When one of its members went to Nashville in the late 1970s, she accompanied him and stayed on when he gave up and went home.

Her experiences in Nashville had the same restless, exploratory quality as her experiences in music. Among the work she did was waiting on tables, setting type, singing on demos for songwriters who sent them to record companies or famous singers, and guiding tours at the Country Music Hall of Fame. She gathered around her a group of fellow hopefuls, organizing potluck dinners at her apartment, and in time got to know many people in the industry. Contacts she made got her spots singing at local clubs and finally a contract with Polygram Records.

The records she made there gave some hint of the distinctive style that was to come and attracted the attention of producer Allen Reynolds, whose clients have included such stars as Don Williams and Garth Brooks. Reynolds guided Kathy away from more or less conventional pop styles to the distinctive personal sound which was to make her famous. Her material characterized by penetrating self-examination and fascinating narrative are what she has become identified with.

The first of her songs to reach the top ten was 'Love at the Five and Dime.' 'Time Passes By' and her first number one hit, 'Going, Going Gone' soon followed. The romantic 'Eighteen Wheels and a Dozen Roses,' with words and music by Paul and Gene Nelson, from the 1988 Mercury album *Untasted Honey*, stayed at number one on the sales chart longer than any other single by a female singer in a decade. Perhaps her best performance from that period was the poignant story-song 'Where've You Been,' written by her husband Jon Vezner and Don Henry. A moving story of an elderly couple remembering what they can of their lives, it had a touching simplicity that met with a warm public response. Her album *Time Passes By*, assembled from her personal favorites, was a success.

Kathy has been honored in the industry with such accolades as the Country Music Association's Female Vocalist of the Year Award in 1989 and 1990, and the same award from the Academy of Country Music in 1990. Both organizations honored 'Eighteen Wheels' as the Single Record of the Year in 1988. Recent CDs have included *Walking Away a Winner* and *Willow in the Wind*. The single 'Lonesome Standard Time' has become a virtual standard by itself. The growing success of Kathy Mattea's career has demonstrated the compatibility of country music with the many other forms which she has incorporated so harmoniously into her own distinctive personal style.

Mavericks, The

While every other young band in Miami was playing rock or dance music in the early 1990s, the group that was to become the Mavericks decided that what they really loved and wanted to perform was country music. With plenty of melody and sparse lyrics they gradually forged a contemporary variation of the great country sound of the 1950s.

The members of the group are Paul Malo, singer, guitarist and songwriter; Robert Reynolds, bassist; Paul Deakin, drummer; and a new addition to the original trio, Nick Kane, guitarist.

Paul Malo fronts for The Mavericks.

The group records for MCA, and their first two albums were *From Hell to Paradise*, and *What a Crying Shame*. The Mavericks have been a surprise success on the charts, with several hit singles, and, via well-produced videos, they have become instant country-hunk idols in a field already well-stocked with such types.

It has been more than production values and promotion, however, that has brought the Mavericks their success: they have achieved a remarkable sound recalling the solid country lyrics and instrumentation of the 1950s. The twin-fiddle, shuffle-beat sound is well mixed with modern country ensembles and contemporary lyrics, and the Mavericks achieve a traditional yet modern sound that serves them well.

Miller, Roger

One of the most talented songwriters in country music history, and one of its most eccentric personalities, Roger Dean Miller was born in Fort Worth in 1936 and raised by an uncle and aunt in Erick, Oklahoma, after his father died when Roger was one. Miller grew up poor and liking country music, particularly admiring the music and comedy of a relative, Sheb Wooley, whose humorous alter ego was Ben Colder.

Miller left school after the eighth

Roger Miller.

grade and bought a guitar, and when he served with the Army in Korea he performed in a country band; he also made the acquaintance of Jethro Burns's brother, who talked Miller into auditioning in Nashville. After the war, Miller did indeed audition his songs and singing for Chet Atkins, but got nowhere. He took odd jobs in Music City and eventually played fiddle with Minnie Pearl's group and drums with Faron Young's Deputies. When he joined Ray Price, Ray – and later Patti Page – recorded Roger's song 'Invitation to the Blues.'

In short order many stars were cutting Roger Miller songs: Ernest Tubb, 'Half a Mind;' Jim Reeves, 'Billy Bayou;' George Jones, 'Heart's in My Dream.' In 1961 he co-wrote 'When Two Worlds Collide' with Bill

Anderson and sang it himself on the RCA label – but as a singer Miller still didn't click.

When he signed with Smash Records in 1964, however, an explosion occurred. He recorded some songs that he and songwriting friends used to jam and scat-sing the nights away with, but on record they proved to be hits coming with unprecedented (and unequalled) rapidity and success: 'Chug-a-Lug,' 'Dang Me,' 'King of the Road,' 'Engine Engine Number 9,' 'Kansas City Star,' 'In the Summertime,' 'England Swings.' 'Do-Wacka-Do' and others. He copped 11 Grammy awards in two years (causing a rules change to prevent such one-man dominance in the future), and in 1966 had his own NBC-TV network show. Although all these records were charted country, they had strong pop appeal as well. And the hits continued, with

Roger cutting songs by other songwriters: 'Where Have All the Heroes Gone?', 'Darby's Castle,' 'Me and Bobby McGee' (he was the first to score big with songs by the struggling Kris Kristofferson), 'Little Green Apples.'

The sudden success propelled Roger to Hollywood and a dependence on drugs, a story he frequently told on television talk sows after he kicked the habit, His hits, however, came with lessening frequency, although he kept busy with many business enterprises – commercials, King of the Road motor inns, vocal parts in the Disney cartoon *Robin Hood*, etc. In 1983 he recorded a duet album with Willie Nelson, *Old Friends*, a tribute to their early days together as drifters and dreamers.

Just as his early associations were with comedians Ben Colder, Jethro Burns and Minnie Pearl, so has humor pervaded the majority of Roger Miller's output. But it was his own brand, a sophisticated literacy that was new to country music. Traditional country themes and chords were mixed with a modern hipness, and behind the humor was seriousness despite an image that was casual in the extreme. Most of the lyrics of his novelty and humor songs were actually cynical, and – somehow appropriately therefore – the early smashes have obscured the excellent, deeper compositions of recent years.

In April of 1985 Roger entered a new phase of his career as *Big River*, a musical based on Mark Twain's writings, with words and music by Roger Miller, opened to critical acclaim on Broadway. The show became the hit musical of the season, and Miller who played Huckleberry Finn's father for a time – won seven Tony Awards, including one for best score. In 1988 he received the Pioneer Award from the Academy of Country Music during its televised ceremonies.

Miller died of cancer in California in 1992. In all, some 500 of his songs were recorded by others. His legacy is bittersweet; well-remembered for his immense talent and lengthy list of accomplishments, he was also regarded even by close friends as unpredictable and sad. His son, Dean, continuing the family tradition, signed a major label deal in 1994, and is a staff writer for Sony/Tree.

Milsap, Ronnie

Born in Robbinsville, North Carolina, in 1944, Ronnie Milsap was a blind child prodigy. He played the violin at age seven, the piano at eight, and the guitar at 12. His initial training was in classical music. But then he turned to rock, and, with three blind friends, formed a rock band called The Apparitions, playing in the Raleigh area.

In college Milsap pursued two years of pre-law studies, but forsook it for music. He did session work in Atlanta and performed at the Playboy Club; in the late 1960s he assembled the house band at TJ's Club in Memphis. He made some recordings, with little success, in the rock and rhythm and blues fields, but in 1973 tried his luck and considerable piano-playing talent on country music, and moved to Nashville.

With Jack Johnson as his manager and RCA as his label, Milsap soon produced a steady stream of ever-bigger hits. Initial sides were in the country mainstream sound, and some were sanitized honky-tonk, like 'The Girl Who Waits on Tables Used to Wait For Me At Home' and 'Stand By My Woman Man.' He could master soulful ballads, like his awesome recording of Kristofferson's 'Please Don't Tell Me How the Story Ends' and 'Too Late to Worry, Too Blue to Cry.' In 1977 Milsap was named the Country Music Association Entertainer of the Year.

Hits continued into the late 1980s, with 'Lost In The Fifties Tonight' earning Ronnie his fifth Grammy. No longer signed to a major record label, he tours heavily during the summer fair season and occasionally during winter. One of his major interests is the Ronnie Milsap Foundation for the Blind, which provides scholarships, offers financial aid to two research centers and assists with career opportunities.

Monroe, Bill

Many uninitiated country music listeners assume that bluegrass music is as old as the hills, a time-honored surviving piece of folk Americana. In fact it is not even as old as Bill Monroe, the man who evolved it, played it, defined it, refined it, named it and remains its chief exponent.

William Smith Monroe was born in Rosine, Kentucky, in 1911. His mother Melissa and uncle Pendleton Vandiver were accomplished fiddlers, and the family was devoted to church music and shape-note singing; Bill was attracted to many forms, including blues and spirituals, as well as old-time mountain music of the region. Uncle Pen taught young Bill to play the guitar, mandolin and fiddle, and soon the boy was accompanying his uncle to dances, with older brothers Charlie (guitar) and Birch (fiddle).

The three Monroe brothers, after the fashion of their musical favorites, Charlie Poole's North Carolina Ramblers and the J E Mainer Mountaineers, formed a string-band ensemble, and in the epochal year of 1927 performed their first broadcasts of music and brother-harmonies. Later in the decade they worked as laborers in the Detroit and Chicago areas and for a while joined a WLS *National Barn Dance* touring show – as dancers! In 1930 they had a successful recording of 'Kentucky Waltz,' and followed with 'Blue Grass Ramble;' the Monroe Brothers then secured radio positions in Gary and

Ronnie Milsap.

Hammond, Indiana. In 1936 Charlie and Bill became a brother act and toured Iowa, Nebraska, North Carolina and South Carolina.

The Monroe Brothers were one of country music's classic brother duet teams, singing mostly sentimental songs in high, tight harmonies, but due to friction they parted in 1938. Charlie, who had fronted the group, formed the Kentucky Pardners and Bill first called his own new group the Kentuckians, then the Blue Grass Boys. In 1939 he joined the Grand Ole Opry.

The Bluegrass Boys became one of

Bill Monroe on the mandolin.

the Opry's most popular acts. Monroe operated a traveling tent show on weekdays, and it included Sam and Kirk McGee, Uncle Dave Macon, DeFord Bailey, a gospel quartet and even an exhibition baseball team to warm up the crowds. Through the early 1940s Bill experimented with his sound. He added an accordion for a while, and a banjo; he urged more solos; he drove the band's music to a more intense cadence; and he pushed his own country tenor to higher registers.

By 1946 Bill Monroe had assembled one of the most unique musical ensembles in American history. His own mandolin was a virtuoso's

delight; Lester Flatt, on guitar, wrote fine mountain music, sang baritone lead, and played a guitar full of Riley Puckett and Maybelle Carter runs; Earl Scruggs played a five-string banjo of astounding, revolutionary brilliance, full of improvisation and syncopation; and Chubby Wise's fiddle played more than traditional hoedowns, contributing mournful, smooth, jazzy and sophisticated stylings.

All of a sudden America had a new music. It had evolved, yes, and its roots were easily traceable. But Bill Monroe's Bluegrass Boys were playing something new. It was driven, intense music. It exploded with bril-

liant solos. It was an integrated ensemble of string instruments that had never actually been combined heretofore. The singing was bluesy, the instrumentation was jazzy, and the name was Bluegrass. The development of bluegrass was logical, but its synthesis was by no means inevitable; it took Bill Monroe's taste and vision to bring it into being. Many great musicians through the years have carried its tenets forward, and Bill generously acknowledges them, but it was, and is, his definition and discipline that has brought bluegrass music to its honored state.

Among the musicians who have been Bluegrass Boys are: Flatt and Scruggs, Wise, Mac Wiseman, Clyde Moody, Howdy Forrester, Jimmy Martin, Don Reno, Carter Stanley, Davie 'Stringbean' Akeman, Red Smiley, Cedric Rainwater (Howard Watts), James Monroe, Sonny Osborne, Gordon Terry, Kenny Baker, Byron Berline and Vassar Clements. The songs most associated with Bill Monroe are 'Blue Moon of Kentucky,' 'Mule Skinner Blues,' 'Molly and Tenbrooks,' 'What Would You Give in Exchange for Your Soul?', 'Will You Be Loving Another Man?' 'Walking in Jerusalem,' 'Footprints in the Snow,' 'I Hear a Sweet Voice Calling' and 'I'll Meet You in Church Sunday Morning.'

Flatt and Scruggs left the Bluegrass Boys in 1948 with Rainwater to form the Foggy Mountain Boys. Although many regard the original Bluegrass Boys-period sound as the best on record, Bill's subsequent recordings into the early 1950s – with Red Smiley, Jimmy Martin *et al* – form some of the purest, loneliest, most haunting bluegrass imaginable; they are performances of pure instrumentation and mournful harmonies.

Bluegrass music suffered hard times during the period when honky-tonk and Nashville Sound trends hit country music and rock 'n' roll invaded the national musical landscape. Bill Monroe never compromised his vision or his sound, and eventually the audiences returned. His disciples have incorporated folk, rock, jazz and electric instrumentation, but he has kept the sound pure. By maintaining such a course his mandolin has become the envy of many. As a microcosm of the bluegrass ensemble sound, he has distilled jigs and reels, bagpipe

sounds and fiddle licks on the ancient instrument. He recalls jazz and blues, and borrows the improvisational drive of Dixieland. Likewise Bill's voice has been emulated universally; the high tenor was present in brother-duets, but Bill Monroe made high-tenor harmonies an irreducible component of bluegrass.

Bill Monroe's concerts are grand affairs. He traditionally invites audience members with instruments (and they bring them in great numbers) on to the stage for a closing jam. For years Bill hosted the Bean Blossom Festival in Indiana, one of the major bluegrass festivals. In 1970 Bill Monroe, who as a creator of a distinct form of American music stands

Bill Monroe – the Father of Bluegrass.

among a select few like Scott Joplin and Bob Wills, was formally inducted into the Country Music Hall of Fame. In 1984 he opened his own Bluegrass Hall of Fame and Museum in Nashville, and was honored for contributions to American culture by President Ronald Reagan. Bill still performs occasionally at the Opry and Bluegrass festivals.

The Father of Bluegrass Music was described by The Solemn Old Judge, George D Hay of the Opry, thusly: 'There is that authentic wail in his high pitched voice that one hears in the evening when Mother Nature sighs and retires for the night.'

Montana, Patsy

Ruby Blevins was born in Hot Springs, Arkansas, and grew up admiring the music of Jimmie Rodgers and Gene Autry, as there were few female country singers to follow, she later said. She attended the University of Louisiana but performed locally on the side. She took her stage surname in honor of Monte Montana, the champion yodeler, when she formed the Montana Cowgirls. Soon thereafter, during a radio performance, Stuart Hamblen christened her Patsy in impromptu fashion. During this time (1932) Patsy also played harmonica and fiddle in Jimmie Davis's band.

From these associations she appeared in a few Westerns with her idol Gene Autry, and then visited the World's Fair in Chicago in 1933. She encountered a male ensemble called the Prairie Ramblers (they had been the Kentucky Ramblers until they adopted a Western Swing sound), and joined the group as lead singer. She and the Ramblers were an act for 15 years, and Patsy was a member of the WLS *Barn Dance* in Chicago into the 1950s. Among her hits were 'Nobody's Darling But Mine,' 'I Love My Daddy Too,' 'I'm An Old Cowhand,' 'Montana,' 'I Only Want a Buddy, Not a Sweetheart.' 'I'm a Little Cowboy Girl' and, in 1935, the first million-seller for a female country singer, 'I Want to Be a Cowboy's Sweetheart.' The Ramblers sometimes recorded risqué songs (without Patsy) as the free-wheeling Sweet Violet Boys, although the stage identities were transparent – occasionally the straight and off-color songs were share sides of the same disc.

In 1946-47 Patsy was featured on ABC radio network's *Wake Up and Smile* program. In later years she included her daughter Judy Rose in her act, the Patsy Montana Trio. Patsy still performs today, in resplendent cowgirl outfits and still in command of an astounding, clear Swiss yodel that helped mark her fame.

Patsy Montana and the Prairie Ramblers were an eclectic, good-times ensemble that reflected disparate musical influences: gospel, cowboy, pop, jazz (they often employed sax and clarinet), purple lyrics, West-

Left: Patsy Montana in her cowgirl duds.

ern Swing, honky-tonk and even polka rhythms. Their sound through the years ranged from string-band ensemble to Western Swing sophistication. In 1970 Patsy Montana received the Pioneer Award from the Academy of Country Music.

Montgomery, John Michael

Only the third country performer (along with Garth Brooks and Billy Ray Cyrus) to have a number one pop album, John Michael Montgomery is one of the sensational new performers of the 1990s.

His first album, on Atlantic, *Life's a Dance*, astonished many in the music industry by selling more than a million and a half copies. The follow up, *Kickin' It Up*, was the surprising pop-album success. He also won an American Music Award for favorite new country artist.

A native of Lexington, Kentucky, Montgomery was the son of an aspiring country singer who lived for the weekends when he could perform; Harold Montgomery featured his wife, Carol, on drums and, when they were old enough, John Michael, his brother Eddie, and sister Becky joined the act.

A bachelor, Montgomery receives a number of marriage proposals in his fan letters from women who admire his good looks as well as his good singing. In a day when many 'hat' acts remind fans of either Merle or George – not an unwelcome trend in itself – John Michael Montgomery stands out as a real individual stylist, a harbinger of solid distinction in country music's future, and of its broadening appeal.

Morgan, George

Born in Waverly, Tennessee, in 1924, George Morgan grew up in Ohio enamored of country music thanks to Grand Ole Opry broadcasts. After a short stint in the Army in the 1940s, Morgan formed a band and played dates on Ohio radio stations. At this time he wrote and performed – though did not yet record – the song that was to be the linchpin of his career, 'Candy Kisses.' It was after he gained prominence as a member of the WWVA *Wheeling Jamboree* and signed a contract with Columbia,

that he recorded the song, which was an instant hit.

In 1948 he joined the Grand Ole Opry, and soon proved that his first hit was no fluke; 'Room Full of Roses' was followed by 'You're the Only Good Thing,' 'Almost,' 'Red Roses for a Blue Lady,' 'Slipping Around' (a duet with Marion Worth), and 'A Red Rose From the Blue Side of Town.' Morgan also sang duets with Rosemary Clooney. Today his daughter Lorrie is a popular New Country singer and is a member of the Opry. Morgan died in 1975 at age 51, after complications from open-heart surgery.

George Morgan sang with a smooth, pop-style voice, but re-

John Michael Montgomery.

George Morgan.

mained with his country audience. While a later generation sensed crossover and ran to New York and Hollywood, George Morgan ran back to Nashville, where his sympathies, and his fans, were.

Morgan, Lorrie

An eloquent voice of romantic tragedy, Lorrie Morgan delivers her melancholy message from a solid base of personal experience; the untimely death in 1989 of her husband and the father of her son Jesse, the talented country singer Keith Whitley, darkened her vision of love and gave great depth to her music.

Lorrie was born with the mixed blessing of being the daughter of a star. Her father George Morgan was a country singer whose hits 'Candy Kisses' and 'Room Full of Roses' were standards. A member of the Grand Ole Opry and a popular singer of duets with Marion Worth and Rosemary Clooney, he inadvertently cast a shadow over his daughter's efforts at establishing a separate career and a distinct musical identity of her own. Another ironic obstacle for Lorrie was her great personal beauty and the stylishness of her clothes, which impelled many to dismiss her as more a model than a performer. But the spunky Lorrie persisted in following her own musical destiny, and her tenacity – to say nothing of her very real talent –

won out. She certainly had the advantage of making connections through her famous father – and the patronage of unabashed admirers like disc jockey and TV host Ralph Emery – but it was her own good voice and personal style that earned her the success she has attained. She was singing on the Grand Ole Opry stage of Nashville's Ryman Auditorium at the age of 12 and went on to open for and back up George Jones on tour. No longer thought of as George Morgan's little girl, she was named a member of the Grand Ole Opry in her own right and was part of the staff of the 'Nashville Now' television show for a time.

Lorrie has followed in her father's footsteps without imitating his pop-oriented style. A traditional country singer, she has had substantial success as a recording artist. Her first albums, made for RCA, went gold and had quite a few number one hits among the singles on them, including the defiant 'Watch Me' and 'A Picture of Me Without You' a remake of her father's standard. A frequent hostess of Opry segments, she

Lorrie Morgan, George's daughter.

proved her acting talent in a 1994 drama that appeared on the Nashville Network. Her CDs have included *Warpaint* and the semi-autobiographical *Trainwreck of Emotion*.

Mullican, Moon

Aubrey Mullican was born in Polk County, Texas, in 1909. When he was eight, his father bought a pump organ so his daughters could learn church music; his son learned to play keyboard blues from listening to local rural bluesmen. He perfected his style on piano and organ and played in church and at dances. As a young man Mullican hoboed to Houston where he worked nights, playing the piano in whore-houses (according to legend, the origin of his nickname Moon – the night work). He formed his own band of regional repute in Texas and Louisiana in the 1930s, and joined Leon Selph's Blue Ridge Playboys in 1940 (when Floyd Tillman was also a member) and, later, Cliff Bruner and the Texas Wanderers.

Mullican's reputation continued to grow. He appeared in a movie, *The Village Barn Dance*, and owned Texas nightclubs in the 1940s. In 1947 he recorded 'New Jole Blon,' a stylized Cajun tune, and followed with three other hits including 'Good Night Irene,' 'I'll Sail My Ship Alone' and 'Mona Lisa.' In 1949 he began a six-year stint as a member of the Grand Ole Opry, and from 1960-63 he was in Governor Jimmy Davis's band. He died of a heart attack in Beaumont, Texas, on January 1, 1967.

Mullican had a remarkable way of playing the piano. His left hand thumped the bass keys, and he picked out melody keys – attacked them, really with two fingers of his right hand. The split-time style was influential with the Ferriday, Louisiana, group of piano players, the cousins Jerry Lee Lewis, Jimmy Swaggart and Mickey Gilley. He was called the 'King of the Hillbilly Piano Players' and performed his songs with boisterous vocals. As he synthesized the music of both his times and his region – blues, boogie-woogie, country, honky-tonk, Western swing, and Cajun – he was clearly an inspiration to the emerging rockabilly sound.

Right: Moon Mullican at the piano.

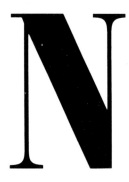

N

Nelson, Willie

Born in Fort Worth in 1933, Willie Nelson was raised by his grandparents in the central Texas town of Abbott. He learned the guitar, which both grandparents played, and, after high school, enlisted in the Air Force. Subsequent to his service he attended Baylor University for two years but dropped out and held

Country music poet Willie Nelson.

various salesmen's jobs, including door-to-door hawking of vacuum cleaners, encyclopedias and Bibles. Finally Willie, drawn to the music business, spent more than seven years as a disc jockey at radio stations in Texas, Oregon and California. He also wrote songs and played local gigs on his guitar whenever he had a chance.

In 1960 he moved to Nashville. He sold the rights to some of his songs, including 'Family Bible' and 'Night Life' (for $50 and $150, respectively). His friend Hank Cochran introduced Willie to Ray Price, and soon Willie was the regular bass guitar player in Price's Cherokee Cowboy Band. It was at this time that Nelson the songwriter started to make an impact; his compositions were being recorded by big stars, and turning into big hits. They included 'Night Life' (Price's single), 'Hello Walls' (Faron Young), 'Crazy' (Patsy Cline) and 'Funny How Time Slips Away' (Billy Walker), all in the early 1960s.

Also despite the legend that Nashville rejected his singing, Willie had two top ten singles himself in 1962; 'Touch Me' and 'Willingly.'

Willie joined the Grand Ole Opry in 1964, and had an active schedule of recording for RCA. His most creative albums were *Yesterday's Wine*, a spiritual-cosmic concept album; and *The Words Don't Fit the Picture Any More*, which contained the first version of 'Good Hearted Woman.' However, Willie was dissatisfied with Nashville life, and when his house burned down it confirmed his wanderlust. He returned to home turf of Texas in 1972. Willie opened up a club in Austin, and simultaneously reacted to and fostered the new 'Austin Sound,' a synthesis of country and rock, but really a fresh affirmation of independence and innovative scoring.

He established the long-running Fourth of July picnics at Dripping Springs, presenting country and rock singers and attracting hundreds

of thousands of fans. He recorded albums for the R&B label Atlantic, one of which, *Phases and Stages*, is possibly his best. A concept album about the breakup of a marriage, one side is from the husband's side and the flip side reflects the wife's point of view. Then, in a creative deal with Columbia Records, Willie cut another concept album, *Red Headed Stranger*; the album and a hit single from it, 'Blue Eyes Crying in the Rain,' were massive hits.

Shortly afterward, RCA hurried up a re-release of songs by Willie, along with some by Waylon Jennings, Jessie Colter and Tompall Glaser, *Wanted: The Outlaws* was an even bigger album than *Stranger*, and it cemented the Outlaw image campaign, furthered by Nelson's headbands and long hair after they had gone out of general fashion.

In addition to a constant stream of top singles, Willie has cut some notable albums, including two gospel LPs, *The Troublemaker and Family Bible*; a tribute *To Lefty* (Frizzell) *From Willie*; several landmark pop-standard albums including *Stardust* and *Somewhere Over the Rainbow* and albums from his movie soundtracks. Willie also became a respected actor, and his credits include *The Electric Horseman, Honeysuckle Rose, Barbarossa* and *The Songwriter*.

Nelson is a non-pareil songwriter of infectious melodies and sensitive lyrics; he is one of the legitimate poets of country music. His guitar picking is masterful (one of his trademarks is the battered old guitar with holes worn in the top, and scratched signatures of all his early Nashville friends). And as a singer he is in the Floyd Tillman tradition of sliding notes and off-the-beat cadences perfectly matching the genuine blues of his nasal tenor.

One of Willie's major contributions to the industry has been starting the trend of having artists from other labels cross over for duet albums. This has led to some classic combinations, not the least of which are Willie's own impressive and creative collaborations. His duet albums have included those with Waylon Jennings, the rock singer Leon Russell, Roger Miller, Webb Pierce, Hank Snow, Faran Young, Ray Price and Merle Haggard.

Willie Nelson is still going strong.

During the depression that hit America's smaller, family-owned farms, Nelson organized 'Farm Aid' concerts with star-studded performers and satellite TV hookups. The concerts raised more than $6 million.

Only the tidal wave of contemporary singers and stars, hunks and cowgirls, black hats and white hats, could threaten to dislodge Willie Nelson from top-of-the-chart prominence, and indeed this almost happened: in the early '90s he recorded some albums for very minor labels, experimented in obscure musical corners (more pop standards, Spanish music, retreads – always fresh and welcome – of his own early writing) and toured less. After the IRS garnished most of his wealth and property, he recorded *The IRS Tapes* (later a CD set) with just him performing his self-penned songs on his guitar. In *Moonlight Becomes You*, a 1994 CD on the small Texas label Justice, Willie speaks a personal message to fans about major labels' disinclination to record anything but the latest trend.

But Willie is now back with major labels (Epic, most recently), touring (solo, after several years with the Highwaymen – Cash, Jennings, and Kristofferson), and a frequent fixture on television (his own specials on the Nashville Network and guest appearance on others' shows and specials). His craggy countenance should always be front and center in country fans' consciousness, and his talents as writer and performer never show signs of flagging.

Nitty Gritty Dirt Band, The

This group has undergone many shifts in personnel, a name change (and a return to its original name), has a wide variety of influences and owns its own audience. But the Nitty Gritty Dirt Band has been devoted to country and traditional music, and one project of theirs, if not their records, assures them a place in the history of country music.

The band's origin was in Long Beach, California in 1965. Guitarists Bruce Kunkel and Jeff Hanna formed a folk song group in high school, and after graduation added Jimmie Fadden (autoharp and harmonica), John McEuen (banjo and fiddle) and two

others to form the Nitty Gritty Dirt Band. When John's brother Bill joined the group as manager and producer, they began to play small dates – evolving from a Jim Kweskin-type novelty group to more serious folk/traditional sounds – and finally were paired as opening acts for big-name stars playing the West Coast.

In 1967 they had a hit record with 'Buy For Me the Rain,' and followed up with 'Hard-Hearted Hanna,' a jug-band anthem. But they hit their stride in 1970, recording Jerry Jeff Walker's 'Mr Bojangles.' In 1972 they shifted more to country and had hits with Hank Williams's 'Jambalaya' and Doug Kershaw's 'Diggy Liggy Lo.'

It was also in that year that the Aspen Recording Society mounted one of the most ambitious projects in country music, historically more important than even universities or institutions have yet attempted. *Will the Circle Be Unbroken* was a three-record concept album with the Band and some of the most significant names in country music: Maybelle Carter, Roy Acuff, Earl Scruggs, Merle Travis, Jimmy Martin and others. Besides preserving classic performances of classic material, the recordings captured out-takes, conversations and laughter in relaxed moments.

During the 1980s the Dirt Band (as they briefly renamed themselves) concentrated on more country than folk, albeit mainstream country rather than the bluegrass and traditional modes honored in their *Will the Circle* project.

Nolan, Bob

Born Robert Clarence Noble in New Brunswick, Canada, in 1908, Bob Nolan grew up liking music and writing poems for his school newspaper – a rare early avocation among the country songwriters. He moved to Arizona at 14 and, in Hollywood in 1931, joined the Rocky Mountaineers, an instrumental ensemble. With Leonard Slye and Tim Spencer, the Pioneer Trio was formed, later to become the Sons of the Pioneers; Nolan usually sang lead.

This group defined a style that set a standard for countless imitators, and although cowboy music had been a distinct tradition, the Sons of the Pioneers synthesized what be-

came the public's perception of the form and established its definitive conventions. Much of this was due to Bob Nolan. His gentle high baritone was as distinctive as the group's unique harmonies – but, mostly, his songwriting set the tone for modern cowboy music.

When Len Slye became Roy Rogers and left the Sons to make movies, the group continued to make records and star on a weekly radio show. But they also maintained a schedule of personal appearances, and went into the movies themselves. They played in Gene Autry singing Westerns, and those of Charles Starrett, and were prominent for years in Roy Rogers movies. In many films Nolan played a leading role and received co-star credit.

Nolan retired from the Sons in 1949 but continued to record with them until 1957. He was somewhat disenchanted with the business and rejected the lifestyle of incessant traveling and having to write songs on deadline. In his last years he wrote poetry, sometimes abstract, and returned to the recording studio in 1979 – the year before his death – to cut an album of superb cowboy songs. His voice had hardly changed from his active years.

Bob Nolan was beautifully impressionable and sensitive. Moving to Arizona from the Canadian backwoods as a teenager, he was awed by the majesty and solitude of the desert; he would walk alone for hours under the Western skies. Between takes of his last album, he rested in a corner of the studio listening to tapes of spring rainfall and mountain streams. Nolan's feeling about the West – its landscape, history and very symbolism – was also mystical.

Consequently the music he wrote, for all its commercial demands, contained some virtual hymns in honor of the West. His classic compositions include: 'Tumbling Tumbleweeds,' 'He Walks With the Wild and Lonely,' 'Cool Water,' 'The Touch of God's Hand' and 'Wandering.' Nolan's voice complemented his melodic, often reverential songs – his was a gentle, unadorned baritone. And to call him a poet of the American West is not hyperbole; it is what he was, first and foremost, for all his other considerable talents.

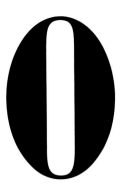

Oak Ridge Boys, The

The Oak Ridge Boys had its genesis in a 1940s quartet, the Country Cut-Ups, that performed at the Oak Ridge Laboratories in Tennessee where nuclear research was being conducted and workers couldn't leave the site for security reasons. The group turned gospel and took the name the Oak Ridge Quartet. It disbanded after World War II and re-formed in the 1950s in Nashville with new members. The Oaks underwent many personnel changes, although they steadily increased their gospel audience.

The oldest Oak, in terms of service, is Duane Allen, who joined the gospel quartet in 1966. The group soon garnered awards in the gospel field with hits like 'Where the Soul Never Dies,' 'Just a Little Talk with Jesus,' and up-tempo versions of other standards. Its current membership was completed when Richard Sterban, tenor, and Joe Bonsall, bass, joined the group.

As their success increased, acrimony within the gospel music establishment did too. There were charges that the Oaks simply weren't religious. Bonsall replies: 'Our only goal was to make gospel as prestigious as any other kind of music.' They formally turned secular in 1974. Johnny Cash invited them to open for him in Las Vegas. They did session work with rock/folksinger Paul Simon. They played more Las Vegas dates and then Roy Clark added them to his act and took them on a tour of Russia.

In 1977 one of their singles finally put their secular career on a super-star-level track: 'The Y'All Come Back Saloon;' it was a country hit that established their identity and harmo-

The Oak Ridge Boys.

nies. 'Crying Again' was another success. In 1978 the Oaks were named Country Music Association Vocal Group of the Year, and the Academy of Country Music bestowed a similar honor. Since then they have had hits with the moody 'Sail Away' and the rocking 'Elvira,' an old Dallas Frazier song.

One of the most durable partnerships in country for years, the Oaks lineup changed amid personal difficulties in 1987. William Lee Golden left the group, replaced by Steve Sanders, the group's former guitarist. They are no longer signed to a major record label.

O'Day, Molly

She was born Laverne Williamson (in Pike County, Kentucky, in 1923) and performed as Mountain Fern and Dixie Lee before taking the stage name Molly O'Day. She would make a widely respected name for herself before quitting the ranks of commercial country music.

Molly was influenced by the music of the Coon Creek Girls when she was growing up, and her first professional performances (at 16) were singing and playing twin banjos with her brother Skeets. In 1939 they joined the Cumberland Mountain Folks, who had just changed their sound to Western, but Molly's Southeastern/mountain vocals were so compelling that the outfit returned to mountain music. Its members included Johnny Bailes and Molly's future husband, Lynn Davis.

Through the 1940s Molly played on countless radio shows and made many recordings for Columbia. In 1946 Mac Wiseman joined the group as a bass player, and soon thereafter Molly became the first performer to discover Hank Williams. She learned one of her classic songs, 'Tramp on the Street,' from him and Hank wrote many songs, mostly gospel, for her. Hank was associated with Molly for three years before he burst into America's musical consciousness.

In 1950 Molly O'Day chose to record only gospel music, and her spiritual inclinations were reinforced when she contracted tuberculosis and defeated the disease through her faith. She abandoned commercial recording in 1952 to become an evangelist in the Church of God.

In the late 1940s when country music was becoming more pop-oriented, O'Day revived the distinctive mountain singing style. Her voice was a pure, plaintive mountain-wail, chilling, emotional and sincere, reminiscent of Roy Acuff when he was in his 1930s prime. The legendary talent-hunter Uncle Art Satherly (British-born recording executive and discoverer of Gene Autry, Bob Wills, and Acuff) said that Molly O'Day was the greatest woman country singer of all time. Among the many hits of her brief recording career were: 'Tramp on the Street,' 'Don't Sell Daddy Any More Whiskey,' 'Poor Ellen Smith,' 'Black Sheep Returned to the Fold,' and 'Matthew Twenty-Four.'

Molly O'Day died at the age of 69 at her home in Huntington, West Virginia, in December 1987.

Osborne Brothers, The

Among the most popular and innovative of all bluegrass stylists, Sonny and Bob Osborne have created their own version of progressive bluegrass. Where many others have ex-

The Osborne Brothers: Bob and Sonny.

perimented with folk, rock, jazz and swing elements, it seems odd that very few have combined the influence of modern country music; the Osborne Brothers have done so, and with great success.

The brothers were born in Hyden, Kentucky (Bob in 1931 and Sonny in 1937) and grew up listening to country music and the Grand Ole Opry and Ernest Tubb, especially, before bluegrass was developed in the mid-1940s. Bob played with the Lonesome Pine Fiddlers in Beckley, West Virginia, in the late 1940s, and a 12-year-old Sonny guested with his banjo on a Bill Monroe show in 1950. In the early 1950s, as a bluegrass duo, they were teamed with Jimmy Martin; for a while they were settled on radio in Detroit from where, Sonny has recalled, Martin rejected an offer for them to star in the Martha White Flour Show in the South – the gig that eventually went to Flatt and Scruggs – because of a disagreement over $15 in pay.

In 1956 the Osborne Brothers, with Red Allen, were featured members of the WWVA *Wheeling Jamboree*; they soon added Benny Birchfield and later Ronnie Reno and Dale Sledd to their ensemble. In 1959, setting a pattern for future bluegrass performers, the Osbornes played a college date at Antioch College. College folk festivals and bluegrass festivals, in fact, played a large role in resuscitating bluegrass after the onslaught and devastation of rock 'n' roll.

Sonny and Bob joined the Grand Ole Opry in 1964, and continue to tour widely and record. They toured three years with the Merle Haggard road show, and have played at the White Horse.

The unique sound of the Osborne Brothers is a result of their reflected influences, awesome talent, and clever studio/stage techniques. Bob and Sonny are innovators and stylists of the highest order. Bob sings high tenor (probably the highest register in bluegrass today) and, contrary to tradition, will often take the lead vocal. His mandolin technique is the envy of many players, and he pulls fiddle tunes and hornpipe structures from the instrument.

Likewise Sonny will use the banjo for unorthodox functions. He plays in the obligatory bluegrass Scruggs style, but also simulates steel, piano, sax and even drum rhythms from his instrument. And during vocal solos, Sonny will pick single-string countermelodies, almost as a patter.

The Osborne sound included electric instruments and drums in many cases, and a unique feature is their technique of rigging certain instruments and microphones with echo-devices; it achieves a different, fuller sound and is also evocative of mountain music echoing through the misty hills of its origin. On top of all their achievements, the Osborne Brothers also package one of Nashville's liveliest road shows, which has helped popularize and publicize their unique brand of bluegrass music wherever they have traveled around the world.

Through the years their hits have included 'Once More,' 'Tennessee Hound Dog,' 'Each Season Changes You,' 'Midnight Flyer,' 'Ruby (Are You Mad at Your Man)' and 'Rocky Top,' which has become one of the anthems of bluegrass music along with 'Orange Blossom Special' and 'Foggy Mountain Breakdown.' Their addition of electric guitar and drums enabled them frequently to crack the country music charts, which often freeze out bluegrass records. Likewise their lyrics sometimes tend to uptown country and sometimes even honky-tonk.

In recent years the Osborne Brothers have recorded for CMH and Sugar Hill, two of the labels that preserve the tradition as well as the innovative in country music despite Nashville's obsessive homogeneity. For CMH they recorded solo and with Mac Wiseman in superb bluegrass renditions; and lately they have tended to de-emphasize electric elements in favor of a new style of acoustic instrumentation.

Owens, Buck

Alvis Edgar Owens was born in 1929 in Sherman, Texas, into a poor sharecropper's family. His father was determined to escape the Depression's ravages by moving to California as thousands were doing. However, their trailer broke in

Buck Owens and the Buckaroos.

Arizona, so they settled there. At the age of 13 Buck learned to play the mandolin, and later the guitar, and after dropping out of school he became the co-host of a country music television show in Mesa. The show was *The Buck and Britt Show*, and the Buck half was 16 years old.

Later he moved on to become a member of the touring band Mac's Skillet Lickers, and married a singer who had been a member of both shows, Bonnie Campbell. When Buck was 20 they moved to Bakersfield, California, at the urging of two uncles who were on the periphery of the country music business. Buck was a fine guitar player who became a busy sideman and formed his own band, The Schoolhouse Playboys. In the early 1950s he backed up singers on Los Angeles recording sessions, including Tennessee Ernie Ford, Sonny James, Wanda Jackson and Tommy Sands.

Buck was beginning to make a name for himself; actually he was making two names for himself, as he recorded rockabilly songs as Corky Jones. As Buck Owens, he replaced Ferlin Husky as lead guitar player in Tommy Collins' band, and this led to a contract with Capitol Records. But no hits were immediately forthcoming and the troubled Buck divorced and moved to Seattle where he became a disc jockey for a year and a half.

Then his record 'Under Your Spell' caught on, followed by some duets with Rose Maddox that rose to the top ten in 1961. The following year he formed his own group, the Buckaroos, and managed to get his label to allow his band and instrumentation to back him on record. It was a hard honky-tonk sound with brassy, ringing electric guitars and whining steel. It featured the high tenor harmonies of Don Rich . . . and it worked with the public. Buck recorded 'Love's Gonna Live Here' and ultimately had a string of 26 consecutive number one records.

Other typical Buck Owens hits included 'Act Naturally' (which was covered by the Beatles), 'Together Again,' 'I've Got a Tiger by the Tail,' 'Cryin' Time' and 'Waitin' in Your Welfare Line.' He played dates around the world, hosted his own television show in the 1960s (and

Left: Buck Owens performs solo.

later in the 1980s) and co-hosted one of the most popular programs in the history of television syndication, *Hee Haw*.

In the early 1970s Owens experimented with other modes: folk ('Bridge Over Troubled Water'); bluegrass ('Rollin' In My Sweet Baby's Arms') and rock ('Johnny B Goode'). He recorded theme albums (like *I Wouldn't Live in New York City*, an album of city songs) and a *Live in London* set. He was paired for duets with Susan Raye, and later included fiddler Jana Jae in his act.

Buck Owens's sound preserved the strains of honky-tonk that had arisen in the 1950s, and bucked the contemporary trend of lush instrumentation and pop-leaning backups; in fact his determination to stay in Bakersfield was a symbolic rejection of the Nashville Sound. A major part of his sound was the superb harmony of Don Rich, who could anticipate every quaver and slide of Owens's voice (Rich was killed in a tragic motorcycle accident in 1974). Through the years his backup band has included other superb musicians like Doyle Holly, Ralph Mooney and Tom Brumley, son of Albert E Brumley, the great gospel composer.

Ironically much of Buck Owens's great material is now out of print, but as thorough professional, writing and performing classic country songs, his legacy is valuable and important.

The flurry of interest in Buck Owens as a singer and performer that followed the Bakersfield sessions with Dwight Yoakam has subsided. Buck taped a farewell performance concert in Texas for the Nashville Network (that, unlike those of some other stars, seems to have been an actual farewell to the stage) and his only real presence these days is as a grinning host of 15-year-old *Hee Haw* reruns.

Bear Family records of Germany has issued the lifetime recorded work of Buck Owens, and it is unfortunate that no American label has followed suit. Buck's contributions were massive, and are still entertaining. It is to be hoped that, like Haggard, Jones, Nelson, Jennings, and a handful of other greats who can still be active in the field, Buck Owens will be lured from retirement again, and resume an active schedule for yet another generation of fans.

Parnell, Lee Roy

Growing up on a ranch near Abilene, Texas, Lee Roy Parnell had the benefit of knowing the legendary Western Swing artist Bob Wills, an old friend of the family. Wills invited Lee Roy, then six years old, to sing on his radio show, a debut opportunity offered to few in the business, and the boy made good use of it. In 1987 he traveled to Nashville with a job writing songs for Welk Music, and his first album, made for Arista in 1989, was an immediate critical success.

His second album, *Love Without Mercy*, established the young singer's personal style clearly in the public perception. An archetypal 'new traditionalist', he fuses blues, folk, jazz, gospel, and swing into that harmonious mix that distinguishes New Country at its best.

Characteristically, Lee Roy avoids

Lee Roy Parnell.

lush arrangements, beginning a recording session with voice and guitar alone and adding no more than another guitar, drums, bass, and sometimes a piano. Typical of his second album was the sensitivity and reflectiveness of the title song, written by Mike Reid and Don Pfrimmer, but the heart of the album was the traditional country single with gospel undertones, 'The Rock.'

Texas is an important source of New Country music, because many of the styles of country that make up the Texas sound are ingredients of new traditionalism. By weaving together the many strands of this style into a distinctive one of his own, Lee Roy Parnell is a classic voice of his state and its music.

His recent CDs have included *On the Road*.

Parsons, Gram

A seminal figure in the innovative movement of the 1970s that led to a fusion of country, rock, folk and bluegrass, Gram Parsons died an early, untimely death reminiscent of those of Jimmie Rodgers and Hank Williams, but almost too early to establish his legacy. His talent was a promise that he would have become a major figure in country music.

He was born Cecil Connor in Winter Haven, Florida, in 1946. Parsons (he received his second father's surname after his first father committed suicide) grew up liking country, gospel, and rockabilly, and as a teen was a member of several bands, including The Legends, which included Jim Stafford as a member. He then sang and picked with a Greenwich Village folk group, the Shilos, before briefly studying theology at Harvard and forming the International Submarine Band, a country-rock group.

Later he joined the soft-rock/folk group The Byrds, and moved their sounds towards country by influencing the direction of their *Sweetheart of the Rodeo* album; he wrote the single, 'Hickory Wind,' for the landmark, influential disc. For a while Parsons hung out with the Rolling Stones in England, and in 1969 he formed the Flying Burrito Brothers with ex-Byrd Chris Hillman (who had been involved with the Dillards and Clarence White), Chris Ethridge and 'Sneeky' Pete Kleinow.

The Burritos' debut album, *The Gilded Palace of Sin*, contained two classics of the genre they were creating: 'Wheels' and 'Sin City.' Besides Parsons, the group's songwriting sources included elements as diverse as Merle Haggard and Bob Dylan, and the sound was an extremely pleasant fusion of soft rock and bluegrass.

The group recorded several more albums although it endured constant personnel changes, including that of Parsons, who left in 1971 in order to work as a solo. Brilliant albums – *GP* and *Grievous Angel* (featuring his protege Emmylou Harris on vocals) preceded his tragic death after a drug and liquor binge that plagued, and characterized, his all-too-brief personal and professional life. He died in Joshua Tree, California, on September 19, 1973.

His friend Phil Kaufman, road manager for several acts, reportedly fulfilled a mutual pact made with Parsons at the funeral of Clarence White a short time earlier. He stole Parsons' body and cremated it at Joshua Tree National Park. Parsons'

Dolly Parton has enjoyed success as both a country and a pop star.

end was like his being – quick, startling, out of the ordinary.

Gram Parsons had superb talent, taste and vision. For all his gifts as a songwriter, singer, keyboard and guitar player, it can be said that his greatest legacy was an inspiration. He played – and lived – as a rocker, but had an almost reverential regard for mountain music by the likes of the Stanley Brothers and the Louvin Brothers. He introduced old-time music to rock 'n' roll stars, and rock elements to bluegrass players. He planted many of the seeds that are flowering today in country and other forms of American music.

Parton, Dolly

Dolly Rebecca Parton was born in Locust Ridge, Tennessee, in the foothills of the Smoky Mountains, in 1946. The fourth of 12 children in a poor family, Dolly showed an early interest in music and would create tunes that she would ask her mother to write down. At eight she received her first guitar, and she dreamed of being a star.

When Dolly was 13 she began appearing on the Cas Walker Show in Knoxville and cut a record, 'Puppy Love,' for a small label. But the day after her high school graduation she moved to Nashville. She lived at first with her uncle Bill Owens, later a partner in writing and publishing; their composition 'Put It Off Until Tomorrow' was a top ten hit for Bill Phillips in 1966.

Dolly signed her own performing contract with Monument and in 1967 had two hits. 'Dumb Blonde' and 'Something Fishy.' Her later country hits, after joining the Porter Wagoner TV and road shows and the RCA label, included 'In the Good Old Days When Times Were Bad,' 'My Blue Ridge Mountain Boy,' 'In My Tennessee Mountain Home,' 'Coat of Many Colors' and 'The Seeker.' As Miss Dolly on the *Porter Wagoner Show* she acquainted America with her unlikely mix of shy demeanor and forceful vocals, a sexy, superficial appearance and sincere manner. She and Porter recorded some of country music's outstanding duets during their years together.

Everything about their styles – save their rather bizarre costumes and coiffures – was unmatched, but opposites attracted as Porter sang soft, low harmony complementing Dolly's shrill, high leads on classic performances like 'Forty Miles from Poplar Bluff,' 'Jeannie's Afraid of the Dark,' 'Just Someone I Used to Know,' 'Daddy Was an Old-Time Preacher Man' and 'If Teardrops Were Pennies and Heartaches Were Gold.'

In 1973 Dolly left the *Porter Wagoner Show*, although he continued to produce her albums, and she toured with her Family Band of musician relatives and siblings. But three years later she broke all association with Porter and charted a new musical course. Amid massive Hollywood publicity, Dolly Parton went pop, and it paid off for her in terms of crossover success and national acclaim. His first new album title prefigured the shift: *New Harvest, First Gathering*, and her big-selling hits since then have included 'Here You Come Again,' 'Two Doors Down,' 'Great Balls of Fire,' '9 to 5' and a duet with Kenny Rogers, 'Islands in the Sun.'

She also became a movie star in non-country roles; the girl who pined for her 'Blue Ridge Mountain Boy' and sang proudly of her childhood 'Coat of Many Colors' smoked marijuana in *9 to 5* and played a madam in *The Best Little Whorehouse in Texas*.

Dolly's career is categorized by several phases. In the first, she wrote extremely tradition-oriented songs, the best of them rich in tragedy and irony in the mountain manner; the second phase was lyrical, introspective, and autobiographical ('The Bargain Store.' 'Love Is Like a Butterfly,' 'I Will Always Love You') and the third as an all-out appeal for rock and pop audiences. When she wrote those early country songs, she had few equals among country writers or performers – they are simple, pure classics, close to the soil and close to the soul. Considering Dolly's poverty-stricken background, her current success, and her mature self-assurance, she is now where she wants to be.

In 1987 Dolly Parton joined Emmylou Harris and Linda Ronstadt for a long-awaited collaboration album, and the result – *Trio* – was a million-seller that produced four hit singles. It was a return to the root of country music, with primarily acoustical backup. In February 1988 Parton joined erstwhile partner Porter Wagoner briefly for duets on the Grand Ole Opry stage. For the most part, however, her recent moves have been away from country music. In 1987 she switched labels from RCA to Columbia and hooked up with pop producer Steve Goldstein. Her costumes and stage persona, not to mention choice of material became increasingly pop-oriented.

That year she began hosting a big-budget, hour-long TV series, *Dolly*, that featured country acts, trips to her theme park, Dollywood, and tributes from guests and audience members. The show was a flop.

Parton's acceptance by the industry began to turn around again in the 1990s. In 1993 she announced the formation of her own record label, Blue I, and in 1994 she won the Grammy for Best Popular Song for her single, 'I Will Always Love You,' sung by Whitney Houston. She is once again a top-grossing concert act, and is one of a few female performers of her generation who remains attractive to mainstream country radio. In 1994 she recorded a collaboration with Loretta Lynn and Tammy Wynette.

Paycheck, Johnny

Johnny Paycheck's life and career had as many ups and down and happiness and hard times as any of the country songs he sings and writes. Born Don Lytle in Greenfield, Ohio, in 1941, Paycheck grew up devoted to country radio. He bought a guitar as a child and was writing songs by his mid-teens. His talent propelled him into performing at local clubs, and by the late 1960s he was recording some rockabilly sides (as Donny Young) and was a sideman with some of the best country bands of the day – Porter Wagoner, Faron Young, George Jones and Ray Price.

He toured with Jones and was sometimes featured on stage, as his single records gained more fame. In the mid-1960s he founded the Little Darlin' label and recorded some fine honky-tonk music, but within a few years drug and alcohol problems caused him to leave the Jones show and see his own career collapse.

Billy Sherrill of Epic Records was willing to take another chance on the talented Paycheck (who had penned Tammy Wynette's first song, 'Apartment #9' for Sherrill) and Paycheck

vowed to straighten out his life. In the early 1970s, he scored with 'Friend (Don't Take her, She's All I Got)' and followed with 'Mr Love Maker' and 'For a Minute There.'

Paycheck reportedly was bankrupt and wild again in 1976, but bounced back with the biggest hits of his troubled career: 'I'm The Only Hell My Mama Ever Raised' and 'Slide Off Your Satin Sheets,' and, in 1977, two protest-novelty songs that spread his name across all of America's consciousness, 'Take This Job and Shove It,' written by David Allen Coe; and 'Me and the IRS.' In the 1980s he recorded a live album in New York City, a duet album with his old cellmate and soul mate, George Jones, and a tribute album to Merle Haggard with Hag joining in on three cuts.

Every year – seemingly every day – events confirm patterns in Paycheck's life. In 1985 he shot a man in a barroom brawl and received a 9½-year sentence, which underwent a lengthy appeals process. He recorded a gospel album with evangelist John Wesley Fletcher just before the latter was implicated in the Jim Bakker-PTL scandal. And Paycheck can offer considerable personal testimony to the anti-drug 'Just Say No' campaign, with which he affiliated himself in 1987.

High or low, events have not altered Paycheck's unique vocal style, a rockabilly-tinged drive that obviously reflects the on-the-edge aspect of his personality. A constant stylist, he has always chosen – or written – predictably excellent material.

Pearl, Minnie

One of country music's most prominent 'hicks,' Minnie Pearl actually can boast of sophisticated roots. Sarah Ophelia Colley Cannon (born in Centerville, Tennessee, in 1912) studied the classics at Nashville's fashionable Ward-Belmont College and then taught dance for two years. Pursuing her interest in dancing and acting, she became a director of School Theatrical Productions, headquartered in Atlanta.

Part of her duties included travelling to promote her shows, and she began enlivening her speeches with

Country 'hick' Minnie Pearl.

anecdotes about 'Cousin Minnie Pearl' around 1936. By 1940 she was a cast member of the Grand Ole Opry. Grinder's Switch was Minnie's hometown – actually it was a rail crossing near Centerville – and her trademarks were the hat with the price tag, a calico dress, a loud 'How-dee! I'm just so proud to be here!' and endless ruminations on trying to 'ketch a feller.'

Minnie was a cast member of the *Hee Haw* television program, and besides touring with her routine, she wrote a cookbook and launched an ill-fated chain of chicken restaurants. She was elected to the Country Music Hall of Fame in 1975. An annual award to a Country Artist from Music City News is given in her name.

She resides today in a Nashville mansion next door to the governor. A stroke victim since the early 1990s, Minnie receives many well-wishes and dedicated songs from her professional peers at the Opry.

Perkins, Carl

Born near Jackson, Tennessee, on a tenant farm in 1932, Carl Perkins and his family were the only white sharecroppers on the farm. Always interested in music, in 1955 he found himself at Memphis's Sun Recording Studio, and was soon thrown into the rockabilly/rock 'n' roll revolution that was spawned at Sun via such artists as Elvis Presley, Johnny Cash, Jerry Lee Lewis, Roy Orbison, Charlie Rich and Narvel Felts.

Perkins recorded 'Blue Suede Shoes' in late 1955, and it shot to number one in rock, country and pop charts. Driving to New York to accept a gold record for the song on network television, Perkins was almost killed in an auto crash, and spent a year in the hospital recuperating. It was a mixed sort of consolation when he received a note from Elvis Presley saying that Perkins, not he, might have become a superstar if not for the accident.

When Perkins had fully recovered, his career was somewhat cooler than its initial promise. In 1963 he toured England with another rock founder, Chuck Berry; the Beatles paid tribute to Perkins's influence on them. But Perkins had little recording success.

In 1965 his old friend Johnny Cash – who had shared similar drug prob-

Carl Perkins.

lems and career turns – invited Perkins to join his stage show. Perkins remained until 1976, and made appearances on Cash's television program. Perkins, who was always more rockabilly than rock, is still performing and recording, and has returned to country and gospel.

As a writer, performer and guitar player, Carl Perkins is vastly underrated. His songs are classics of their times, whether rockers or hillbilly boogie, at which he excelled (among his compositions: 'Pink Pedal Pushers,' 'Boppin' the Blues,' 'Put Your Clothes On' and 'Perkins Wiggle'). His guitar was the bridge between electrified honky-tonk and shotgun-style rock. He could make it lead or accompany, sing or shriek, all in masterful fashion. Retro projects like *The Survivors*, with Cash and Jerry Lee Lewis have kept Perkins in the public eye.

Pierce, Webb

Born in West Monroe, Louisiana, in 1926, Webb Pierce took to the guitar and country music early, playing at local events and being featured on local radio shows. In the early 1950s he landed a spot as a regular on the *Louisiana Hayride* and took on some talented sidemen, later stars in their own rights; Faron Young, Floyd Cramer, Goldie Hill and Jimmy Day.

Pierce signed with Decca Records and then, in 1952, became a member of the Grand Ole Opry. The following year he left to join the ABC-TV network show *Ozark Jubilee*, where he headlined once a month; in 1955 he was back with the Opry. It was during these years that an incredible string of hits began. Foremost among them were 'In the Jailhouse

hard drinking – life seen from the inside of a smoky bar. Pierce's success, however, was long and fulsome, and sweet. He was, in his prime, a consummate musician and an influential anthem-singer to a lifestyle that composed an important piece of country's audience. Pierce today performs occasionally from his home base of Nashville, where he lives in a house whose backyard boasts a rather notorious guitar-shaped swimming pool.

Presley, Elvis

Elvis Aaron Presley was born to poor parents in Tupelo, Mississippi, in 1935. He sang at an early age, and his parents moved to Memphis when he was 13. After high school graduation, Presley became a truck driver, but wanted to follow a musical career. As legend has it he wanted to

Above: Webb Pierce.
Right: The King: Elvis Aaron Presley.

Now,' 'There Stands the Glass,' 'More and More' and 'Why Baby, Why,' a duet with Red Sovine, with whom he recorded and toured for a time. In 1956 Pierce explored rockabilly with 'Teenage Boogie.'

Between 1952 and 1972 Webb Pierce had major country hits in every year, and 24 consecutive number one songs. He starred in four movies, and even a *Kraft Suspense Theater* drama on network television. Among his other landmark achievements are seven songs simultaneously in the top twelve in 1954, and a career total of more than 40 million records sold. During his heyday Pierce was seven times voted the top country singer.

But his heyday is gone. The distinctive sound that propelled his meteoric success is today passé, almost more obscure to modern ears than old-time mountain music, although the seeds that Pierce sowed have grown and been harvested in many country styles, including rockabilly, the new honky-tonk sounds, and, basically, all electrified country ensembles.

The Pierce sound featured ringing electric guitars, and a whining steel guitar (the first pedal steel in country music). His voice was, as advertised, piercing, and the lyrics' preoccupations were usually hard living and

Elvis's roots were in country music.

1956, and he signed a seven-year, seven-picture deal with Hollywood's Hal Wallis. In 1958 he was inducted into the army, and after his release two years later, maintained a lower-profile schedule of appearances. In 1969 he was obliged to stage a 'come-back' with TV and Las Vegas appearances, and his new wave of hits included semi-country songs by Jerry Reed and Mac Davis. Presley died in his mansion in Memphis, Tennessee on August 16, 1977.

Although his roots were certifiably country, Elvis Presley preserved the most tenuous connection with country music during his musical career. In the rock days, he was obliged (apparently in willing fashion) to distance himself from hillbilly music; he was, after all, the King of Rock 'n' Roll. And later in his career he had turned so pop that rock 'n' roll, much less country music, seemed foreign to him. Recent observers have noted the irony of Presley's phenomenal success. When he was a 'bad boy' in the public's eye, Presley was a shy, polite exemplary country boy in spite of the musical and social revolution he was waging. Later in his career when his musical repertoire was as bland as any pop singer's, his private life was reportedly filled with bizarre self-indulgence and drugs, leading, by most reports, to his death.

But by *all* reports his influence was great, including in his forsaken home, country music. The industry adapted to Presley's revolution in many ways – accommodation, compromise, and even, in some corners, hard-core rejection for purity's sake – for many years, and is still doing so years later.

record a song for his mother's birthday and went to the Sun Recording Studios with the $4 fee to self-record a disc. Owner Sam Phillips heard the session and asked Presley to return.

Phillips had been seeking a person to fulfill his prescription for musical success – a white boy who could sing black – and Presley seemed to fit that bill. His first record was the rocking 'That's All Right Mama,' backed with a decidedly individual interpretation of Bill Monroe's bluegrass classic 'Blue Moon of Kentucky,' either a bright new innovation or country blasphemy, depending on the ear of the listener.

An Opry appearance with Hank Snow was a bust, but Presley toured with Snow to enthusiastic country crowds. He became a member of the *Louisiana Hayride* and acquired a manager, Colonel Tom Parker, who had managed Eddy Arnold. Presley was billed as the Hillbilly Cat, but he soon proved bigger than any gimmick designed to put him over. He was booked to perform at a C&W Disc Jockey Association convention; Steve Sholes of RCA heard him and soon bought his contract from Sun.

His RCA singles were all hits, and he became the leader, the lighting rod, of the new rock 'n' roll, receiving praise and abuse for even more than he was responsible. Presley was a star attraction on the *Dorsey Brothers* and *Ed Sullivan* TV shows in

Price, Kenny

'The Round Mound of Sound,' as Kenny Price was called by friends having fun at his expanse and expense, was born near Florence, Kentucky, in 1931. He was raised on a Boone County farm, and, like many other country singers, learned to play music on a mail-order guitar. Soon he was playing local dances and was a home-town favorite.

During the Korean War, Kenny played with Horace Heidt's USO Band, and after returning from Korea he enrolled in the Cincinnati Conservatory of Music. Unable to stray from his roots, however, Kenny joined the WLW *Midwestern Hayride* in 1954, first as lead singer with its group, the Hometowners, then as a solo act.

For a local label he recorded two songs that gained national hit status, 'Happy Tracks' and 'Walkin' On New Grass.' He was signed by RCA in 1969 and more hits followed over the next few years: 'Biloxi,' 'The Sheriff of Boone County' and 'Sea of Heartbreak' among them. He also recorded a splendid tribute album to Red Foley, with Chet Atkins playing Foley's guitar.

Kenny's voice was, indeed, similar to Foley's – warm, smooth, and a deep, rich baritone. He was an accomplished comedian, having been a prominent *Hee Haw* staffer for years on television. He also sang solo numbers on the program, and was the bass singer in the classic Hee Haw Gospel Quartet that preserves the old-time gospel harmonies of the Delmore Brothers and others. An album released by the quartet features the voices of Kenny, Grandpa Jones, Buck Owens and Roy Clark.

'The Round Mound of Sound' hosted the Nashville Network program *Wish You Were Here* with his wife Donna before his death of a heart attack at his home in Florence, Kentucky, in August 1987.

Price, Ray

Ray Price has been one of the most influential stylists in country music, and one of its biggest-selling stars. The pop moves he pioneered once served him well, and now might haunt him as his fine vocals are now in search of an audience. But it is significant that he is making a comeback in the country field, not the pop field.

Born in Perryville, Texas, in 1926, he grew up on a farm, served in the Marines and attended North Texas Agricultural College in Abilene as a veterinary major. Through all these activities Ray listened to and sang country music; in 1948 he sang as The Cherokee Cowboy on the KRBC *Hillbilly Circus*. The next year he joined the *Big D Jamboree* in Dallas and released a record, 'Jealous Lies,' which received national exposure when the CBS network picked up the program.

In 1952 Ray signed with Columbia Records and joined the Grand Ole Opry. He was befriended by Hank Williams. Hank would often crash in Ray's apartment and when he missed concert dates (as he often did) Ray would cover for him. After Hank died, several of Hank's Drifting Cowboys became members of Ray's band, The Cherokee Cowboys. 'Release Me' and 'I'll Be There' were two of Ray's big hits at this time.

Until 1956 Ray's vocals sounded much like Hank Williams's – as did those of many country singers. But in that year, on the single 'Crazy Arms,' Ray created a new sound that proved enormously influential and

Ray Price and the Cherokee Cowboys.

The legendary Ray Price.

became a trademark style of his for a decade. He introduced a loping 4/4 bass beat, a shuffle rhythm on drums, a single or twin Texas fiddle and a different vocal style – a slightly deeper voice that stretched to high, slightly off-register quavering vibratos. Ray Price arrived in a big way. His hits in this style included; 'My Shoes Keep Walking Back to You,' 'Heartaches By the Number,' 'Burning Memories,' 'Don't You Ever Get Tired of Hurting Me,' and 'Night Life.'

In 1967 the musically restless and innovative Price switched modes again, recording 'Danny Boy' with a 47-piece orchestra. His vocalisms were unchanged, but the environment was and, although the record was a big seller, many country stations refused to play the song. Nevertheless Ray stayed the course, supported by fans, and in 1970 he matched up with a rising songwriter, Kris Kristofferson. The hits they produced broke sales records and ushered in a new era of country music – thoughtful lyrics packaged in lush, uptown production. Among Ray's hits of this period and this collaboration were 'For the Good Times,' 'I Won't Mention It Again'

and 'I'd Rather Be Sorry.' 'You're the Best Thing That Ever Happened to Me' also scored in the early 1970s, and became an anthem for lovers through its sensitive lyrics and tender production.

Through these years Ray Price was eight times voted *Billboard* magazine's Top Country Vocalist. But as the pop-country sound abandoned all vestiges of country, and as other Texas musicians incorporated rock 'n' roll modes for an 'outlaw' sound, Ray found his audience declining. He turned to gospel music, recording some fine albums for Myrrh, and went into semi-retirement on his Golden Cross Ranch in Texas, following his early love of raising horses. He has since returned to performing, however. He and Willie Nelson recorded an album of their Texas-flavored songs; he acted in the Clint Eastwood movie, *Honkytonk Man*, and signed with the Eastwood-Snuff Garret country label, Viva Records.

Always an individualized stylist, Ray has had many disciples, including Johnny Bush and Ray Pennington, who sing in his style. He has helped the careers of many country performers through encouragement and apprenticeship in his Cherokee Cowboys, including Willie Nelson,

Roger Miller, Johnny Paycheck, Buddy Emmons and Johnny Bush. Besides his many award-winning albums are many concept LPs, including *Night Life* and tributes to Hank Williams and Bob Wills.

Ray Price, a man who forged two stylistic revolutions in one musical career, actually had crooner tendencies going back to his first hit, 'Jealous Lies.' And, appropriately, the style of his mature period embodied his two strains; Ray's soft voice is as lush as a string-section backup, but his high notes are vocal equivalents of the honky-tonk steel guitar. Ray Price made himself into a country legend that lives on today. In 1993 Ray recorded an acclaimed CD, *Memories That Last* with Faran Young.

Pride, Charley

The Pride of Sledge, Mississippi, was born in 1938 as one of 11 children. As a boy he picked cotton and listened at night to country music radio, particularly the Grand Ole Opry on weekends. But Charley Pride loved baseball, too, and aspired to a career in sports. As a young man he played in the Negro American League, moonlighting by singing in local shows during trips.

In 1963 he was working as a smelter in Montana, and singing on the side. It was during a local gig that Red Sovine heard him singing 'Lovesick Blues,' the Hank Williams favorite. Sovine urged Charley to go to Nashville, but Pride hesitated, because he was still a member of the New Yorks Mets organization. But music prevailed, as did Sovine and Red Foley, who led the way to an audition with Chet Atkins of RCA. In the beginning of 1966 his first record, 'The Snakes Crawl at Night,' was released, and it became a big hit.

RCA was a bit nervous about the handling and reception of Pride; although he didn't sound so, he was black. But then or now there has been virtually no resistance among the Southern/rural/country audiences to this singer who would become the first major black country star. Pride followed with other big hits, including, 'All I Have to Offer You is Me,' 'I'm So Afraid of Losing You Again,' 'A Shoulder to Cry On,' 'Is Anybody Goin' To San Antone' and 'Wonder Could I Live There Any More.'

With songs like 'Kiss an Angel Good Morning' and 'Amazing Love' he started a slide toward pop sounds, which led to songs like 'You're My Jamaica.' On the other hand, Charley can still preserve a rockabilly/honky-tonk tradition in songs like 'Mountain of Love.' He has also recorded two fine gospel albums and a tribute album to Hank Williams.

Charley Pride has lent a helping hand to newcomer artists like Ronnie Milsap, Johnny Russell, Johnny Duncan and Gary Stewart through the years. His own fine deep baritone and solid country singing style are responsible for Charley Pride's enormous success; he was named the Country Music Association Entertainer of the Year in 1971.

Charley Pride's musical evolution could be taken from one of his hit's titles: 'I'm Just Me.' His career is rebounding as of late; in 1994 he became a member of the Grand Ole Oprey, and a Branson theater bears his name.

Puckett, Riley

George Riley Puckett was born in 1894 in Alpharetta, Georgia. At age three months he contracted an eye infection that was mistreated, and Puckett became blinded for life. He developed a marvelous proficiency on banjo and, especially, guitar that led him to radio station WSB in Atlanta in 1922.

He joined with Gid Tanner to record the first country string-band music on disc in 1924, and he preceded Jimmie Rodgers by three years in blue-yodeling, on the record 'Rock All Our Babies to Sleep.' That same year the Lick the Skillet Band was formed, and in 1926 Pappy McMichen joined his fiddle to Puckett's guitar and Tanner's fiddle to form the trailblazing group The Skillet Lickers. Puckett's lead guitar was important to their sound, as were his bluesy vocals and comic touches.

Puckett remained with the Skillet Lickers until the early 1930s, and then left to perform on radio stations in Georgia, West Virginia, Kentucky and Tennessee. For a time he was a member of the *Boone County Jamboree* on Cincinnati's WLW. And when he died in 1945 he was a member of the Stone Mountain Boys on WACA in Atlanta.

Riley Puckett made two important contributions to early country music. His voice was smooth and beautiful, a controlled balladeer's that was as comfortable with the raucous mountain music that the Skillet Lickers perpetrated as with the uptown, early poptunes he was also fond of playing. In addition, his masterful guitar playing – full of clever and forceful bass runs - influenced many later greats like Charlie Monroe, Lester Flatt and Mac Wiseman. Pappy McMichen once claimed that Columbia Records declined to sign Jimmie Rodgers because they already 'had it all' with Puckett.

Charley Pride.

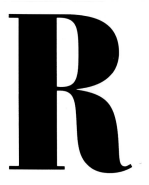

Rambo, Buck and Dottie

The Rambos are among the premier singers and songwriters in country gospel music. Buck was born in Walnut Grove, Kentucky, one of 13 children, and his future wife Dottie was born in nearby Camp Breckinridge. Dottie answered a call to ministry and music at the age of 12 and began touring. It was at one of her engagements that she met Buck, and later, when he was 18 and Dottie 16, they were married.

Eventually Buck learned the guitar and joined his wife's musical ministry. When their daughter Reba was 13 she joined the group and has since gone on to become one of the most prominent singers in the contemporary Christian Music field. The Rambos' lively concerts sometimes resembled revival meetings, and for a time they specialized in all-night gospel sings. They have recorded extensively and appeared on television, particularly on their own programs for the Trinity Broadcasting Network.

Perhaps the most significant contribution of the Rambos has been the songs that Dottie has written; she has penned more than 1500, and Buck and Dottie perform only her music. Among the classics associated with Buck and Dottie Rambo are 'He Looked Beyond My Fault,' 'I've Never Been This Homesick Before,' 'Holy Spirit, Thou Art Welcome,' 'Sheltered in the Arms of God' and 'We Shall Behold Him.'

Raye, Collin

Collin Raye comes by his musical talent naturally; the son of Lois Wray, a performer in Arkansas and Texas who once opened a flatbed-truck show for Elvis, Jerry Lee Lewis, Johnny Cash, and Carl Perkins, he and his brother Scott formed a band that achieved considerable local fame in the Northwest and in Reno while he was still in his teens. The Wray Brothers recorded on the Mercury label.

Born Floyd Wray in DeQueen, Arkansas, and raised in Texarkana, Collin became a single act after working with his brother and got a contract with Epic when he was noticed by producer Jerry Fuller. His debut album, *All I Can Be*, was a success, highlighted by its hit title song, which included harmony by Vince Gill. Collin's vocal style features an impressive span in pitch from a rough lower range to a delicate tenor almost as high as Gill's. Other hits from the album were the moving love songs 'Love, Me,' which was nominated for the Song of the Year Award by the Country Music Association in 1992, and 'In This Life.' *Extremes* was a follow-up CD.

Collin has been lucky – or discriminating – in his choice of sidemen. Working with him on his hit first album were Herb Pederson and Jay Dee Maness of the Desert Rose Band, Fred Tackett of Little Feat, steel player Paul Franklin of Dire Straits, and others of equal distinction.

Reed, Jerry

Jerry Reed Hubbard was born in Atlanta in 1937. He worked briefly in cotton mills, but early on showed his talent for music, playing guitar in schools and in local clubs when he was young; in 1955 he signed with Capitol Records. No hits resulted – neither did they from a later contract with Columbia – but Reed made his mark as a writer. In the 1950s he penned rock hits for Brenda Lee and Gene Vincent, and in the 1960s wrote 'Guitar Man' for Elvis Presley.

He moved to Nashville and became a busy session player and backup musician on tours. Reed's guitar playing is nothing short of phenomenal, with brilliant fingering and a total command of the guitar and its Reed-stretched limits. His proficiency attracted the attention of Chet Atkins, who signed Reed to RCA and activated a massive publicity campaign to promote him.

Among Reed's first albums were *Nashville Underground* with songs like

Above: Jerry Reed.
Right: Collin Raye.

'Tupelo Mississippi Flash' (a humorous sendup of Presley and the world's reaction to him) and 'A Thing Called Love,' a surprisingly (for Reed) subdued and tender love ballad; the *Guitar Country* album, with songs like 'Blue Moon of Kentucky,' 'Sittin' On Top of the World' and 'Are You From Dixie' and the *Cookin'* album, with 'Alabama Jubilee' and Shel Silverstein's 'Semi-Great Predictor.'

These albums established Reed's credentials as a singer, songwriter and instrumentalist. His singles of the early 1970s that established him as a superstar – 'Amos Moses' and 'When You're Hot, You're Hot' – were novelty songs in a comic black dialect that went to the top of country and pop charts. At the same time Reed was a regular featured guest on the popular television program, *The Glen Campbell Goodtime Hour*. In 1974 he co-starred in a movie with Burt Reynolds (and other country singers including Don Williams), *W W and the Dixie Dance Kings*; it began a long association between Reed and Reynolds. They also starred in *Gator*, and the immensely popular *Smokey and the Bandit* movies.

Jerry Reed, who is married to Priscilla Mitchell, country singer and singing partner of Roy Drusky, has continued to record country music in spite of his Hollywood activities. Some are novelty ('Lord Mr Ford'), some are trendy ('East Bound and Down', a truck-driving song) and many are his straight-out, Reed-picking, dazzling pieces of country like 'Sugar Foot Rag.' An infectious, sometimes overwhelming personality pervades his invariably upbeat music.

Reeves, Jim

James Travis Reeves was born in Galloway, Texas, in 1924. He picked up a guitar as a youth and loved the music of Jimmie Rodgers. At the age of nine he performed on a 15-minute radio show in Shreveport. But a close second in his affection was baseball, and Reeves was drafted as a pitcher by the St Louis Cardinals. However a leg injury he suffered in 1947 settled the decision for him: to make music his career.

Jim Reeves in a recording session.

Reeves performed briefly with Moon Mullican in Beaumont, Texas, before cutting some records in 1949 and moving to Louisiana. He obtained a job with radio station KWKH, home of the *Louisiana Hayride*, but as an announcer, not as a singer. When a locally produced record, 'Mexican Joe,' rose to national prominence, however, he was signed as a singer on the prestigious show. This was 1953, and Reeves's success kept building: another local-turned-national hit, 'Bimbo,' a record deal with RCA and, in 1955, regular staff status on the Grand Ole Opry. In 1957 he had a daily television show on ABC.

At this stage Jim Reeves was a hard-core country singer in the honky-tonk tradition. He sang in a strident voice, pushed to its highest register, and he acquired a growing circle of fans. By the early 1960s, however, he better fit the new nickname applied to him, 'Gentleman Jim.' He lowered his voice to its comfortable range, and replaced the sparse honky-tonk backup with lush strings, smooth guitars and a mellow vocal quartet, usually the Jordi-naires. The arrangement was a harbinger of the Nashville Sound, and record sales responded by going through the proverbial roof.

His mellow versions of songs that still contained country lyrics, chord progressions, and thematic preoccupations made the combination right (as opposed to later country-pop efforts where none of the three ingredients were country). Among the classic performances of Jim Reeves are 'Four Walls,' 'Am I Losing You,' 'He'll Have To Go,' 'I Love You Because' and 'Welcome to My World.' In 1962 Reeves conducted a successful world tour, and starred in a movie about South Africa, *Kimberly Jim*.

In 1964, while flying to Nashville in a private plane, Jim Reeves was killed. He has continued as a recording artist, however, as his widow Mary has released unsold cuts and repackaged old songs, often with chart-topping success. Decades later Jim Reeves records were still hitting the charts, and through the miracle of studio electronics, he was even singing duets with Deborah Allen, who was a youngster when Reeves

died, and Patsy Cline ('Have You Ever Been Lonely'), who also died in a plane crash in the 1960s. Their duet release was assembled from the two singers' versions of the same song. There have been more than 30 hits by Jim Reeves since his death, more than he placed during his 'first' career.

Reno, Don

Don Reno, a bluegrass tenor singer and innovative banjo picker, was born in Spartanburg, South Carolina, in 1927. Gaining proficiency on the banjo, he played with the Morris Brothers locally at the age of 12, and the following year joined Arthur 'Guitar Boogie' Smith, where he remained for three years. Just before entering the service in World War II he formed a group called the Carolina Hillbillies with Hank Garland and others.

In 1948 Bill Monroe invited Reno to replace Earl Scruggs in the Bluegrass Boys, a big assignment. But Reno's flashy, energetic banjo style is remarkable by any standards and was equal to the task. He remained with Monroe for a year and a half before forming his own band, the Tennessee Cut-Ups. In 1950 guitarist Red Smiley joined, and the group became one of bluegrass' premier ensembles. Smiley's smooth voice and agile guitar was a perfect counterpart to Reno's high tenor voice and driving banjo.

The Cut-Ups continued as a group, but were periodically interrupted by disbandings, often caused by Red Smiley's poor health. In the mid-1950s Reno had rejoined Smith briefly (during which time they composed 'Feudin' Banjos,' later, as 'Dueling Banjos,' a bluegrass instrumental standard alongside 'Orange Blossom Special'). Smiley died in 1972, and was replaced as harmony lead by Bill Harrell, the mandolinist who joined the band in 1955. Two of Reno's sons have played with the band and a third, Ronnie, has been a member of Merle Haggard's Strangers.

Don Reno's influential banjo stylings were marked by faultless playing and innovations like adapting his three-finger roll to aural steel guitar and electric guitar modes. He frequently adapted standards to bluegrass, and infused jazz elements.

Charlie Rich – a soulful pianist.

Rich, Charlie

Born in Colt, Arkansas, in 1932, Charlie Rich took to the piano early, and his taste in music was jazz of the Stan Kenton variety. He played tenor sax in a high school band, and took one year's worth of music courses in college before he served in the Army. During the Korean War he was stationed in Enid, Oklahoma, where he joined the base jazz combo, The Velvetones; he married the group's vocalist, Margaret Ann. After the war Charlie took up farming but Margaret Ann urged him to pursue music.

He played in local Memphis clubs and at one, the Sharecropper, he was heard by Bill Justis, A&R man at Sun Records. This was in the mid-1950s, when Sun was the center of the rockabilly and rock 'n' roll universe. Rich was hired to back other singers like Johnny Cash and Roy Orbison, but concerning his own solo career he was reportedly advised to 'learn to play as badly as Jerry Lee Lewis.'

By 1960 he did have two moderate hits to his name, 'Lonely Weekends' and 'Breakup.' For the next five years Charlie played on various labels with little success until he scored with 'Mohair Sam' on Smash/Mercury, and then came another dry spell. Margaret Ann encouraged him as his wife and songwriting partner during a spell of playing small clubs.

Then in 1968 Billy Sherrill of Epic Records decided to do something with Rich's enormous talent; one of Charlie's problems may have been the difficulty in categorizing his work – jazz, blues, country – and rather than compromise any segment, Sherrill merely arranged and promoted it better. Success no longer seemed elusive. In 1970 he had a hit on Margaret's composition 'Life's Little Ups and Downs,' simply one of the finest country songs ever written, a ballad about a worker failing to

Charlie Rich – The Silver Fox.

get a raise, the disappointment his wife might feel and the fact the she wouldn't mind because she loved him so much. The song is emblematic of the audacity of country music in addressing real-life concerns as no other music does.

In 1972 Charlie recorded two Kenny O'Dell songs that propelled him to superstardom: 'I Take It On Home' (an anthem of fidelity that is musically the stronger of the two), and 'Behind Closed Doors.' Confirming the 20-year overnight-success story of Charlie Rich was the massive follow-up hit 'The Most Beautiful Girl,' co-written by Sherrill. Charlie was named Top Male Vocalist by the Academy of Country Music in 1973 and Entertainer of the Year by the Country Music Association in 1974.

Charlie Rich continued to record country songs, but progressively veered more toward pop, reflecting, perhaps, his Las Vegas image when superstar time arrived. He recorded an acclaimed gospel album, *Silver Linings*, and has seen all his old record companies re-release every possible cut he made in a studio.

Charlie's voice is a hoarse baritone that inevitably stretches into higher registers. It can growl and croon when needed, but his real appeal is on the keyboard. Charlie Rich is the most soulful pianist in country music, something akin to Ray Charles. His blues and jazz touches only enrich his country repertoire, underpinning the emotion and sentiment in the country lyrics. His 'countrypolitan' shift is seen as less opportunistic – in country fans' eyes – than that of Dolly Parton or Crystal Gayle or Kenny Rogers, because his jazz and pop credentials were authentic from the start, just like his country identity. Like so many other stars of country music, Charlie bridged the gap between various styles, and was and still is able to please all audiences.

The Silver Fox really marginalized himself as far as country music is concerned when he went so heavily into the pop scene, especially with glitzy Vegas lounge shows. The loss of major label affiliation and media exposure preceded the wave of new stars with New Country and New Traditionalist sounds and he removed himself. Country was just part of Charlie Rich's portfolio – but an irreducible element. There was a reminder of this fact – and a happy musical gift to his loyal fans – with 1992's small-label CD *Pictures and Paintings*, featuring jazz, pop, blues, and country, with Charlie and his piano backed by a small combo. It is well that he continued to be himself, in his final years of performing. Charlie Rich died suddenly on July 25, 1995, at the age of 63.

Riders in the Sky

Riders in the Sky is a comedy ensemble that performs Western music; or perhaps they are a classic cowboy-harmony trio that injects comedy into their act. The three members are Doug Green, Fred LaBour and Woody Paul, who described themselves thusly and respectively: Ranger Doug, The Idol of American Youth; Too Slim; and Woody Paul, which is evidently not a stage name. Doug plays rhythm guitar, writes some of the group's songs, and yodels. He is the front man for the group, but he is also Douglas B Green, one of the most respected of country music historians, with more than 500 articles and reviews and several books to his credit; he directed the Oral History Project of the Country Music Foundation. Too Slim is the lead singer and plays upright bass, and Woody Paul sings harmony and plays banjo and fiddle.

For all their self-effacing humor, Riders in the Sky perform creditable Western music in the Sons of the Pioneers tradition and blends affection and satire. In the 1990s the group has hosted television series on TNN.

Ritter, Tex

Although he entered the Western music field with more sophisticated credentials than most singers, Tex Ritter probably captured the spirit of real cowboy songs better than most. He was born Maurice Woodward Ritter in Panola County, Texas, in 1905. Raised on a ranch, he enrolled as a law major at the University of Texas where he associated with J Frank Dobie, the Western folklorist, and John Lomax, collector and archivist of cowboy songs. Ritter developed a unique lecture-and-song presentation, 'The Texas Cowboy and His Songs,' with which he toured the nation.

After taking his presentation to Chicago, he tarried to further his law studies at Northwestern, and went

to New York in 1930, determined to carve out a career in music. He secured a role in the Broadway play *Green Grow the Lilacs*, singing cowboy ballads and understudying Franchot Tone; Rodgers and Hammerstein later based the classical musical *Oklahoma!* on the production. The play was one manifestation of New York's faddish fascination with things Western, and Ritter was able to capitalize on the trend. He appeared on WOR radio's *Lone Star Rangers*, and hosted *Tex Ritter's Camp Fire* and the *WHN Barn Dance*.

In 1933 Ritter cut his first records, and three years later appeared in his first film, *Song of the Gringo*; by the 1950s he had been featured in more than 80 movies and TV shows. Set-

Tex Ritter (at the mike).

tling in California, Ritter co-hosted the *Town Hall Party* radio dance with Johnny Bond, and added tours and concerts to his recording and film work. Among his many hit records through the years were: 'Somehow,' 'There's a New Moon Over My Shoulder,' 'Jealous Heart,' 'Have I Told You Lately That I Love You,' 'The Wayward Wind,' 'Rye Whiskey,' 'Boll Weevil' and 'Deck of Cards.' Perhaps his two biggest singles were 1952's 'Do Not Forsake Me Oh My Darling,' from the film *High Noon* and 1961's 'I Dreamed of a Hillbilly Heaven.'

In his later years Tex Ritter was a resident of Nashville and became a traveling ambassador of country music. He was elected to the Country Music Hall of Fame in 1964, and joined the Grand Ole Opry in 1965.

Tex Ritter died on January 2, 1974 at a Nashville jail where he was arranging bail for a band member. It was a passing that was somehow closer to dying with one's boots on than most of his fellow cowboy performers could claim. Ritter's music was like that too; his voice was not the smooth crooner of Autry, Rogers, the Sons and other singing cowboys. He was gravelly, lower-register, and seemingly unpolished in matters of timing and phrasing – no doubt closer to how cowboys actually sang, when they did. Likewise his material probably reflected the real feelings of working cowboys (which were not always love songs under a prop moon) – death, dust, despair, boredom, bitter humor and cynicism. In these ways Tex Ritter was probably the most representative singer of the authentic American cowboy song.

Robbins, Marty

Marty Robbins was born in Glendale, Arizona, in 1925, of mixed Italian and Indian descent. His father taught him the harmonica, and his grandfather – who had been a traveling medicine man – taught him cowboy songs. Marty was also inspired by Gene Autry's singing-cowboy movies.

When he grew up, Marty sang in Phoenix clubs and hosted a local radio show, *Western Caravan*. Little Jimmy Dickens, passing through on a tour, heard Robbins sing and

Marty Robbins.

recommended him to Nashville. Robbins signed with Columbia Records in the early 1950s, and joined the Grand Ole Opry in 1953. His hit records started in country ('I'll Go On Alone') and detoured to teenage music ('A White Sport Coat and a Pink Carnation'); he then moved to his beloved sphere of cowboy songs ('El Paso,' 'Big Iron' and 'Devil Woman'); ballads ('Ribbon of Darkness') and heart songs ('My Woman, My Woman, My Wife'): Marty also proved adept at blues ('Don't Worry 'Bout Me)', a song that pioneered the raspy electric-guitar sound that was to be a hallmark of hard rock) and rockabilly ('That's All

Right'). His other styles included pop, folk, Mexican, gospel and even Hawaiian, and other hits included 'Singing the Blues,' 'El Paso City,' 'Among My Souvenirs,' and 'Some Memories Just Won't Die.' Between the late 1950s and early 1980s there was hardly a year that Robbins did not have a top ten song.

Such activity was reflective of Robbins' personality. He possessed a great sense of humor and would engage in badinage with other musicians, offstage folk and audience members during a performance. He would abandon his guitar to play the piano and then leap up to sing cowboy songs with his little Mexican-style guitar and a Sons of the Pioneers-type harmony group. A tradition when he played the Opry was to have him close the show; Robbins would invariably sing, play and talk far beyond closing time to the evident consternation of MCs.

Robbins' personal life was just as colorful. He was an avid race-car enthusiast, and achieved top NASCAR ratings. He drove his car 'Devil Woman' in many major events and endured several harrowing accidents. He also endured several major heart attacks before succumbing to a massive seizure in December of 1982, just two months after being inducted into the Country Music Hall of Fame. Robbins had appeared widely on television, and had roles in 10 movies as well. His talented son Ronny continues the Robbins name and legacy – one of varied styles, magnetic presence and a devotion to country music and its fans.

Roberts, Kenny

A singer with two nicknames, 'America's King of the Yodelers' and 'The Jumping Cowboy,' Kenny Roberts was born in Lenoir City, Tennessee, in 1927. He was raised on a farm in Massachusetts, and mastered a harmonica at 11. Kenny was performing at age 13, and two years later was part of the Red River Rangers on radio in Greenfield, Massachusetts.

In 1943 he became a member of the Down Homers group on radio in Keene, New Hampshire and in 1946 recorded his first solo record, 'Out Where the West Winds Blow.' After that he was a staffer on the WOWO *Hoosier Hop Barn Dance* in Fort Wayne, Indiana, and appeared on network television. In 1948 Kenny joined the famous *Midwestern Hayride* radio show in Cincinnati, where he recorded his biggest-selling singles, including 'Chime Bells,' 'She Taught Me How To Yodel' and 'I Never See Maggie Alone.'

Later Kenny appeared on Arthur Godfrey TV programs, the Grand Ole Opry, and was connected at various times with *Jamboree USA* on Wheeling, West Virginia's WWVA.

Kenny Roberts actually would jump up and down on stage in his

cowboy costume while yodeling, but his real act was his voice – which was as acrobatic as his routine. Perhaps only Elton Britt was his equal in vocal pyrotechnics of flashy yodels, rapid yodels and long sustained falsetto notes.

Robison, Carson J

Surely one of the most durable of country music's stars, Carson J Robison managed a remarkable career that began with his being the first country singer to perform on a radio station, and ended with recording a rockabilly song in the 1950s. Born in Chetopa, Kansas, in 1890, Robison

Robbins played country, Mexican and Hawaiian music.

was the son of a country fiddler, and he grew up singing and playing old-time music. He made his landmark performance on new-fangled radio in 1921 on Kansas City's WDAF.

In New York City in 1924 he was also a pioneer in country records. Victor first used his talents as a whistler, but his greatest contribution, and success, came in countless pairings over four years with Vernon Dalhart. One reason the duets are countless is because the singers would record the same song many times for rival companies, and use stage names with creative frequency.

Robison then toured the East and Midwest on the vaudeville circuit – he played a fine country guitar and sang in a clear, professional voice – and in 1932 formed a group, The Buckaroos, and then the Carson Robison Trio. In the 1940s and 1950s he settled in Pleasant Valley, New York, where he formed his Pleasant Valley Boys. Besides his pseudonyms (he also wrote as Maggie Andrews and Carlos B McAfee, one of Dalhart's singing names), he also took the nicknames of The Kansas Jayhawk and The King of the Hillbillies. During his career he had also paired with Frank Luther and Buell Kazee.

For all his performing, Robison left his biggest mark as a songwriter in various modes. He favored saga songs in the old British tradition of chronicling disasters and important events (such as 'The John T Scopes Trial'), and had a penchant for comic songs ('Barnacle Bill the Sailor,' which Bix Beiderbecke made into a hit). He even wrote a Western standard, 'Carry Me Back to the Lone Prairie.' Other popular Robison songs included 'My Blue Ridge Mountain Home,' 'Left My Gal in the Mountains,' 'Open Up Them Pearly Gates' and 'I'm Goin' Back to Whur I Come From.' In 1948 he recorded his biggest hit, 'Life Gets Tee-Jus, Don't It?' and in 1956, a year before his death, Carson J Robison recorded a cult favorite, 'Rockin' and Rollin' with Granmaw.'

Rodgers, Jimmie

'America's Blue Yodeler'; 'The Singing Brakeman'; 'The Father of Country Music.' These titles and other honors were bestowed upon James Charles Rodgers, a truly pivotal figure in American music. He was not the first country music star – not by any means the first to record – and had a recording career of a scant six years. But his impact was genuinely revolutionary. His body of work simultaneously fused an amazing disparity of American musical genres, spoke to the very souls of millions of listeners and initiated a form of music that has a vital life of its own two generations later.

Jimmie was born in Meridian, Mississippi, in 1897, the son of a railroad section foreman. Although he briefly pursued other activities, the rails were always close to Jimmie's livelihood and consciousness. But so was music; he had picked up influences from the different parts of the South where the rails would take him, and while he worked himself as a railroader in the mid-1920s, he made several attempts at performing.

A tubercular condition (his mother had died of the ailment when he was four) finally forced him to retire from railroading, which had exposed Jimmie to the elements and physical exertion. The brakeman followed his less strenuous star and took his banjo and guitar to the performing stage, around 1925, as a blackface comedian in a minstrel show. He then became a whiteface entertainer with, and part owner of, a tent show that was tragically destroyed by a tornado. For a short time thereafter, in financial desperation and against doctors' instructions, he went back to railroading.

The Skyland area around Asheville, North Carolina, was famed as a salubrious climate, and Jimmie moved there in 1927. He pursued two activities: city detective (a job arranged by a friend as virtual charity) and singer; he organized a stringband ensemble called the Jimmie Rodgers Entertainers. His 'hillbilly ork' as he called them, secured a brief engagement on local radio, and they became local favorites in spite of bare subsistence remuneration for their playing at dances and fairs.

In August of 1927, Ralph Peer conducted his now-legendary scouting-and-recording session in Bristol, Tennessee, on the Virginia border; Jimmie Rodgers caught wind of the date and made the trip with his band to the makeshift recording studio over a store. At the last moment his three-piece band deserted him and auditioned on their own as the Tenneva Ramblers (named for the two contiguous states). Peer had reportedly met Rodgers once before, through Clayton McMichen in Georgia, and declined to record him because he had another white Southern guitar-playing singer in Riley Puckett. In any event Rodgers persuaded Peer to audition him as a solo on August 4.

The two songs were 'Sleep, Baby, Sleep' backed by 'The Soldier's Sweetheart,' and were moderate sellers. In November Rodgers eked his way north to the Victor Studios in Camden, New Jersey, where he recorded 'Away Out on the Mountain' and 'T For Texas (Blue Yodel Number 1')' – and by 1928 Jimmie was a star of major proportions.

As the South and Southwest discovered the hillbilly music of Jimmie Rodgers (for all his success he was to be a regional artist during his lifetime) he was catapulted to dizzying realms of fame and income. He remained somewhat placid through it all, spending money freely and supporting friends and acquaintances. He may have been fatalistic about the death he knew was near, but he also was simply a plain, honest, regular fellow whose sincerity was a standout part of his performances. That sincerity was clothed in a sharp tenor voice that was adaptable, as rough as some of his roustabout lyrics, and as crooning as other pop-flavored ones. A sloppy sense of timing only added to Jimmie's appeal, as it made him seem closer to home-folk than a slick showbiz entertainer would have been.

The hallmark of Jimmie the Kid's many vocal stylings, of course, was his Blue Yodel, a heart-rending lament that either punctuated lines or served as a coda. It was not the vocal pyrotechnics of a Swiss yodel, but an almost primeval moan – an aural affinity with hard-time rural listeners, especially after the Depression's onslaught.

In rapid succession his hits came, supported by – and in turn nurturing – the rural South's acquisition of record-players. Many songs Jimmie wrote, or adapted, himself, and many he took from other sources; his wife's sister provided many standards. Included among his classic performances are 'My Little Old Home Down in New Orleans,' 'Ben Dewberry's Final Run,' 'Treasures Untold,' 'Lullaby Yodel,' 'Hobo Bill's Last Ride,' 'Mississippi Delta Blues,' 'Any Old Time,' 'Gamblin' Polka-Dot Blues,' 'TB Blues,' 'The Wonderful City,' 'Roll Along Kentucky Moon,' 'No Hard Times,' 'Down the Old Road to Home,' 'Frankie and Johnny,' 'Mule Skinner Blues,' 'Travelin' Blues,' 'My Time Ain't Long,' 'Woman Make a Fool Out of Me,' 'My Rough and Rowdy Ways,'

Jimmie Rodgers – The Father of
Country Music.

Rodgers, The Singing Brakeman.

'California Blues,' 'Everybody Does It in Hawaii,' 'She Was Happy Till She Met You,' 'The Hobo's Meditation,' 'Home Call,' 'Mother, the Queen of My Heart,' 'Waiting for a Train,' 'Why Did You Give Me Your Love,' 'My Carolina Sunshine Girl,' 'In the Jailhouse Now,' 'Nobody Knows But Me,' 'Why Should I Be Lonely?' 'Miss the Mississippi and You' and 'I'm Sorry We Met.' Most of his records were million sellers, and his backup represented an incredible array of musical styles – his own guitar, country musicians picked up while recording on the road, the Carter Family in duets and even Earl Hines and Louis Armstrong.

In all, Jimmie Rodgers recorded 111 songs, 13 of them numbered in the 'Blue Yodel' series, although he yodeled on many more songs. He toured with the great humorist Will Rogers, made a movie short for Columbia (1929's *The Singing Brakeman*), and made numerous radio appearances, including regular spots in Texas, where he moved for his health.

In 1933 Jimmie traveled to New York to record a series of 24 records; it was time for a new catalog, and he needed to replenish the income that was coming and going so fast. But he also sensed it would be his last recording session, and he wanted to cut as many records as he could to provide security for his wife and daughter. Tuberculosis had taken its toll, and a special cot was provided in the Victor Recording Studio so Jimmie could rest between takes. Only 12 songs were recorded before Jimmie's lungs hemorrhaged; he died in the Taft Hotel on May 26, 1933. A special funeral train returned Jimmie Rodgers' body to Meridian, its whistle at a sad, low moan. All along the route crowds large and small gathered along the track to pay respects.

Today the Rodgers Gravesite and Park is a virtual shrine of country music. However, his records – which continue to sell all over the world – and his legacy are the real, living memorials. Also, through the years many artists have preserved the Jimmie Rodgers sound. Among these are Ernest Tubb, Hank Snow, Elton Britt, Jimmie Davis, Gene Autry, Cliff Carlisle, Eddie Noack and Merle Haggard. Jimmie was the first artist elected to the Country Music Hall of Fame, in 1961.

Much has been made of the influence of rural black music on Jimmie; his primary exposure was from black rail workers. Indeed the emphasis on blues, the lyrical structures and especially the allusions in many songs illustrate a strong influence; but it was part of a larger fusion that Jimmie effected. He dwelt as much on the sentimental songs of the rural white South, on the 'hillbilly' traditions whose label he adopted, and even on pop songs of the time. There were Dixieland influences, and mountain music strains as well; he used the bottleneck guitars of black bluesman, but also borrowed them from the Hawaiian musicians touring the South (his own ill-fated tent show had been a Hawaiian novelty). Likewise, Jimmie's Blue Yodel reflected both the Bavarian yodel that was a brief fad in the Deep South and Texas, and the blues-drenched field shouts of blacks. He borrowed AABC lyric patterns from rural blues, a device that has curiously been unused by his successors.

Jimmy Rodgers is the Father of Country Music because he combined disparate modes that were not otherwise fated to be used; in his records can be heard mountain music, cowboy ballads, jazz and blues. In his sentimental preoccupation there was a real melding of Tin Pan Alley and Tin Pan Valley; in his rough and rowdy songs was a whole thematic school that had been seldom tapped by white rural singers. His residence in Texas and occasional Western dress seems to be responsible for many country stars' styles; Bill Monroe, for instance, who is hardly a cowboy, has for years sported a cowboy hat.

Indeed it was the thematic preoccupations of Jimmie Rodgers, more than his music – pervasive as its influence was – that made him the Father of Country Music. As the Carter Family – who also recorded during that fateful August week in Bristol – spawned the schools of old-time, religious, bluegrass, sentimental and harmony music within country, Jimmie Rodgers is the musical godfather to blues, jazz and pop influences, honky-tonk, Western Swing and solo singers. Many copied his stylings but no enduring Jimmie Rodgers School remained. Rather his bequest is virtually all of what is known today as country music.

Rodriguez, Johnny

Juan Raul Davis Rodriguez was born in Sabinal, Texas, in 1952. At the age of 17, Johnny was arrested for rustling and barbecuing a goat. With little else to do in jail but sing, Johnny was heard by a Texas Ranger, who recommended him to a local music promoter. Happy Shahan. Soon Johnny was performing at the local Alamo Village, where he was eventually introduced to Tom T Hall. Hall helped arrange a Mercury Records contract for Rodriguez, and invited him to front Hall's band, The Storytellers. In early 1973, when Johnny's first record, 'Pass Me By,' debuted, he and Hall played Carnegie Hall in New York City.

It was a good omen: Rodriguez was immediately accepted, and he followed with a consistent string of hits. His voice is squarely in the Lefty Frizzell mold, and he has shown himself very capable of handling somber ballads and shuffle-beat honky-tonk songs. Johnny's backup has always been economical and mainstream country; he's at his best when counterpointed by a fiddle or twin Texas fiddles.

His other hits have included 'Jealous Heart,' 'Easy Come, Easy Go,' 'I Wonder If I Ever Said Goodbye' and 'Down on the Rio Grande.' His English is without a perceptible Spanish accent, but he frequently interposes Spanish verses in songs.

Rogers, Kenny

Born in Houston in 1937, Kenny Rogers played guitar as a youngster,

Johnny Rodriguez.

and would sometimes get together with the young Mickey Gilley. In high school he formed a rockabilly band, The Scholars, and cut an album for the local Carlton record label.

After high school, Rogers joined a jazz ensemble, the Bobby Doyle Trio, where he sang and played bass; another album, for Columbia, followed. Rogers then landed a spot with the jazzy-pop group, The Kirby Stone Four. In 1966 he graduated to the popular folk-singing New Christy Minstrels, moving to Los Angeles; the next year he broke away with another Minstrel and two other singers to form The First Edition (later, as Rogers assumed more of a lead role, Kenny Rogers and the First Edition) to explore the avenues of soft rock.

With the First Edition, Rogers had impressive chart success with songs like 'Ruby, Don't Take Your Love to Town' (written by Mel Tillis) and 'Reuben James.' Their popularity was such that in 1971 they hosted a syndicated television series, *Rollin' on the River*. But by 1975 the group's success had waned, and it dissolved.

Thereafter Kenny Rogers bounced back with a vengeance. He met and married Marianne Gordon (a *Hee Haw* girl) who helped him cope with the hard times. In 1977 he recorded a song, 'Lucille,' that went to the top of all music charts and has since sold over four million copies. He followed it up with a country duet with Dottie West, veteran of the genre (she had recorded with Jim Reeves and Don Gibson); 'Every Time Two Fools Collide' was a major hit. Their other duets included 'Anyone Who Isn't Me Tonight' and 'Till I Can Make It On My Own.' Before he switched to a virtually exclusive pop format, Rogers recorded two classic 'story songs' in the time-honored country tradition: 'The Gambler' and 'Coward of the County.'

Acting has for all intents and purposes replaced singing as Rogers's primary career. On the strength of his success with *The Gambler* TV movies (currently four sequels to the original), he has appeared in and/or produced several western-themed shows. In addition, his hobby of photography has expanded to include two published works: *Kenny Rogers' America* and *Your Friends and Mine*, a volume of celebrity portraits.

Image problems surfaced for Rogers in 1992, when a scandal involving his romantic life brought down his marriage. His business interests include a chain of fast-food restaurants, Kenny Rogers' Roasters, a line of western clothing and performances in Branson, Missouri.

Rogers, Roy

Born Leonard Slye in Cincinnati in 1911, Roy Rogers grew up on the farm the family bought in Duck Run, near Portsmouth in southern Ohio. His favorite pastimes included riding horses, playing guitar like his father and watching Tom Mix films and other cowboy movies. In the late 1920s he learned cowboy music and became a caller at local square dances.

In 1930 Slye hitch-hiked to California and became a peach picker in Tulare. But music called and he joined a quintet of cowboy musicians, the Rocky Mountaineers. He also played with other ensembles, including Uncle Tom Murray's Hollywood Hillbillies, the O-Bar-O Cowboys, and the Texas Outlaws; and he formed a short-lived group called the International Cowboys. In 1934 he established the singing group the Pioneer Trio with Bob Nolan and Tim Spencer, later calling it the Sons of the Pioneers when the Farr Brothers, Hugh and Carl, joined.

The Sons of the Pioneers fused a variety of influences into what we know today as cowboy music – as old as traditional trail songs, and as new as the on-demand Hollywood movie melody. In fact the Sons of the Pioneers occasionally played in some of those movies, including those of Gene Autry. They were performing regularly on a Los Angeles morning radio program when the word came that Gene Autry had left Republic Pictures, leaving a vacancy in lead-cowboy roles there. Slye auditioned, had his name changed (first to Dick Weston) and, as Roy Rogers, a new career awaited. He debuted in *Under Western Skies* in 1938, for Republic.

Between then and 1955, Rogers, as 'The King of the Cowboys,' starred in 88 films, and the Sons were often there to co-star and sing with him. In 35 of the movies his leading lady was Dale Evans, who married Rogers in 1947 after his first wife died. The couple achieved their greatest fame

as stars of their own television show, 101 episodes of which were filmed between 1951 and 1954. Roy and Dale made many records and personal appearances; their biggest record was their theme song 'Happy Trails to You.'

Rogers suffered a heart attack in 1958, which curtailed his activities. However he founded a museum of his memorabilia in the Mojave Desert town of Apple Valley; founded a chain of fast-food restaurants bearing his name and hosted a syndicated television series called *Roy Rogers Presents the Great Movie Cowboys*. While his recording output has been limited in recent years, Roy released several singles and the album *Hoppy, Gene, and Me* in the 1970s. In 1991 he recorded *Tribute* on RCA. The album paired the cowboy hero with some of the biggest names in the country today, including Clint Black, Willie Nelson, Kathy Mattea and The Kentucky Headhunters. A committed Christian, Roy Rogers has also recorded some gospel albums alone and with Dale Evans, and appeared on the Christian Broadcasting Network.

Although his primary duty in his original groups, including the Sons of the Pioneers, was comic relief, Roy Rogers had a fine singing voice and an outstanding yodel. He and Bob Nolan established the stereotypical sound of cowboy harmony vocalists – tenor (in Roy's case) or baritone, gentle tone, unadorned style and an evident sincerity. By singing and beating bad guys in movies and TV, Roy Rogers became a virtual icon to a generation of American youth.

Ronstadt, Linda

Occasionally visitors to country music can perform some classic interpretations and reveal a genuine affinity for country idioms; Linda Ronstadt is in the forefront of that group. Born in Tucson, Arizona, in 1946, she grew up loving the music of Hank Williams before discovering Elvis Presley. She spent one year at the University of Arizona before moving to California at age 18.

She formed a group called the Stone Poneys that had a major hit with 'Different Drum.' After the group dissolved in 1968, Linda went

Legendary cowboy singer Roy Rogers.

Left: Dolly Parton, Linda Ronstadt and Emmylou Harris collaborated on *Trio*. *Above:* Linda wins a Grammy.

played with her formed the Eagles; she switched labels, and took on Peter Asher as producer. She also included more rock and pop in her repertoire, and in those markets her records sold in massive quantities. She holds a record as the biggest-selling female vocalist in the history of music.

In the public eye she was a popular recording artist and romantically linked with presidential hopeful Governor Jerry Brown of California. But her musical creativity led her in 1980 to play Mabel in a New York production of *The Pirates of Penzance*; she then recorded a couple of albums of lush pop standards arranged by Nelson Riddle; and in 1985 she played Mimi in the New York Shakespeare Festival's production of *La Boheme*.

In 1987 Linda finally participated in a project long discussed with Emmylou Harris: a collaboration – with Dolly Parton in this case – wherein traditional songs and basic harmonies could be explored. The result was *Trio*, one of the most impressive creative projects of the decade; the traditional-sounding collection featured classics of gospel music as well as Jimmie Rodgers and Johnny Russell songs. It won major awards in the industry, sold a million copies, and produced four hit singles, three of which went to number one.

Linda's exceptionally eclectic range of interest and talent have continued to expand, though her latest efforts see very little airplay. Foregoing more commercial avenues in favor of projects that suit her artistic interests, she has released and toured in support of two critically-acclaimed Spanish-language albums that allow her to explore her Mexican-American heritage.

Linda Ronstadt possesses a voice that may be alternately brassy and sensitive, the mistress of – among many other forms – a rockabilly drive or a tender country ballad. Through the years Linda has also utilized some of the best country musicians in concert and on record, including Randy Scruggs, Mike Auldridge, Byron Berline, J D Souther, Weldon Myrick, Buddy Emmons, Jimmie Fadden, Herb Pederson and Emmylou Harris. She has also sung harmony on bluegrass records of The Seldom Scene.

solo and signed a recording contract with Capitol. Here she asserted her early country predilection, and recorded two outstanding country-oriented albums, *Hand Sown/Home Grown* covered a wide range of country and rockabilly, with country backup. Such numbers included 'We Need a Whole Lot More of Jesus and a Lot Less Rock 'n' Roll' by Wayne Raney (who had been a sideman with the Delmore Brothers); 'Silver Threads and Golden Needles' and 'Break My Mind.'

Her followup album, *Silk Purse*, contained Ronstadt versions of songs popularized by Hank Williams, Mel Tillis, and Mickey Newberry, as well as the gospel 'Life Is Like a Mountain Railway' and her debut of Gary White's 'Long, Long Time.' And her next albums, even as she was shifting more towards rock, contained songs by Johnny Cash and Hank Williams, and the country standards, 'Crazy Arms' and 'I Fall to Pieces.' In the late 1960s Linda had been a cult favorite, filling places like the Cellar Door in Washington, but hardly more than that. But the cross-pollination – and her own talent – changed things; sidemen who

Scruggs, Earl

Born in Shelby, North Carolina, in 1924, Earl Eugene Scruggs grew up in the Flint Hill area where the three finger banjo technique was played in country music. It was a radical departure from the banjo's traditional role as a strummed or rhythm instrument. Charlie Poole had dabbled in the technique and localite Snuffy Jenkins had pioneered it, as had Rex Brooks and Smith Hammett, a relative of Earl Scruggs. But it is Scruggs who practically owns the instrument because of his stylistic innovations – the dazzling fingerwork, lightning speed, and musically sophisticated syncopation.

Scruggs could play the five-string banjo at five, and he was performing publicly with his brothers two years later. By 15 he was on radio in North Carolina, playing with the Carolina Wildcats, and later in South Carolina with the Morris Brothers. Scruggs was a textile worker during World War II, after which he joined Lost John Miller on Knoxville radio and on Nashville's WSM. When Miller retired from touring, Scruggs was in need of work and was hired by Bill Monroe to succeed Dave 'Stringbean' Akeman – a flailing-style banjo player of the old Uncle David Macon school – in the Bluegrass Boys.

The addition of Earl Scruggs was the last essential element that Bill Monroe needed in his bluegrass equation; he had been evolving mountain music since his days with brother Charlie Monroe to a more driven, high-harmony, technically proficient instrumental sound. The Bluegrass Boys who greeted the young Scruggs included Monroe with his virtuoso mandolin and high-tenor voice; Lester Flatt, songwriter and guitar-picker and Chubby Wise, jazz-tinged fiddler.

Until 1948 the Bluegrass Boys recorded some of the finest music in the American folk field; they performed on radio and toured widely. But it was Monroe's incessant road schedule that led Scruggs to quit the group in 1948. He was followed later by Lester Flatt, and when they were playing together on Mac Wiseman's *Farm and Fun Time* radio show in Bristol, Virginia, they decided to form their own bluegrass ensemble. With Wiseman, Bluegrass Boy alumnus Howard Watts (stage name: Cedric Rainwater, later a bass player with Hank Williams) and Jim Shumate on fiddle, the Foggy Mountain Boys were formed, named for the Carter Family song, 'Foggy Mountain Top.'

If anything, Flatt and Scruggs surpassed Bill Monroe, at least in public fame. This was due in part to their eventual bookings on college campuses and the folk-festival circuit, but in 1951 they toured with Ernest Tubb and Lefty Frizzell. Two years later they picked up Martha White sponsorship on radio and tours, and in 1955 hosted a television program and joined the *Grand Ole Opry*. In addition, Flatt and Scruggs gained exposure by releasing the 'Ballad of Jed Clampett' from TV's *Beverly Hillbillies* (they also played themselves on the popular show), and performing the theme music from the movie *Bonnie and Clyde*. Flatt and Scruggs survived the temporary decline of bluegrass during the rock 'n' roll onslaught better than any other bluegrass group.

Their major hits include 'Foggy Mountain Breakdown,' 'Salty Dog Blues,' 'Roll in My Sweet Baby's Arms,' 'Earl's Breakdown,' 'Flint Hill Special' and 'I'm Working on a Road.' Alumni of the Foggy Mountain Boys include Josh Graves, who left the Bluegrass Boys to make the dobro an integral sound of the music with Flatt and Scruggs, and Benny Martin, fiddler.

Through the 1960s, the Foggy Mountain Boy's sound became a bit sluggish perhaps due to a musical contempt bred by familiarity. Certainly the tastes of Flatt and Scruggs were diverging; Flatt preferred traditional tunes and themes while Scruggs, enjoying the urban folk festivals and bringing his rock-musician sons into the ensemble, was experimenting with other modes. The pair

split in 1969 and Flatt indeed explored more basic, traditional forms while Scruggs followed his sons' tastes.

The Earl Scruggs Revue was formed, with sons Randy on guitar, Gary on bass and rhythm and Steve on keyboards. Their father continued to play his patented three-fingered riffs over a hybrid of bluegrass and rock music. That technique, now virtually universal among banjo players, uses the thumb and the next two fingers in a constant picking of strings wherein the melody is surrounded by a virtual torrent of counterpoint and syncopation. Scruggs developed the Scruggs Tuner Peg that stretches notes and changes pitch on specialty numbers; he has also written a book on the banjo and supervised the design of instruments. In 1971 Scruggs performed on banjo and guitar on the landmark album set, *Will the Circle Be Unbroken*.

Ultimately Earl Scruggs's contributions are supremely important to the sound of bluegrass music. Before his masterful technique was introduced, the banjo had devolved into a comedian's instrument, practically a novelty relic like the autoharp, honored in the breach and virtually relegated to geographical pockets of the US.

Some critics have compared the 'glory days' of Bill Monroe's band and those of Flatt and Scruggs and judged the Foggy Mountain Boys to display more intensity. This is debatable, for no one has played with more intensity, nor driven his band musically harder, than Bill Monroe. The real difference in the two superb ensembles is that Monroe was always more functional; he placed more emphasis on lyrics, on songs. Monroe's players would take solo licks, and improvisation was valued, but Flatt and Scruggs played more ensemble instrumentals. There seemed to be more music for music's sake – and, after all, Earl Scruggs ranks as one of the purest musical talents in all of country music history – so perhaps it was inevitable that Flatt and Scruggs broke up. Flatt was the traditional mountain man, and Scruggs is the ultimate musician, always experimenting and ever taking delight in playing the five-string.

The Earl Scruggs sound – his dis-

New Country's Ricky Van Shelton.

Ricky Van Shelton

A rural background in a town called Grit, Virginia, would seem ideal for a country musician, but Ricky Van Shelton developed a taste for The Beatles and The Rolling Stones while working as a pipe fitter. Only when his brother talked Ricky into driving him and his friends to a Blugrass concert one night did the country bug bite him. He's been driving the same classic Ford Fairlane 289 and following the New Country road ever since.

The road took him and his wife Bettye to Nashville, where he worked days at whatever jobs he could find and looked for the chance to perform in local clubs. In time a demo tape found the right ear: someone at CBS Records heard it and offered him a contract. His warm baritone, rugged good looks, and classic country sound made him a natural. His first album, *Wild Eyed Dream*, shot up to the million-sale mark, establishing it as platinum, and the ones that followed – *Loving Proof, RVS III, Backroads*, the gospel album *Don't Overlook Salvation*, and the anthology *Greatest Hits Plus* – did the same. His singles were no less successful. Among the cuts to make number one on the country charts were 'Don't We All Have the Right,' with words and music by Roger Miller, 'I'll Leave This World Lovin' You,' with words and music by Wayne Kemp, and 'I Meant Every Word He Said.' Ricky has also been successful with such videos as the one he did with Dolly Parton of their duet 'Rockin' Year.'

ciplined variations, joyful riffs, and familiar codas – will remain forever as an integral part of country music.

His success in clubs and record stores has been reflected at the award ceremonies. The Academy of Country Music named him Top New Male Vocalist in 1987, and the next year the Country Music Association gave him its Horizon Award, Music City News named him Star of Tomorrow, and the Nashville Network voted him Favorite Newcomer. In 1989 he was selected Best Male Vocalist by the CMA. In 1990 and 1991, fans chose him for the Nashville Network-Music City News Entertainer of the Year Award. Recent hits have included 'A Bridge They Didn't Burn' and 'A Couple of Good Years Left.'

Shepard, Jean

A premier exponent and defender of honky-tonk musical traditions, Jean Shepard was born in Paul's Valley, Oklahoma, in 1933, and raised in Visalia, in California's San Joaquin Valley, where she moved with her family at the age of 10. Her first musical activities were in a girls' glee club, and at the age of 14 Jean sang with the Melody Ranch Girls at local dances and shows.

Soon Jean was part of the Bakersfield musical scene, where musical activity and innovation was second to Nashville only in terms of volume; in the 1950s and early 1960s it had its own 'sound,' and produced a host of talented singers and songwriters. Hank Thompson heard Jean sing, and his recommendation resulted in a Capitol Records contract; by 1953 she was a member of the *Ozark Jubilee* with Red Foley, out of Springfield, Missouri. In that year she recorded 'Dear John Letter' with Terry Preston (Ferlin Husky, another Bakersfield product), a song that went to the top of country record charts. Husky became Jean's legal guardian so they could tour and promote the song; Jean was a minor and could not cross state lines otherwise.

But when she attained her majority in 1955, she joined the *Grand Ole Opry*, and in 1959 married country singer Hawksaw Hawkins, who died four years later in the plane crash that also took the lives of Patsy Cline and Cowboy Copas. She is now mar-

Ricky Skaggs.

ried to Benny Birchfield, who once played with the Osborne Brothers.

Jean Shepard's major hits have included 'Forgive Me, John,' (a follow-up to 'Dear John Letter'), 'Satisfied Mind,' 'With His Hand in Mine,' 'Seven Lonely Days,' 'Come on Phone,' 'Another Lonely Night,' 'Slippin' Away' and 'At the Time.' She continues to tour widely, and is concerned with packaging many acts that play to local audiences. Jean is a talented and entertaining performer, and continues as a regular act on the *Opry*. Jean sings with a hard but pleasant voice, straightforward in her interpretations of heartache, honkytonk and up-tempo songs. She also possesses one of the most remarkable yodels in all country music.

Skaggs, Ricky

His first national hit record was 'Don't Get Above Your Raising,' and it appropriately has been a guidepost to the subsequent career of Ricky Skaggs. He has become a country superstar and bucked all of the industry's trends by preserving mountain and bluegrass flavors in his music.

Ricky Skaggs was born in Cordell, Kentucky, in 1954, and his family's free time was spent on mountain music and religion. His father taught Ricky the mandolin at age five, and the family played at local fairs and in churches. When Ricky was but seven he played on stage with the Stanley Brothers, and soon thereafter with Flatt and Scruggs on the *Martha White* television program. When he was 15 he and Keith Whitley hosted

two local radio shows: a bluegrass show on Saturday, a gospel show on Sundays.

The music that most inspired the musician in Ricky was that of the Stanley Brothers, and a dream came true when he joined Ralph Stanley when he was 15. The association lasted two years, at which time Ricky quit, temporarily discouraged by the music business and his financial woes. He became a boiler operator in the Washington, DC, area.

Soon, however, he was swept up in the 'newgrass' ferment centered in the Washington area. He joined the Country Gentlemen for two years (recording a solo album, *That's It*), and met Linda Rondstadt and Rodney Crowell, who were then absorbing bluegrass and country. He also met Emmylou Harris, whose Hot Band he was later to front to widespread acclaim. Ricky joined J D Crowe and the New South for a while, and then formed his own bluegrass group, Boone Creek. He recorded his second album, *Sweet Temptation*, followed by others, including *Skaggs and Rice* (with Tony Rice) for Rounder and Sugar Hill, two of the boldest and brightest of the independent record labels in country music.

In 1977 Ricky joined Emmylou Harris, and played a large role in the production of her landmark bluegrass tinged album *Roses in the Snow*. It took his own contract with Epic Records to ignite Ricky's career, for his style and material did not change when he joined the major label. His fortunes did, as he won awards from the Country Music Association, the Academy of Country Music and the Music City News, including Best Male Vocalist from CMA in 1982, for songs like the above-mentioned 'Don't Get Above Your Raising' (an old Flatt and Scruggs song), 'You May See Me Walking,' another Flatt and Scruggs song, 'Crying My Heart Out Over You,' 'I Don't Care,' and 'Heartbroke.' In 1981 Ricky married Sharon White of the innovative bluegrass family The Whites, and shares their appetite for Western Swing and diverse influences; Ricky also veers towards rockabilly in certain numbers he performs. But he maintains a largely bluegrass ensemble (albeit progressive), and is mightily proud

Bluegrass and gospel are Skaggs' fortes.

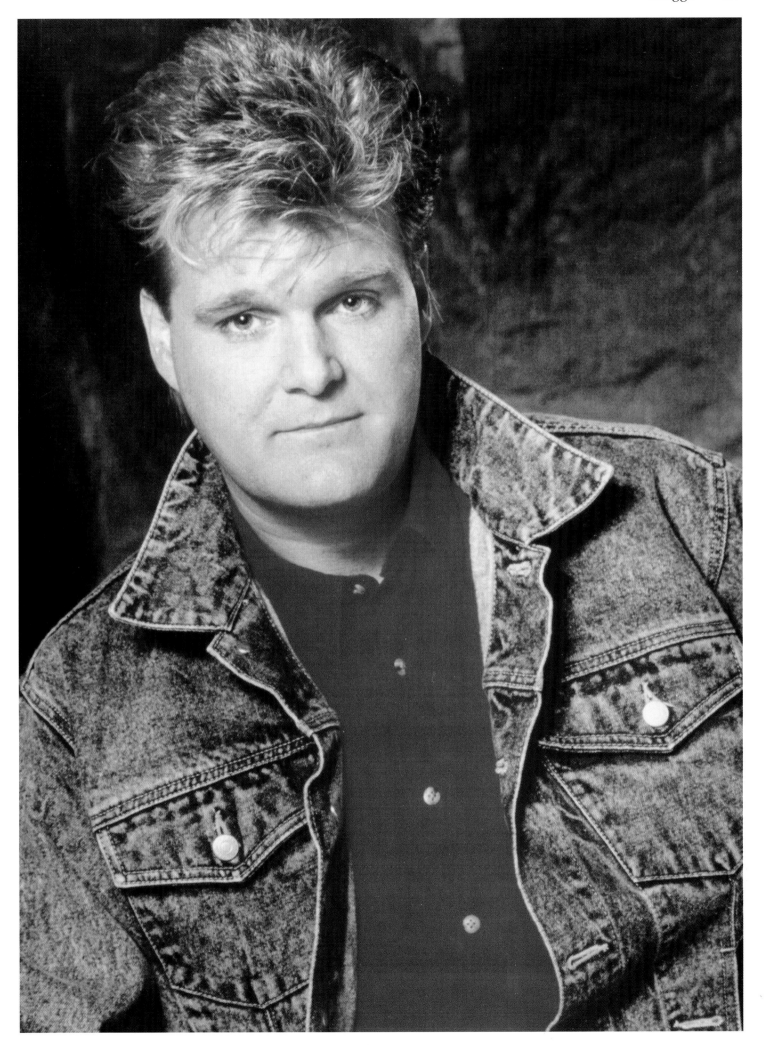

of the raising he received in music. Ricky, who joined the Grand Ole Opry in 1982, is a veritable wizard on the mandolin, fiddle, banjo and guitar, and possesses a beautifully clear high tenor that is appropriately reminiscent of the old-time and mountain singers of the Appalachians whose music he preserves so tastefully.

Skaggs was voted Entertainer of the Year by the Country Music Association in 1985. A 1987 album, *Love's Gonna Get Ya!* was judged too pop by Skaggs and, evidently by some fans, since sales were off his usual hot pace, so he returned to pure country sounds with his next album, *Comin' Home to Stay*. This release featured sounds of bluegrass, country, gospel, and a little rockabilly, and re-established Skaggs as a major figure in the New Traditionalist wave.

A committed Christian, Skaggs endorsed the 1988 presidential candidacy of Pat Robertson, planned a 'worship and praise' event in Nashville featuring thousands of musicians and singers, and traveled to Nigeria for an evangelical conference.

Ricky's musical and spiritual lives have become even more entwined during the '90s. Still an extremely popular concert draw, he devotes a great deal of time to television ministry, witnessing and gospel performance. He also recorded a disc featuring a reunion of Newgrass Revival members in 1994, and hosts the syndicated radio show *Simple Life With Ricky Skaggs*.

Skillet Lickers, The

One of the most interesting congregations in country music history, the Skillet Lickers was a rough, rowdy, crazy bunch of pickers and singers who performed everything from fiddle breakdowns to minstrel songs to vaudeville comedy routines. They were among the first of country's recording stars and recorded 565 discs in approximately a half-dozen years of existence.

The group was founded by Gid Tanner, a North Georgia hoedown fiddler who was a chicken farmer by trade. They performed briefly as the Lick the Skillet Band in the mid-1920s, but when master fiddler

Pappy McMichen joined in 1926, the group became Gid Tanner and the Skillet Lickers. The personnel at that time was: Tanner and McMichen, fiddles; Riley Puckett, guitar; Fate Norris, banjo; Lowe Stokes and Bert Layne, fiddles; and Ted Hawkins, mandolin.

Tanner actually fronted the group and led his own cheering section of shouts and ejaculations, like Bob Wills was to do in Western Swing years later. His fiddle was rough and wild in comparison with the smoother, more mature fiddle of McMichen. Riley Puckett played a strong lead guitar and sang in a bluesy fashion.

Rivalling their popular music in public acceptance was the Skillet Lickers brand of comedy. It was rural, broad and bawdy; 14 spoken routines, the ongoing 'A Corn Likker Still in Georgia,' were huge sellers. The group's musical hits, among hundreds of sides, include: 'Down Yonder,' 'Ida Red,' 'Sally Gooden' and 'The Wreck of the Old '97.' After Lowe Stokes lost his hand in a bar brawl in 1931, the Skillet Lickers broke up, although they recorded once again in 1934. As pioneer country recording artists, the Skillet Lickers let their exuberance show through and gave a taste to record buyers of just how much fun country music could really be.

Smith, Carl

Carl Smith grew up in a part of the country that seemed to ordain his career in music. He was born in 1927 in Maynardsville, Tennessee, the birthplace of Roy Acuff, and four miles 'over the hill' from where Chet Atkins was born. He was indeed devoted to country music from an early age, and saved pennies to purchase his first guitar.

In the 1940s Smith secured a spot on WROL radio in Knoxville (with Molly O'Day, Archie Campbell and others) and by 1950 he was a member of the Grand Ole Opry, where he remained for eight years. In 1951 he signed with Columbia Records, and soon became one of the major country music stars of the 1950s. Carl's hit records included 'Let's Live a Little,' 'If Teardrops Were Pennies,' 'Let Old Mother Nature Have Her Way,' 'I Overlooked an Orchid,' 'Hey Joe,' 'Don't Just Stand There,'

'There She Goes' and 'Ten Thousand Drums' (a saga song about the Revolutionary War). In all, through the 1970s, when his career cooled, Carl Smith sold 15 million records.

Smith appeared in three movies and on TV's *Four-Star Jubilee* over the ABC network; he also hosted *The Carl Smith Country Music Hall*, a program syndicated worldwide.

Smith's voice is a smooth baritone, similar to, but a bit rougher than, Eddy Arnold's. He employed a honky-tonk instrumentation in much of his work, however, resisting the lush backdrops that tempted Arnold. Western Swing influences could also be heard in Smith's music, as well as traditional modes. He sang for a time with the Carter Family, and married June Carter; their daughter Carlene Carter is a country star of the '90s. Today he is married to country singer Goldie Hill, and has mostly retired to his expansive ranch in Tennessee.

Smith, Connie

Born in 1941 in Elkhart, Indiana, as one of 14 children, Constance June Smith was raised in West Virginia and Ohio. After she married and settled in Ohio, she sang country music as an amateur and even made some local TV appearances. In 1963 she won a talent contest in Columbus, Ohio, and was thereby 'discovered' by Bill Anderson, who was ultimately responsible for Connie being signed by RCA. He also wrote her first song, 'Once a Day,' a monstrous hit that spent two and a half months on the top of country music charts. In 1965 she became a member of the *Grand Ole Opry* and was suddenly a major country star.

Her hits came in rapid succession and with strong sales: 'Then and Only Then,' 'Ain't Had No Lovin',' 'Just One Time,' 'Cincinnati, Ohio,' 'If It Ain't Love,' 'Ribbon of Darkness,' 'Run Away Little Tears,' 'Just For What I Am,' 'Even the Bad Times are Good' (with Nat Stuckey), 'Come Along and Walk With Me,' 'Too Much to Gain to Lose,' 'I Never Knew What That Song Meant Before,' 'That's the Way Love Goes,' 'Ain't Love a Good Thing,' 'Dallas,' 'I Got a Lot of Hurtin' Done Today' and 'Lovin' You.' She also recorded tribute albums to songwriters Bill Anderson and Dallas Frazier, as well as a remarkable collection of little-known Hank Williams gospel songs.

As Connie has frequently testified, however, instant stardom was almost impossible to cope with; she endured two failed marriages and personal crises. She has also frequently testified that being a born-again Christian salvaged her life. For years she has included at least one gospel song on every album, and for a long time recorded and sang only gospel music. She has appeared with evangelists Billy Graham and Rex Humbard, delivering her testimony as well as her songs. She has refused to play in clubs where alcohol is served, a sacrificial challenge to a country singer, and continues as an Opry star.

The possessor of a powerful voice, the diminutive Connie Smith delivers her songs with emotion and force; sometimes it seems that her clear alto vocals hardly need a microphone. She is a great vocal stylist. Indeed many consider Connie Smith the finest female voice in country music. In the mid-1990s she has now tried her hand at songwriting.

Smith, Fiddlin' Arthur

Generally regarded as the best of the old-time fiddlers, Arthur Smith was born in 1898 in Bold Springs, Tennessee. He learned to play the fiddle at five, and when a young man he got a job on the North Carolina and St Louis Rail Road – 'The Dixie Line' – where he picked up different fiddle styles along the route. On the line he met another employee, Harry Stone, who also was a part-time announcer on Nashville's WSM radio. It was arranged for Smith to audition for the station's Grand Ole Opry, and in 1927 he was added to the roster of the fledgling program.

Smith played as a solo and joined other acts, such as Jack Shook and the Missouri Mountaineers. He toured and recorded with the great Delmore Brothers, and, with Sam and Kirk McGee, recorded as the Dixieliners, after Smith's old railroad affiliation. In 1935 Smith cut his first record, 'Fiddler's Dream,' and in the 1940s he went to Hollywood to make movies and cut records with Jimmy Wakely, which displayed his ability to slide from country to Western. In

the 1960s Smith toured northern cities under the aegis of the Newport Folk Foundation.

Arthur Smith was in total command of his instrument. He played a smooth, mature fiddle that could be moved to incredible feats – acrobatic, complex fingering, an energetic drive, bits of other tunes cleverly admixed without warning, and wild octave jumps. Arthur Smith's fiddle techniques are still admired throughout the South.

Snow, Hank

Hank Snow, The Singing Ranger and one of the real individualists of country music, was born Clarence Eugene Snow in Brooklyn, Nova Scotia, Canada, in 1914. The victim of a broken home and child abuse, Hank left home at 12, pursuing such activities as fishing and working as a cabin boy on an ocean freighter. But as a youth he liked Western movies and the records of Jimmie Rodgers, so he aspired to a career as a performer.

In 1934 he sang as Hank the Yodeling Ranger on the *Canadian Farm Hour* over Halifax radio, and two years later signed with RCA Records as a Jimmie Rodgers sound-alike, performing ballads and country songs with a clear yodel. For years, however, RCA considered Hank only a Canadian talent, and didn't market his country records in the US. In 1944, in an attempt to counter that situation, Hank moved to Dallas at the invitation of Ernest Tubb, who had also begun his career inspired by

Fiddlin' Arthur Smith, one of the best of the old-time fiddlers.

Jimmie Rodgers records. In Texas and on the staff of the *Wheeling Jamboree* in West Virginia and elsewhere, however, Hank failed to make a major impact.

In 1949 RCA issued its first US release of a Hank Snow song (he was billed only as Hank, The Singing Ranger) but the next year, under his full name, he made country music history by writing and recording one of the biggest hits in history. It was a train song, squarely in his idol's tradition: 'I'm Movin' On.' Hank's song still holds a record; it was number one for 26 weeks, and in the top ten for 14 months. The next two decades, his busiest, were to see 61 hit records for Hank Snow, including 'Marriage Vows,' 'I've Been Everywhere,' 'Rhumba Boogie,' 'The Golden Rocket,' 'Now and Then (There's a Fool Such As I),' and 'Merry-Go-Round of Love.' Through the years Hank also recorded strictly instrumental albums (as a soloist and with Chet Atkins) and cut three tribute albums to Jimmie Rodgers that are among the finest of such material; one Rodgers album contains transcribed recollections of Albert Fullam, a trainman who knew and worked with Rodgers.

In the mid-1950s Hank furthered the career of Elvis Presley by hosting his appearance on his own *Grand Ole Opry* segment (Hank had joined the Opry in 1950 when 'I'm Movin' On' broke), and including Presley in his tour package. Through the years

Hank has featured superb musicians in his band, the Rainbow Ranch Boys, including fiddler Chubby Wise (who had also been with Bill Monroe's first bluegrass aggregation, and is also a fine jazz and Western Swing fiddler) and steel guitarist Kayton Roberts.

The latter-day singing style of Hank Snow is a challenge to describe. Hank's voice is nasal, and he will employ vocal slides from his resonant bass to brassy high notes before settling in on vibrato tones. His phrasing is precise, almost clipped, and, like his instrumental work, displays a devotion to perfectionism; Hank often uses a music stand with a score during his performances, even when signing his standards.

Hank Snow was inducted into the Country Music Hall of Fame in 1979, a position he surely deserves for his unique contributions and amazing career. He owns the longest continuing contract in the history of recorded music; RCA signed him through 1987, more than 50 years with the label.

In the 1980s Hank directed his energies toward the Hank Snow Foundation for the Prevention of Child Abuse and Neglect of Children, an outgrowth of his own harrowing childhood experiences. Hank's concern has led him to many TV talk shows and extensive fundraising and research work to fight the epidemiological problem.

Sons of the Pioneers, The

This classic vocal group did for Western music what Bill Monroe did for bluegrass music – defined a style of music, creating and sustaining a tradition that has lived through originators and countless disciples. The Sons of the Pioneers derived their sound from a mixture of traditional camp and trail songs, popular country dance music, and Hollywood movie requirements – a pastiche that sounds so engaging and natural that it seems to have been around forever.

The personnel did not just happen to be at the right place at the right time. The Sons of the Pioneers have been blessed with incredible songwriting talent and vocal harmonies.

The group started in 1933. Leonard Slye, member of the all-instrumental Rocky Mountaineers hillbilly band, decided to form a vocal group, believing that the future of country music was with singers, not instrumentalists. He put an ad in a local Los Angeles paper, and soon was joined by Bob Nolan. After some shuffling of style and personnel, the pair was joined by Tim Spencer – via another newspaper ad – and the trio joined the Texas Outlaws on their KFWS radio show as The Pioneer Trio. In 1934 they were joined by American Indian brothers Hugh and Karl Farr, who played, respectively, fiddle and guitar, and the group's name was changed to Sons of the Pioneers. In 1936 guitarist and tenor Lloyd Perryman joined the group.

It was at this time that the group struck out on its own, becoming featured performers on the *Hollywood Barn Dance* on KHS radio; members of the group also sought work in the local movie industry and appeared individually or together. When Gene Autry left Republic Pictures in 1937, Slye was given the stage name of Roy Rogers and promoted into a major cowboy star. Although he had to leave his singing group, he arranged for the Sons of the Pioneers to appear as actors and singers in many of his movies.

The records that the ensemble recorded through the years – and performed in movies, in concerts, and on their radio programs - form a virtual textbook of what we know today as cowboy music. Although very few of the Sons grew up with horses (or were even born in the West), these men were poets and singers of incredible sensitivity, their lyrics and harmonies producing sharp evocation of the cowboy's life – his daily toil, his dreams, his bitterness, his faith. Some of their many classic titles include 'Cool Water,' 'Tumbling Tumbleweeds,' 'He Walks With the Lonely,' 'The Touch of God's Hand,' 'Ridin' Home' and 'Way Out There,' all written by Nolan. Spencer wrote many memorable songs as well, including classics that were also covered by other singers: 'Room Full of Roses,' 'Cigareets, Whusky and Wild, Wild Women' and 'The Everlasting Hills of Oklahoma.'

Hank Snow, The Singing Ranger.

In addition to the original Sons mentioned above, other members of the group have included 'Slumber' Nicholas, Pat Brady (later the comic sidekick on Rogers's TV show), Ken Curtis (later playing Festus Hagan on TV's *Gunsmoke*), Dale Warren, Roy Lanham, Billy Armstrong, Rusty Richards, Billy Liebert, Rome Johnson, Ken Carson, Doye O'Dell, Duece Spriggins, Tommy Doss, Shug Fisher, Luther Nallie and Dale Morris.

The influence of the Sons of the Pioneers cannot be overstated. Their songs helped cement an imagery in American folklore that is as strong as any other. But the unique lyrics and, especially, their tuneful, gentle harmonies left a legacy that influenced musicians, singers and songwriters ever since their heyday. Besides all the real and would-be cowboy singers who simply *have* to sound like the Sons of the Pioneers, their influence can be heard in Marty Robbins, the Glaser Brothers and even the Statler Brothers. The original sextet was inducted into the Country Music Hall of Fame in 1980, and the group, with new personnel, continues to perform and record today. They began performing regularly in Branson, Missouri, in the early '80s, moving to the Foggy River Boys Theater in 1985. The group was named to the Grammy Hall of Fame the following year.

Sovine, Red

Woodrow Wilson Sovine was born in Charleston, West Virginia, in 1918, learned the guitar at a young age, and was devoted to some of the nation's pioneer country music radio stations as he grew up. In 1935 he joined the Carolina Tar Heels in Charleston, and then moved to the *Wheeling Jamboree*, heard over WWVA in West Virginia and beamed over the entire Northeast of the US and Canada.

Sovine joined the Echo Valley Boys in 1947, and two years later succeeded Hank Williams on both the *Louisiana Hayride* and Hank's *Johnny Fair Syrup Show* on radio. At the *Hayride* he struck an association with Webb Pierce that saw them write, perform, record and tour in tandem; in 1945 both joined the Grand Ole Opry. Two of their classic duets were 'Why, Baby, Why?' and 'Little Rosa.'

It was another decade, however, before Sovine found his groove, and that was with the twin specialities of recitations and truck-driving songs. In 1964 he recorded 'Giddyup Go,' a tearjerker about a trucker's little boy; three years later he cut the classic 'Phantom 309,' a story about a trucker who swerved to his death instead of hitting a busload of school-children. Sovine's rough-hewn bass voice, dripping with genuine tears, made the sentimental recitation all the more emotional.

Predictable as the fact that country fans love to weep was that Sovine would dominate truck-driving themes when the CB craze hit, and indeed he produced the masterful (and, once again, emotional) 'Teddy Bear,' about a crippled boy whose life was lived via his CB radio. Recitations and sentimental story-songs are as old as the very roots of country music, and Red Sovine, who died in 1980, was the master of the form during his generation.

Stanley Brothers, The

They were born in the part of Virginia that spawned the Carter Family: Carter Glen Stanley in McClure in 1925, and Ralph Edmond in Stratton in 1927. Indeed they grew up absorbing the music of the Carters and other traditional mountain and old-time music. In 1946 they formed the Stanley Brothers and the Clinch Mountain Boys, and started the *Farm and Fun Time Show* on radio in Bristol.

The Stanleys were among the first groups to turn bluegrass after Bill Monroe synthesized the style; Ralph Stanley always claimed he learned the three-finger banjo technique from local pickers like Snuffy Jenkins, not Earl Scruggs. And although they became prominent bluegrass musicians, they always maintained an old-time and mountain repertoire, a distinction that is sometimes lost. The Stanleys' tight harmonies and unadorned instrumentation were reminiscent of Grayson and Whitter, Mainer's Mountaineers, the Blue Sky Boys and, of course, the Carter Family. The Stanleys' music was rough-hewn but gentler and homier than that of Bill Monroe, their singing filled with evident conviction and emotional simplicity.

The Stanleys recorded 'Molly and Tenbrooks,' a song they heard Monroe perform, before the Bluegrass Boys actually cut it. In the early 1950s Ralph left the act to pursue a career in veterinary medicine (during which time Carter played with Bill Monroe) but the group re-formed and compiled an enormous catalog of recorded music. Their memorable songs include: 'Clinch Mountain Backstep,' 'Little Glass of Wine,' 'White Dove,' 'The Fields Have Turned Brown,' 'Lonesome River,' 'The Darkest Hour Is Just Before the Dawn,' 'Rank Stranger,' 'Tragic Romance,' 'Shackles and Chains,' 'Man of Constant Sorrow,' 'Two Coats' and 'Hard Times.'

Among the many fine musicians who have played with the Stanleys have been Pee Wee Lambert, George Shuffler, Ricky Skaggs, Keith Whitley and Curly Ray Cline. Ricky Skaggs, now a superstar in his own right, and Emmylou Harris have revived Stanley Brothers standards on record in recent years.

Carter played a guitar in the Maybelle Carter style and Ralph, banjoist, possesses one of the finest high tenor voices in country music. Through the years gospel music formed perhaps half of the Stanley's repertoire, which was recorded on labels like Columbia, Rich-R-Tone, Mercury, King, Wango (for many of the gospel cuts), Rimrock, Rebel and County Sales of Floyd, Virginia, which has made a treasure trove of traditional music available to fans. Copper Creek Records of Roanoke has undertaken an archival task of issuing recordings of the Stanleys' more obscure performances, including concert transcriptions.

Carter died suddenly in 1966, but Ralph continues to perform and has honed his own style of banjo and vocals as a soloist.

Statler Brothers, The

Kurt Vonnegut has called them America's poets. Their identification is with nostalgia – Saturday morning moving-picture shows, childhood memories, screen cowboys and country music favorites – the warm moments of our shared, and personal, pasts. But the Statler Brothers' specialty is evoking emo-

tions through their songs – not only memories, but humor, wisdom, sadness, and joy as well. Listeners are immediately comfortable with a Statler Brothers song because they seemed to have lived the lyrics or can empathize with someone who has. That indeed makes them poets in the grand sense, and it also makes them among the finest writers and singers in country music history.

The Statler Brothers are not Statlers nor are they all brothers. All were born in or around Staunton, Virginia – Harold Reid in 1939 and his brother Don in 1945; Phil Balsley and Lew DeWitt in 1939. Growing up in the Shenandoah Valley between the Allegheny and Blue Ridge mountains, Harold, Phil and Lew sang together occasionally beginning in 1955. They sang gospel music and their idols were the Blackwood Brothers and Hovie Lister and the Statesmen. They disbanded in 1958 but reorganized in 1960 when Don joined the group. The early names for the quartet were the Four Star Quartet and the Kingsmen; the Stat-

ler name came from a box of Statler facial tissues on the table when they were discussing the need for a new name ('We could just as easily have become the Kleenex Brothers,' Harold remembers).

Through country music promoter Carlton Haney they met Johnny Cash at a little hillside country music stage called Watermelon Park in Berryville, Virginia, in 1963. Cash agreed that he could use the Statlers in his show, and for nine months they pursued him by telephone. After this 'gestation period' they were invited to join the Cash show, where they remained until 1972, including on Cash's network television program.

In 1965 the Statlers, recording for Columbia Records, scored a massive country and pop hit with 'Flowers on the Wall,' a nonsense song of rejected romance written by Lew. They followed up with some other more modest hits, including 'You Can't Have Your Kate and Edith Too,' and a gospel album, but basically Columbia did not exploit or promote the

The Statler Brothers in the early days.

Statlers. In 1970 they switched to Mercury Records where Jerry Kennedy's tasteful production combined with a creative explosion of quality songwriting by the Statlers. They were also given great creative latitude, from repertoire to album design. The Statler Brothers flowered, sometimes off the wall, but always on the mark.

Their first song for Mercury, 'Bed of Roses' was a hit, and has been followed through the years by a dizzying array of other popular successes: 'Pictures,' 'Do You Remember These,' 'Since Then,' 'The Class of '57,' '1953-Dear John-Honky-Tonk Blues,' 'Monday Morning Secretary,' 'The Boy Inside of Me,' 'Thank You World,' 'Susan When She Tried,' 'The Strand,' 'What Ever Happened to Randolph Scott,' 'I'll Go to My Grave Lovin' You,' 'Do You Know You Are My Sunshine,' 'Your Picture in the Paper,' 'I Was There,' 'Thank God I've Got You,' 'The Movies,' 'Silver Medals and Sweet Memories,'

The Statlers: Jimmy, Don, Harold, Phil.

'Nothing as Original as You,' 'How to Be a Country Star,' 'Who Am I To Say,' 'Here We Are Again,' 'Charlotte's Web,' 'In the Garden' and 'Atlanta Blue.' In 1985 their song 'Elizabeth' was voted Song of the Year by *Music City News*. It was written by Jimmy Fortune, the Statler's new tenor singer, replacing Lew DeWitt, who left the group for health reasons in 1982 and has since died.

For years the Statlers won the Country Music Association and Academy of Country Music Vocal Group category awards, as well as many other industry accolades. Their *Best of the Statler Brothers* albums remained on record charts for more than four years and has sold more than two million copies. Since leaving Cash, they have headlined shows all over the world, also performing at the White House and with Billy Graham Crusades.

The Statler Brothers have recorded several theme albums. Their *Old Testament* and *New Testament* albums are thoughtful treatments of messages in the Scriptures, and they have also created comedic alter egoes with great success. Lester 'Road Hog' Moran and His Cadillac Cowboys are a prototypical local country ensemble mangling the airwaves on Saturday radio shows and dreaming of a Nashville break. The Statlers recorded and performed various routines and an album, *Alive at the Johnny Mack Brown High School*. The Road Hog bits are hilarious and truthful (in one song of four lines they combine the garbled lyrics of 'Hello Walls,' 'Hello Darlin',' and 'Time Slips Away'), with fans all over the country swearing they know the disc jockey who's being lampooned.

There have been syndicated Statler Brothers television specials, and they have frequently hosted and been featured guests on award shows. Their TNN television show, *The Statler Brothers* (begun in 1991), is continually ranked number one. Until recently the Brothers hosted a Fourth of July Picnic in Staunton, attracting thousands of fans.

The Brothers sing in a basic four-part gospel quartet sound (Don, lead and MC; Phil, baritone; Lew/Jimmy, tenor; Harold, bass and comedy). Their backup is purposefully simple and, on record, largely acoustic.

The Statlers' material is roughly equal parts nostalgia/sentiment and love songs, with an interesting undercurrent of songs from the darker side of life – girls gone wrong, tragic affairs and the like. Their special genius in writing (most of their songs are original) and performing is making the mundane seem as special as it really is, or should be, to listeners. Songs like 'Pictures,' 'The Class of '57,' 'Do You Remember These,' and 'The Boy Inside of Me' are seemingly routine lists of recalled memories. But when listed by the Statler Brothers they are vital fragments of life, almost forgotten items, but no less precious for that. Other singers can try to take listeners to the stars, but the Statlers have a rare gift of bringing you back home and reminding you that's where you always wanted to be.

Stevens, Ray

Born Ray Bagsdale in 1939 in Clarksdale, Georgia, Ray Stevens first performed music in a rhythm and blues band, plied comedy and worked as a disc jockey in his local Albany, Georgia, area. He received a bachelors degree in music at Georgia State University.

In 1962, from his home base in Nashville, he began to record a string of successful singles, although none of them were country. His specialty became the novelty song, like 'Ahab the Arab' and 'Gitarzan.' Between the hits he worked as an arranger and producer, and even after he scored with major serious records, like 'Everything Is Beautiful,' he would return to novelties like 'The Streaker.'

Ray Stevens.

In 1970 the *Ray Stevens Show* was a seasonal replacement for Andy Williams's network variety hour (Stevens had earlier appeared on Williams's program), and he featured comedian Steve Martin and singer Mama Cass Elliot among his regulars. In the late 1970s Stevens recorded an album of pop standards with country instrumentation and scoring. Most notable among the cuts was the hit 'Misty.'

Like many country performers with waning record sales and radio accessibility (but a substantial number of loyal fans), Stevens turned to television as his main marketing tool in the mid-to-late '80s. His sales with this tactic have been phenomenal; proof that the popularity of novelty songs remains high despite the lack of radio support. Stevens is extremely successful in Nashville real estate ventures.

As an innovator and talented performer, Stevens has made his mark. His repertoire is as versatile as his talents are varied. 'Mr Businessman' was a political sermon, and 'Everything Is Beautiful' was virtually a humanist hymn. 'Turn Your Radio On' paid tribute to a fine traditional gospel song, but through all his music Ray Stevens seems almost more interested in the instrumentation and arrangements than the words. Indeed his talent dazzles: some of his records contain only Ray Stevens, playing, via overdubbing, every instrument with incredible technical brilliance.

Stone, Doug

Inspired by influences as diverse as rocker Frank Zappa and country legend George Jones, Georgia native Doug Stone has created an upbeat country sound that resulted in four gold and two platinum albums out of his first six Epic and Columbia albums. From 1990 through 1995 he had eight number-one singles, and during that time period none of his singles ranked lower than the top five.

Stone has written some of his own music, almost all attesting to his love of traditional-country lost-love and pain songs. He began his career as a teenager in his hometown, Newnan, Georgia (near Atlanta), singing first in skating rinks and later in a bar by night while working as a mechanic

by day. But full-time country singing was not long in coming.

His hits include '(I'd Be Better Off) in a Pine Box,' 'Fourteen Minutes Old,' 'Too Busy Falling in Love,' 'Why Didn't I Think of That,' 'Little Houses,' 'Come In Out of the Pain,' 'Warning Labels,' and his biggest song to date, 'A Jukebox with a Country Song.'

A heart attack several years ago temporarily slowed Doug Stone down and shocked his fans, but he has bounced back with one of the liveliest stage shows this side of Garth Brooks.

Stoneman, Pop and the Stoneman Family

Possibly the only country artist who spanned the eras from cylinder recordings to stereo, Ernest V Stoneman was also a walking history book

Above: Doug Stone – a lively performer.
Right: The Stonemans through the years.

of country music, performing various modes of country music in his career. He played the banjo, jews harp and harmonica.

Born in a log cabin near Iron Ridge, Carroll County, Virginia, in 1893, Pop Stoneman heard the pioneer recording of 'The Wreck of the Old 97' by Henry Whitter, whom he knew, and traveled to the Victor Recording Studios in New York, claiming he could sing it better. He did indeed sing it, in addition to his first major hit, 'The Sinking of the Titanic' (September 1, 1924), and eventually more than 200 other sides for Victor through the 1920s. Although he favored saga songs, Stoneman recorded country, old-time, gospel, novelty and even Tin Pan Alley songs under eight different names in those years. Between 1925 and 1929 he also toured on the Keith Vaudeville Circuit.

The Depression put him out of work, and he took a job as carpenter in the Washington, DC, Naval Yard. Although he didn't record at all between 1934 and 1957, he and his growing family performed frequently at Washington clubs and events. A 1957 album for Folkways drew him out, and in 1962 the Stonemans played the Grand Ole Opry. They were thereafter guests on many TV shows and had their own program, *Those Stonemans*, in the late 1960s. (Pop's TV debut was actually in the mid-1950s when he won $20,000 on a quiz show, *The Big Surprise*).

Of his 23 children, 13 survived and all became musicians. Prominent among them are Roni, who became a banjo player and comedienne on *Hee Haw*, and Scotty Wiseman Stoneman, a fiddler. Making up the Stonemans, a group that still performs and records (for CMH) are also Patti on autoharp; Donna, mandolin; Van, guitar; and Jim, bass. It is a top bluegrass ensemble.

Pop Stoneman, who died in 1968, was a vital figure in country music. He preserved hundreds of old-time songs that might otherwise have been lost but for his collecting obsession. He was 'there' at crucial points in the development of country music; he accompanied Uncle David Macon and Riley Puckett on recordings, and claimed to have given Al Hopkins the name 'Hill Billies' to record under, thereby naming an American style of music. He was perhaps the most representative performer of the Galax style of traditional rural music (from Virginia) – pure old-time style of White music uninfluenced by jazz or blues.

Strait, George

George Strait began his life on a ranch and continues to live on one; a son of the soil, he has retained his contact with it throughout his stellar public life. He was born in Poteet, Texas, and grew up in the neighboring town of Pearsall, where his family raised cattle. He studied agriculture in college without serious thought of abandoning it for a career in music, and he returned to help with the 1,000 head of cattle at the family ranch.

But although there was no particular musical inspiration from his parents, who, as he recalls, 'didn't even have a phonograph,' music had got into his blood while he was still in high school. He mastered the guitar by himself from a Hank Williams songbook and became a member of a garage rock 'n' roll group, and he fronted a country music band while serving in the army in Hawaii. Although fully expecting to go back to ranching when he graduated, he was interested enough to post a notice on his college bulletin board looking for a band to sing with. He found one in the Ace in the Hole, a group of classmates who made him its lead singer and whom he still uses as a back-up.

He did not go back to the ranch but kept his hand in music with occasional local dates in the surrounding area. He emulated his hero Bob Wills by singing Western Swing, and followed the lead of Merle Haggard and George Jones with traditional country music. He also followed Jones in recording for the venerable 'Pappy' Dailey, the producer with whom Jones had started long before. A club in San Marcos where Ace in the Hole played provided him with an even better contact. Its owner, Erv Woolsey, was impressed by the young singer's direct, traditional style and, when he became an executive at MCA Records, offered him a contract.

George's first album with MCA had the ingenious title *Strait Country*, making good use of the artist's name and accurately defining his honest, unadorned style. It found an appreciative audience and included the Top Ten hit 'Unwound,' a simple Texas two-step that struck a responsive chord in an audience perhaps becoming jaded with the 'urban cowboy' craze. Harking back to the roots of country music, it was respectful and authentic without being trite, and it was a huge success. In the years that followed, George has seen more than 40 singles recorded by MCA climb to the number one position on the country charts. His songs are full of sentiment, melancholy, and humor and include such varied styles as romantic country ballardry, up-tempo Western Swing, and honk-tonk. Among his hits have been 'Love Without End, Amen,' 'Does Fort Worth Ever Cross Your Mind,' the 1984 'You Look So Good in Love,' 'Ocean Front Property,'

'Famous Last Words of a Fool,' and the cleverly named 'All My Ex's Live in Texas,' with words and music by Sanger D and Lyndia J Shafer.

George Strait has been widely credited for his music in the industry. He was named Top Male Vocalist by the Academy of Country Music in 1984 and 1985 and by the Country Music Association in 1985 and 1986. The ACM named him Entertainer of the Year in 1989, and the CMA paid him the same honor in that and the following year.

Personally, George is withdrawn to the point of being reclusive. Especially since the death of his daughter in an automobile accident in 1986, he has rarely granted interviews, and he never exploits his celebrity. Although he occasionally sneaks into clubs to hear what's happening on the music scene, he keeps a low profile. This is in part from modesty, but mainly from a genuine attachment to the land and a desire to protect the simple life he lives on it. His passion for ranching is reflected in the annual Roping Classic he organizes; he is himself a roper of some talent and hopes one day to compete at a rodeo in the event.

If he is not gregarious, George is an active professional, with frequent and sold-out public appearances. A cool, even detached performer, he has always followed his own musical principles, pursuing and reanimating the traditional sounds of country music in its various aspects even when it was out of fashion and professionally unprofitable to do so. His aesthetic integrity has paid off, for himself and for the industry. He continues to stretch his music and his talents; he starred in the movie *True Country* in 1993. Recent hits include the singles, 'Easy Come, Easy Go,' and CDs *Chill of an Early Fall* and *Lead On*.

Stuart, Marty

Marty Stuart revealed his musical ability and identity as a child. Born in Philadelphia, Mississippi, he was hired to play the mandolin with the Sullivan Family, a prominent bluegrass gospel group, when he was 12. At 13 he went on to join the legendary Lester Flatt's touring group. He was a protege of Flatt's for eight

Right: George Strait.

years until the master's death in 1979. Six years with Johnny Cash followed. Marty became a part of the 'bluegrass fusion' movement, performing on guitar and mandolin with such notables as Vassar Clements, and began to make a name for himself. His first album, *Marty With a Little Help from My Friends*, was self-recorded on the Ridge Runner Records label, and it was followed by *Busy Bee Cafe* with Sugar Hill, a regional recording studio. By the mid-1980s, however, the excellence of his bluegrass music had attracted enough attention to win him a contract with Columbia Records in Nashville.

These albums were not successes, however. One was never issued and the other was promoted so indifferently that it did nothing for the artist's career. Discouraged, he went back to Mississippi and the Sullivan Family for a time until he felt once more in touch with his traditional

Marty Stuart – a New Traditionalist.

heritage. Fortified, he determined to take another shot at Nashville. This time was the charm; he got a contract with MCA Records and had a sensational run of successful albums: *Hillbilly Rock*, *Tempted*, and *This One's Gonna Hurt You* were all hits. Travis Tritt collaborated with him on 'This One's Gonna Hurt You (For a Long, Long Time), and the two performed together in 'The Whiskey Ain't Working,' a number one hit on a Tritt album. The song was widely praised as the freshest new work in contemporary country music, and the pair won the 1992 Vocal Event Award from the Country Music Association.

A keeper of the flame, Marty Stuart is a classic example of the 'new traditonalist.' Deeply rooted in country music, he has been a part of gospel, bluegrass, and rockabilly traditions since he was a child and has never lost sight of his origins.

Another tradition he keeps alive is that of donning sequined outfits – latter-day Nudie suits for which he is noted.

The remarkable Stuart can – and has – switched gears from performing hard-rocking country on the Grand Ole Opry one week and the next week playing bluegrass and gospel on the mandolin and singing harmonies with Vince Gill, Ricky Skaggs, and Alison Krauss.

All of Marty's hit singles have accompanied memorable videos; 'Let There Be Country' is a recent example. A recent CD is the collection *The Marty Party*.

J. D. Sumner and The Stamps Quartet

The strong link between country and gospel music was expanded and strengthened by Elvis Presley when he chose backup singers such as J. D. Sumner, who with his Stamps Quartet had become a driving force in the gospel field.

Sumner became one of Presley's

closest friends, and following the 'King's' death Sumner found his music more popular than ever because of his close working associations with the man who revolutionized rock 'n' roll. 'He left us a portion of his popularity,' Sumner has said.

The smooth, lilting melody of Sumner's quartet is still heard on Presley recordings and over the years there have been may pure gospel records by the Stamps Quartet on such labels as Sun and Starday. Only

Stuart in a rhinestone-studded jacket.

the Blackwood Brothers have influenced as many gospel and country-gospel acts as have the Stamps – including the now obligatory cascading deep voice behind the harmonies so associated with the legendary J. D. Sumner. The Stamps were featured performers in an acclaimed TV-marketing video success: *All Day Singing and Dinner on the Ground*, a jam of more than 40 gospel, country and southern gospel artists, released in 1995.

Swaggart, Jimmy

One of the biggest-selling gospel music artists in musical history, Jimmy Lee Swaggart was born in 1935 in Ferriday, Louisiana. Jimmy's uncle was Lee Calhoun, a rich and powerful Louisiana landowner who was never a Christian but did pay for the erection of a frame Assemblies of God Church in Ferriday. Jimmy had a Pentecostal upbringing, as did cousins Jerry Lee Lewis and Mickey Gilley.

There was backsliding enough in his teens, however. Jimmy and Jerry Lee frequently shoplifted from local stores. They stole away to clubs, and played piano music, learned from honky-tonk country records by Moon Mullican, and from a local barrelhouse player, Old Sam. The driving, boogie, left-hand bass fascinated the young cousins. Jimmy and Jerry Lee played at churches together – until they were asked to cease their provocative catting of the rhythms – and at many dances.

Nevertheless Jimmy remembered his promise to become a minister at the time of his conversion. His parents became evangelists, and in 1953 he decided to enter the ministry. He became a street-corner and campmeeting preacher. He quit his regular jobs in 1958, with no prospect of income other than faith, but was denied ordination by his denomination in 1959.

It soon became apparent that his cousin's repute in the secular world was giving people pause, especially since Jimmy frequently mentioned Jerry Lee Lewis – now the king of rock 'n' roll – in his services. It gave Jimmy pause too, when he was scarcely surviving as a traveling evangelist and Jerry Lee was earning thousands of dollars a week. Jerry Lee arranged a contract to inaugu-

rate a gospel line of records with the prestigious Sun label that had discovered him and Presley, Cash and others, but Jimmy felt led to reject this offer.

The decision was hard, for progress seemed slow – but it was steady. He self-recorded some albums (including one at Sun, but just for use of equipment) that gradually gained an audience on Christian radio stations. His crusades – some lasting for weeks – were attracting larger crowds. In 1969 he began his *Campmeeting Hour* radio program of music and preaching, and it soon was broadcast on hundreds of stations. In 1971 and '72 he recorded the years' top-selling gospel albums (*This Is Just What Heaven Means to Me* and *There Is a River*, respectively). In 1973 he inaugurated his television program, which at its height appeared on 700 stations worldwide.

Jimmy Swaggart's musical style is old-fashioned Holy Ghost revival-type playing. (While he plays country gospel, other singers in his troupe perform other types of Christian music; the purpose, according to Jimmy, is to draw different people to the message.) There is the keyboard-pounding, glissando-filled style of his youth, but the Gospel is always paramount. In fact he rejects Christian music that does not contain glory and salvation messages upfront.

By 1985 Jimmy Swaggart had recorded nearly 50 albums, and regularly sold in excess of half a million of them yearly. His television ministry of music and sermons is broadcast to dozens of countries, and he expanded the Jimmy Swaggart Evangelistic Association in many directions – a monthly magazine, schools and childrens' centers around the globe, a satellite television network, the Jimmy Swaggart School of the Bible in Baton Rouge, Louisiana. He was, by several surveys, the most-watched television evangelist in America, and he credits his first love, gospel music, with attracting many eventual converts in their first, curiosity-filled sampling of his TV program.

A member of country music's most fascinating family, Jimmy Swaggart ultimately reached more fans, as America's premier country gospel artist, than his cousins Jerry Lee

Lewis and Mickey Gilley did with their followers.

Among the songs most identified with Jimmy Swaggart are 'Some Golden Daybreak,' 'God Took Away My Yesterdays,' 'Meeting In The Air,' 'I Want to Praise the Lord,' 'At An Altar of Prayer,' 'You Don't Need to Understand,' 'Sweet, Sweet Spirit,' 'Down the Sawdust Trail,' 'Had It Not Been,' 'The Healer,' 'Friendship with Jesus,' 'Jesus Will Outshine Them All,' 'Just Over in the Glory Land,' 'We Shall See the King,' 'There is a Fountain,' 'Sweet Holy Spirit,' 'Power in the Blood,' 'He Brought Me Out of the Miry Clay,' 'Whole Lot of People Goin' Home,' 'Heaven's Sounding Sweeter All the Time,' 'Learning to Lean,' 'I'll Fly Away,' 'I Shall Not Be Moved,' 'The Best of the Trade,' 'Somewhere Listenin',' 'Sometimes Alleluia,' 'He Washed My Eyes With Tears,' 'I'll Be Satisfied' and his long-time theme, Jimmie Davis's 'Someone to Care.'

In February 1988 Swaggart confessed – after being exposed – to unspecified 'sins' in a televised and much-publicized speech (witnesses had photographed him at a motel with a prostitute who claimed she posed nude for the evangelist). The scandal rocked his ministy, which had been reportedly receiving $140 million per year in contributions.

Swaggart's parent denomination, the Assemblies of God, imposed a year's banishment on his ministry – including the music and television portions – and two years of rehabilitation. The singing preacher rejected the admonition (although it was, to the letter, a regimen advocated by Swaggart himself a year earlier when he wrote about fallen church leaders), and he was stripped of his credentials. After three months of what turned out to be self-imposed absence from stage, TV screen, and pulpit, Swaggart returned to public performances.

Without a doubt, his ministry was crippled. The scandal's damaging effects were compounded by its following in the wake of fellow television singer-evangelists Jim and Tammy Bakker's downfall of the previous year. It seems viewers do indeed believe in forgiveness, because now that Swaggart is back on the air, he again boasts a large and ever-growing audience.

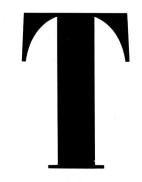

Tanner, Gid

Born in Thomas Bridge, Georgia, in 1885, James Gideon Tanner was raised on a chicken farm. At 14 he inherited a fiddle from an uncle and soon mastered its playing, performing at local fairs and dances.

In the 1920s Tanner participated in a fiddle contest with the legendary Fiddlin' John Carson, and was heard by record scout and producer Frank Walker of Columbia Records. On March 7, 1924, in New York City, Tanner and blind guitarist Riley Puckett – playing, ironically, a banjo – performed what is arguably the first country string-band music on record. Back in Georgia, Gid Tanner organized a band of friends to play traditional, breakdown and comedy material. It was originally called Ye Olde Home Town Band, after the cartoon panel by Lee Stanley. The name was later changed to the Lick the Skillet Band, and, when fiddler Clayton McMichen joined in 1926, Gid Tanner and the Skillet Lickers.

The Skillet Lickers gained enormous popularity on record and in touring, both in concerts and on radio broadcasts. Tanner, although a fiddler, was more a front man and would punctuate the solos with patter. His fiddle playing was of the wild, hoedown variety, a North Georgia style that has been preserved by many players through the years. The high-spirited jokester Tanner would also lead the old-time comedy routines, which sometimes rivaled the music for the public's favor.

His band was dissolved in the early 1930s but Gid Tanner continued to record with individual members and other musicians. For all his fame and his enormous influence – as a fiddler and as a pioneer country recording artist with more than 500

records to his credit – Tanner always considered himself primarily a chicken farmer. He never gave up the family farm, and it is where he earned his livelihood in the closing years of his life. Gid Tanner died on May 13, 1960.

Thompson, Hank

Henry William Thompson was born in Waco, Texas, in 1925. His first musical love was the harmonica, an instrument on which he won contests; he then mastered the guitar. In the early 1940s he performed on local radio as Hank the Hired Hand and, after serving in the Navy in World War II and briefly attending Princeton, Hank formed the Brazos Valley Boys and scored some regional hits on Southwest record charts.

Tex Ritter heard Thompson record and arranged for a Capitol Records contract. Thompson upgraded his band to Western Swing proportions and fronted what was arguably the 1950s' best country big-band ensemble. He survived the decline of such aggregations by concentrating on honky-tonk themes, and thereby became a major recording artist. Among his hits were 'Humpty-Dumpty Heart,' 'Whoa Sailor,' 'Wild Side of Life,' 'The Oklahoma Hills,' 'Six Pack to Go' and 'Cab Driver.' 'Wild Side of Life' was the enormous hit that called upon the durable country melody that has served 'The Prisoner's Song,' 'I'm Thinking Tonight of My Blue Eyes' in a slight variant, 'Great Speckled Bird' and the 'answer song' to Thompson's hit, 'I Didn't Know God Made Honky Tonk Angels,' through which Kitty Wells opened up country music to female soloists.

Hank Thompson's superb musicianship and arrangements – his late '60s album *Hank Thompson Salutes Oklahoma* is one of the great big-band Western Swing recordings – have marked him as a talented innovator. He is the first artist to have recorded in high fidelity, in stereo, and 'live' before a concert audience. His voracious and eclectic musical taste has also led him to record albums of Mills Brothers and Nat King Cole tunes. Thompson's voice is a crisp, sure baritone at home with his usual honky-tonk fare or his musical forays into other fields, handling both with elan.

Mel Tillis in 1981.

Hugh Cherry has quoted Tex Ritter about a man whose career he helped launch: 'Hank Thompson took a six-pack of beer and a book of Mother Goose and made a career.'

Tillis, Mel

Melvin Tillis was born in Tampa, Florida, in 1932, and was raised in nearby Pahokee. He began writing country songs while in the Army, and after discharge was able to sell some in Nashville, although he was initially not considered seriously as a singer. Mel suffers from a stutter that theoretically dates from a malarial bout at the age of three, and although it virtually disappears when he sings, its existence made record executives extremely wary.

Besides, his songs were making hits for others, so Mel was pigeonholed; after arriving in Nashville in 1957 his biggest hits were Bobby Bare's 'Detroit City' and Kenny Rogers's 'Ruby, Don't Take Your Love to Town.' He also wrote hits for Burl Ives, Brenda Lee, Jimmy Dean, Johnny Ray, Theresa Brewer, the Everly Brothers, Tom Jones and Dean Martin.

In the mid-1960s he recorded some of his own songs and steadily built up a reputation with a list of ever-higher charted records. Since then his hits have included: 'Who's Julie,' 'Stateside,' 'These Lonely Hands of Mine,' 'Old Faithful,' 'Heart Over Mind,' 'Brand New Mister Me,' 'I Ain't Never,' 'Sawmill,' 'Midnight, Me and the Blues,' 'Coca Cola Cowboy' and 'Southern Rain.' His determined ascent resulted in frequent guest appearances on the Porter Wagoner and Glen Campbell television programs, and a string of duets with Sherry Bryce and Nancy Sinatra. Mel turned his stuttering into a comedy prop (winning industry awards for comedy as well as songwriting and singing), and saw these diverse gifts propel him to Entertainer of the Year honors at the CMA's 1976 awards.

Mel Tillis is frequently a guest on television talk shows, and has appeared in several movies. In Burt Reynolds' *WW and the Dixie Dance Kings* he played himself and a gas-station attendant; and in 1985 he and Roy Clark co-starred in *Uphill All the*

Way. He also appeared in a country video with Glen Campbell in 1985, plugging their duets.

After his Entertainer of the Year award, Tillis's material began to reflect significant (but subtle) pop influence. His act and recordings, however, retained a good measure of the pure country flavor on which he built his career – Mel delivered Tommy Collins songs in classic '50s honky-tonk fashion on a 1985 *Tonight Show* performance. In 1993 he announced plans for an $18 million facility in Branson, Missouri, that would house fully-equipped televi-

Mel Tillis.

sion and recording studios. Completed the following year, the complex has become one of the resort community's most popular tourist attractions.

Tillis's own recording efforts have been minimal in recent years; the notable exception being an appearance on daughter Pam's highly successful *Sweetheart Dance* album.

Tillis, Pam

An independent mind and a free spirit are the characteristics that set Pam Tillis apart and give her a commanding place in contemporary country music. The daughter of the

famous country music songwriter, singer, actor, comedian Mel Tillis, Pam experienced the problems that often plague the children of celebrities. Some respond by becoming pale imitators of their celebrated parents; other recoil from the spotlight and accept obscurity, still others rebel and seek out other paths to success. Pam followed the third course; a troubled teenager with a face scarred from an automobile accident, she kept aloof from country music to explore alternative musical styles like disco and punk rock.

She didn't make much of a go of it, though, and finally gave in to the call of her family tradition and returned to Nashville. She became a session singer and a songwriter of extraordinary originality and verve, and her songs made hit records for such singers as Ricky Van Shelton and Highway 101. When she received a singing contract from Arista in 1990, she proved she had inherited her father's vocal ability after all: Her first album, *Put Yourself in My Place*, included the single 'Don't Tell Me What to Do,' which so perfectly expressed the spirited performer's attitude that it made number one on the charts almost at once and was nominated as the Single of the Year by the Country Music Association in 1991. The next year the CMA nominated her single 'Maybe It Was Memphis' for the same honor, and the singer was also nominated for the CMA's Horizon Award in both those years. A solidly established figure in contemporary music, Pam has woven all the styles with which she experimented in her rebellious years into a seamless fabric of country music.

Her stage shows and country videos reveal a spirited and uninhibited liveliness that happily infects all of her up-tempo songs.

Tillman, Floyd

A superb country songwriter and a unique stylist, Floyd Tillman was born in Ryan, Oklahoma, in 1914, and was raised across the Red River in Post, Texas. His early musical attraction was Western Swing and jazzy influences, and in 1935 he joined Adolf Hofner's band in San Antonio. Floyd also played with the Mark Clark Orchestra, and formed

Right: Mel's daughter, Pam Tillis.

Singer/songwriter Floyd Tillman.

the Blue Ridge Playboys with Pappy Selph, with whom he pioneered the innovative, jazz-influenced, lead role of the electric guitar.

The composer of more than 200 songs, Floyd Tillman has written hard honky-tonk, cheating and no-nonsense country lyrics, and has found great crossover appeal, with cover versions by some of the top pop singers in the field. Among his hits are 'Makes No Difference Now' (a song to whom he sold Jimmie Davis half the rights, and which was covered by Bing Crosby), 'I'll Keep On Lovin' You' (also recorded by pop singer Connie Boswell), 'Gotta Have My Baby Back' (on which Ella Fitzgerald had her own hit as well), and 'Slippin' 'Round' (a hit for Jimmy Wakely and Margaret Whit-

ing when Tillman's own label was afraid of the reaction to a song about cheating).

Floyd's other classics include 'I'll Never Slip Around Again,' 'I Love You So Much It Hurts' and 'This Cold War With You.' Floyd was the virtual originator of honky-tonk music; his songs were exceptionally popular, and his style of writing and singing were both very influential.

His writing displays his early interest in swing and jazz, with bluesy notes and minor-key shifts. Given his thematic preoccupations, it's a perfect matchup with traditional country sounds and instrumentation (even in the electric-guitar era of East Texas honky-tonk, Tillman records would utilize mandolins). Floyd's vocal style is at once audacious and engaging. His timing is casual, his phrasing lazy and his on-key per-

formance rates something around a C+. But Floyd is a stylist of the first rank, and his personalized lyrical slurring is an appealing component of his songs. Bing Crosby and Ella Fitzgerald could do versions of his outstanding songs, but the emotional, powerful tunes are still Floyd Tillman's.

Tippin, Aaron

Aaron Tippin comes across as a '90s type of guy – a body-building hunk; a sensitive, soft-spoken personality; and possessing a wealth of talent that he manages shrewdly in his career.

But as contemporary as he looks and sounds on songs like 'Read Between the Lines' and his video-paired 'There Ain't Nothin' Wrong With the Radio,' he also asserts at every opportunity his affinity with the older forms of country – farther back than rockabilly, to Jimmie Rodgers-era vocal techniques. In the manner of Larry Gatlin and Reba McEntire, Tippin uses his voice as an instrument, not so self-indulgently as to intrude on the lyrics.

Lyrics are important to Tippin, for he broke into the Nashville music business as a staff writer with Acuff-Rose Publishing. He also walked the trail that once guaranteed anonymity in country music but now often portends success – that of demo singer. Tippin would record versions of songs offered to big stars, sometimes sung in the style of certain established personalities, sometimes applying all his skills to showcase the song and its lyrics as best he could. Such a discipline forces an artist to meet every challenge in interpreting songs, provides him with a wealth of studio experience – and can get him noticed along Music Row.

Born in Pensacola, Florida, and reared in Greenville, South Carolina, Tippin followed the route of other New Country artists like Vince Gill and Ricky Skaggs by cutting his performance teeth on bluegrass as well as mainstream country. And, after considering a career in aviation, Tippin spent weekends driving from his home in Kentucky to Nashville scaring up work and contacts (following the route of another dedicated aspirant at the time, Billy Ray Cyrus, who traveled to Nashville every weekend from West Virginia).

Tippin's first single, for RCA, was the very successful 'You've Got to Stand for Something'; an acclaimed CD of the same name also marked Tippin as a star of the future. Indeed his subsequent CD releases have been notable hits: *Read Between the Lines; Call of the Wild*; and the introspective *Looking Back at Myself*. His video 'There Ain't Nothing Wrong With the Radio' was a major hit in sales and country video surveys.

Tippin has been touring to packed houses; much of the audience is com-

Aaron Tippin is also a body-builder.

posed of frantic female fans, who presumably are interested in, at least, his arms, a pair of massive hamhocks that are accentuated by Tippin's stage uniform of tight, short-sleeved T-shirts.

Tompall and the Glaser Brothers

The Glaser Brothers were all born in Spalding, Nebraska – Tompall in 1933; Charles, 1936; James, 1937 – and their rancher father Louis taught the boys to play guitar and sing. By the

late 1940s the trio of brothers had their own local television show, and in the mid-'50s appeared on TV's *Arthur Godfrey's Talent Scouts*, which led to their meeting Marty Robbins. Robbins signed them to record on his own label and sing backup on some of his records, notably on his *Gunfighter Ballads and Trail Songs* album wherein the Glasers sang Sons of the Pioneer-style harmonies.

As a trio, Tompall and the Glaser Brothers first recorded folk music, then country. They toured with Johnny Cash in the early 1960s, and joined the Grand Ole Opry in 1962. Among their hits as a group were 'She Loves the Love I Give Her,' 'Odds and End,' 'Baby, They're Playing Our Song' and 'The Last Thing On My Mind.' Their outstanding concept album *Award Winners* included an interpretation of 'Help Me Make It Through the Night' and a documentary tribute to Bob Wills via his theme 'Faded Love.'

Tompall and the Glasers specialized in tight, gentle, airy harmonies. Tompall sang lead; Jim, tenor; and Chuck, baritone. In the late 1960s and early 1970s they captured a host of vocal-group awards, and were cited as the *Record World* Group of the Previous Decade. They wrote songs for other singers and even became involved in record production and music publishing, with three companies under their aegis.

In 1972 the brothers split, with each maintaining an active role in country music. Tompall became a single act (scoring hits with 'Charlie' and 'Put Another Log on the Fire'), forming the Outlaw Band and being included on the *Wanted: The Outlaws* LP that proved a quantum leap in the careers of Willie Nelson and Waylon Jennings. Chuck became more involved in record production and other behind-the-scenes activity; he managed Kinky Friedman and the Texas Jewboys. He later suffered a stroke from which he was slow to recover motor functions.

The Brothers were back together again in 1978 and in 1981 scored a hit with a unique version of another Kristofferson song, 'Lovin' Her Was Easier Than Anything I'll Ever Do Again.' But two years later they had split again to pursue separate careers. In 1985 Jim had a stupendous hit with his single 'You're Getting To Me Again.'

Travis, Merle

Merle Travis is the name most closely associated with the country guitar in an industry where the guitar is as common as drinking water. He was born in Ebenezer, Kentucky, in 1917, where his father was a coal miner. Merle learned guitar from coal miner Mose Reger, who also taught Ike Everly, master picker and father to the Everly Brothers. The picking style that Merle developed includes a running bass played on the thumb, melody riffs with the higher fingers, syncopation and precise instrumental phrasing. With his style Travis influenced an entire generation of guitarists.

In 1935 Merle played with the Tennessee Tomcats, and two years later joined the seminal Georgia Wildcats

Merle Travis – a master picker.

of Clayton 'Pappy' McMichen. He joined the staff of the new *Boone County Jamboree* on WLW in Cincinnati, before it became the *Midwestern Hayride*. Among the co-stars were the Delmore Brothers and Grandpa Jones, and the four often teamed as the Brown's Ferry Four gospel quartet. It was on WLW, incidentally, that Chet Atkins heard Merle play, inspiring his own influential guitar style.

Merle joined the Drifting Pioneers and was featured on NBC's *Plantation Party*. After World War II he moved to California where he backed Tex Ritter, played on recording sessions and appeared on Cliffie Stone's *Hometown Jamboree*; he also played with Jimmy Wakely's band. Merle acted in several movies, including *From Here to Eternity*, wherein he played a guitar-picking sailor.

One of the pioneers of the electric

guitar, Merle also designed the first flat-guitar, the solid-body style that is now common, particularly in rock music. As a guitar virtuoso – although his love remained for country music – Merle experimented widely with musical styles. He played hillbilly, boogie, blues, pop, Tin Pan Alley, mountain, bluegrass, honky-tonk, Western Swing, Cajun and jazz, and, through Atkins, his sound can be cited as contributing to the Nashville Sound.

His many recorded hits included his own compositions of 'Sixteen Tons,' 'Sweet Temptation,' 'Divorce Me C.O.D.,' 'So Round, So Firm, So Fully Packed,' 'Dark as a Dungeon' and 'Smoke! Smoke! Smoke! (That Cigarette)' (co-written with Tex Williams). He performed definitive versions of 'Nine-Pound Hammer,' 'I Am a Pilgrim' and 'John Henry.' He also sang, with Eddie Kirk and Tennessee Ernie Ford, a superb cover of the Delmores, 'Blues Stay Away From Me.'

The versatile, essential Merle Travis was inducted into the Country Music Hall of Fame in 1977. In his past years he recorded duets with Chet Atkins, and many solo and combo efforts (with Joe Maphis and others) for the heritage-conscious CMH label. He died in Okalahoma in 1983.

Travis, Randy

An epitome of the history of 'new traditionalism,' Randy Travis's career dramatizes the rocky road the new form had to travel to gain acceptance. In his unwavering faith in the traditional sounds of country music, he has served the industry very well as both pioneer and prophet; and, like most prophets, he was for many years without honor in his own New Country.

Randy had a rough road of his own to travel. He was born Randy Traywick in North Carolina. His love for country music did nothing to keep him out of trouble, and he was in one scrape after another throughout his youth. At 17 he had reached a crossroads: looking at five years in the state penitentiary for breaking and entering, he won a talent contest sponsored by a Charlotte honkytonk called Country City USA. Lib Hatcher, the club's manager, was taken with the boy's promise and

talked the judge into releasing him into her care. She became his manager and, when her husband divorced her, his wife.

Her faith was not awarded for quite a while. They moved to Nashville and he worked in the kitchen of the Nashville Palace, a club she managed. In time he performed there, now billed as Randy Ray, and did a few records produced by singer Joe Stampley, but attracted little attention. He was going against the tide of pop, and his style was dismissed as out of date. But Randy never bowed to fashion; defiant in lifestyle, he was equally independent in music. He persevered in following the traditional sound of country music – his vocal stylings are of the Lefty Frizzell sound – and refused to bend to popular taste. Music City responded by ignoring both his demo tapes and his live performances.

But if the professional establishment was steadfast in closing its ears to the Randy Travis sound, there was a silent public that was getting ready for it. At last someone took a chance; although Warner Bros had turned him away before, a new producer

there named Kyle Lehning made an album of Travis songs. The appropriately named *Storms of Life* filled a need in the music market that no one knew existed. It was an unprecedented smash, the first debut album in country music history to go platinum, and it held the number one spot on the charts for a dozen consecutive weeks.

The industry couldn't do enough to make up to Randy for its previous neglect. He won numerous Grammies and every country music award there was, and he was made a member of the Grand Ole Opry. His second album, *Always and Forever*, did almost as well as his first, bringing him his second platinum and ranking number one for 10 months.

He was treated like an innovator when in fact the changes he introduced to country music were a return to its original sources. His dignifed demeanor, natural good looks, and classical country voice were in the great tradition. When the still youthful Randy Travis made the album *Heros and Friends*, a homage to the undying values of country music, he sang with a gallery of

Randy Travis – New Country superstar.

legendary veterans who recognized him as one of them, including Merle Haggard and George Jones. Other recent CDs have included *High Lonesome* and *Wind in the Wire*. Singles have included 'It's Just a Matter of Time' (a cover of the Brook Benton standard), 'I'd Do It All Again with You' and 'This Is Me.'

Trevino, Rick

A country piano player with the skill of Rick Trevino is a rare artist today, and in fact, going back to the marvelous Moon Mullican some 40 years ago, there haven't been all that many of them: Marty Robbins; cousins Jerry Lee Lewis and Mickey Gilley; Mike Reid; Ronny Milsap; Floyd Cramer – and you have it.

Handsome young Trevino, a third-generation Mexican-American, was born in Austin, Texas, and his first single and album were recorded in both Spanish and English. The Spanish album *Dos Mundos* was released on Sony Discos Records, went gold in Spain and was also popular in the American Southwest.

His first hit on Columbia was 'She Can't Say I Didn't Cry,' and was followed by 'Honky Tonk Crowd' and 'Doctor Time,' which quickly became Trevino's signature song.

Trevino's parents were both musicians and they taught him the value of hard work. Also gifted athletically, Trevino turned down a baseball scolarship to Memphis State University to concentrate on his music. His most recent single 'Just Enough Rope,' indicates that Trevino (who, as a country music Latino, follows in the footsteps of Johnny Rodriguez and Freddy Fender) will be a superstar.

Travis Tritt.

Tritt, Travis

James Travis Tritt, who dropped his first name for the evocative alliteration of the remaining two, began his career as a soloist with a church choir in his native Marietta, Georgia. A self-taught guitarist at 8 and a songwriter by 14, he formed his first musical attachment to such Southern rock stars as the Allman Brothers, Lynyrd Skynyrd, and the Marshall Tucker Band, but he experienced the impact of the traditional country music of such heroes as Merle Haggard and George Jones. He grew up in a home of working people and himself held blue-collar jobs, and he knew the pain of failed marriages that of his parents and two of his own. The two themes – labor and heartache – were to provide him with material for some of his most powerful and poignant music.

Travis sang in small clubs in Georgia until he was noticed by a Warner Bros representative, Danny Davenport. The connection was enough to get him started; it brought him a contract with Warner Bros, which tried to induce him to change his new first name to avoid confusion with their singer Randy Travis. Ken Kragen, who manages such stars as Kenny Rogers and who organized 'We Are the World' and 'Hands Across America,' became his manager.

The resurgence of traditionalism in country music had already begun by the time Travis made his debut album, *Country Club*, in 1990, so its New Country sound was nothing entirely new. With the promotion of Warner Bros, the skillful management of Kragen, and the high caliber of Travis's Southern rock and traditional country performances, it was no wonder that the album was a success, but few anticipated the success it attained, reaching the level of platinum in little more than a year. Fortunately, his second album's name, *It's All About to Change*, was no omen; Travis's share of the country music market did not change but if anything grew greater. The album climbed to the dizzy heights of double platinum, and four of its singles reached number one on the country charts. His third album, *t-r-o-u-b-l-e*, includes what has become a working-class anthem, 'Lord Have Mercy on the Working Man.' A model of traditional country music, it has a background chorus featuring George Jones, Tanya Tucker, Porter Wagoner, T. Graham Brown, Brooks and Dunn, and Little Texas. Travis's wry comments on a type of Southern preacher, 'Bible Belt,' became a part of the sound track of the 1992 film *My Cousin Vinny*; and his cover of an old Elvis Presley song, 'Burnin' Love,' was used in the James Caan movie *Honeymoon in Vegas*, made the same year.

Travis's music is appreciated by the country music community as well as by the general public. On one day in 1991, he performed Southern rock at Charlie Daniel's Volunteer Jam and that evening received the ultimate honor for the other element of his performance repertoire when

he joined an exclusive fraternity by becoming the youngest member of the Grand Ole Opry. The following year he received a nomination for the Country Music Association's Male Vocalist of the Year award. His song 'Here's a Quarter (Call Someone Who Cares)' received a nomination for Song of the Year, and he and Marty Stuart won the Vocal Event Award for their No Hats Tour. A versatile performer, Travis appeared with Kenny Rogers in the TV movie *Rio Diablo* the same year.

Travis Tritt never succumbed to the lure of the pop influence on country music when he formed his style, but remained squarely centered in the traditions of the un-adorned variety, and allowed the drive and vitality of rock 'n' roll to enter his sound. But if he stands slightly outside the 'new traditional-ist' group, his allegiance to the root values of country music is unwaver-ing. Recent single hits include 'Fool-ish Pride' and 'Outlaws Like Us,' and his newest CD is entitled *Ten Feet Tall and Bulletproof*.

Tubb, Ernest

One of the great personalities in country music, and for nearly two generations the quintessential country touring performer, Ernest Dale Tubb was born in Crisp, Texas, in 1914. After hearing 'T for Texas' he became hooked on Jimmie Rodgers almost to the point of obsession, and resolved to make music his life. He acquired his first guitar at age 20, and secured a spot on San Antonio radio; it was there he met Carrie Rodgers, the widow of Jimmie Rodgers. She encouraged Tubb by lending him one of the Singing Brakeman's guitars and arranging for his first recordings ('The Passing of Jimmie Rodgers' and 'Jimmie Rodgers' Last Thoughts'); she even managed his career for a while.

Tubb operated a dance hall and ran a beer distributorship before signing with Decca in 1939. He was sponsored by Universal Mills as a touring artist (taking a nickname after one of their flours: The Gold Chain Troubador) and was featured

Ernest Tubb.

on radio in Fort Worth. In 1941 Tubb kicked off a minor career in the movies, appearing in *Fighting Bucka-roo*; later he had a prominent role in *Ridin' West* and *Jamboree*.

It was in 1942 that Tubb entered the country superstar ranks with 'Walkin' the Floor Over You,' a self-penned song that has since become a standard and was covered by such pop artists as Bing Crosby. The next year he was invited to join the Grand Ole Opry, where he pioneered the use of electric instruments and showcased his classic honky-tonk string of hits: 'Slippin' Around,' 'Blue Christmas,' 'Goodnight Irene,' 'I Love You Because,' 'Half a Mind,' 'Thanks a Lot,' 'It's Been So Long, Darlin',' 'Mr and Mrs Used-to-Be,' 'I'll Always Be Glad to Take You Back,' 'Try Me One More Time,' 'Driving Nails in My Coffin' and 'Waltz Across Texas.' Through the years he sang duets with the Andrews Sisters, Red Foley and Loretta Lynn.

'ET,' as he was called, hosted a splendidly produced television program in the late 1950s (many of the segments were again broadcast in the mid-1980s) and for years hosted the *Ernest Tubb Record Shop Show* immediately after *Grand Ole Opry* WSM broadcasts on Saturday nights. The shop is a Nashville landmark, and the show, picked up live from a crowded portable stage in a corner of a shop, for years showcased new talent.

Showcasing new talent was one of Tubb's specialties. Many country music stars, including Jack Greene and Cal Smith, were alumni of his band, the Texas Troubadors; he also featured the cream of sidemen, such as Billy Byrd on steel guitar. His affection for fellow performers was matched by his devotion to his fans. As a road-show singer, Tubb became practically an institution. Even in his advanced years, he played perhaps 300 dates a year – saying hello, shaking hands, and singing his songs at high school gyms, small clubs, American Legion halls and open-air country stages. In a day when carefully manicured-and-packaged 'superstars' were signing agreements to play domed stadiums and Las Vegas showrooms and network television specials, ET stayed closer to his loyal fans than anyone.

Musically Tubb pioneered the sock-style of guitar, spit-out electric leads and riffs. It was an exigency of playing honky-tonks, where one had to be heard above crowd noise and compete with the blaring, amplified sound of juke boxes. His voice was rough and undisciplined in the extreme. Many contemporary fans are unfamiliar with his early work, where his voice was higher, sweeter and indeed cloer to Jimmie Rodgers. But much of his later recording contains an individual style that is no less (and perhaps more) attractive for all its inexact phrasing and missed notes. When you 'visited' ET through his music, you were not going to a mansion with polished marble floors and fancy drapery; you were in a log cabin – rough, homey and honest.

Ernest Tubb's last recorded work was the *Legend and Legacy* album on First Generation Records, wherein a host of singers joined duets with ET

Tanya Tucker began singing at 13.

out of pure affection and homage to a classic country singer, including Willie Nelson, Merle Haggard, Loretta Lynn, Vern Gosdin, Johnny Cash, Conway Twitty and others. He also joined Hank Williams Jr and Waylon Jennings in a song dedicated to ET and the 'slick' world's passing-by of the music and performing lifestyle he represented: 'Why Don't You Leave Them Boys Alone (Let Them Sing Their Songs).' Ernest Tubb was elected to the Country Music Hall of Fame in 1965. This country genius died in 1984.

Tucker, Tanya

A versatile singer equally at home in several modes, Tanya Tucker has had at least two distinct careers in her short but rich professional life. A native of Seminole, Texas, she was encouraged by her parents to go into music. Her mother, Delores Taylor, was herself in the industry – she wrote songs for Elvis Presley and discovered Johnny Rivers – and sent Tanya to Columbia/Epic Records executive Billy Sherrill at 13. By the time the talented youngster was 16 she had recorded five albums that placed in the Top Ten.

Tanya was at the cutting edge from the beginning, her precociously sensuous voice rendering lyrics considered *risqué* even for adults when she was still an adolescent. In 1972 she made the charts with 'Delta Dawn,' whose lyrics by Alex Harvey and Jerry Collins were, in those pristine days, considered scandalous. The next year the equally suggestive Curly Putman song 'Blood Red and Going Down,' a crossover country-and-Western and pop tune, added to her reputation, as did 'What's Your Mama's Name, Child?' Other Columbia releases of the time included the provocative 1974 'Would You Lay With Me (in a Field of Stone)?' with music and lyrics by David Allen Coe, and 'The Man That Turned My Mama On.'

She strayed increasingly from her country music roots in the late 1970s, but her career as a rock singer failed to gel. By the beginning of the next decade she was almost broke, and her personal life was also beginning to crumble. She became a regular figure in the tabloid press, with several failed relationships including a broken engagement to Glen Camp-

Tucker is still winning awards after over 25 years of performing.

bell, until finally she dropped from the scene.

After a few years of relative silence, Tanya returned to music in 1986 to record for Capitol (later renamed Liberty) Records. Restored to vitality, she was also renewed in her devotion to country music. She had never abandoned the form completely, since country songs often backed up even her rock numbers, and through the 1970s she had made such pure country songs as 'San Antonio Stroll,' 'Don't Believe My Heart Can Stand Another You,' 'A Cowboy-Lovin' Night,' 'Pecos Promenade,' and 'Texas (When I Die).' In 1987 she had a real country hit with the album *Love Me Like You Used To* for Capitol, and she seemed to be back on track. Her return to her country roots was not completely smooth – in 1988 the tabloids reported her entering the Betty Ford Clinic for alcoholism and cocaine dependency – but she bounced back stronger than ever when, that same year, 'I Won't Take Less Than Your Love,' with words and music by Paul Overstreet and Don Schlitz and recorded with Overstreet and Paul Davis, reached number one on the country charts. Her return to country has been applauded by the public and the industry. The CMA nominated her for three consecutive years as Top Female Vocalist and selected her in 1991.

Twitty, Conway

Born Harold Lloyd Jenkins in Friars Point, Mississippi, in 1933, Conway Twitty was the son of a Mississippi River pilot; he learned the guitar at age five and formed a band, the Phillips County Ramblers, at 10, and soon thereafter had his own radio show in Helena, Arkansas. While in high school he considered the ministry as a profession, and was also attracted by baseball, earning a contract offer from the Philadelphia Phillies organization.

In the army he formed a rock 'n' roll band (The Cimarrons), and in the mid-1950s recorded some rock sides for Sun Records under the name Harold Jenkins and the Rockhousers (these were released only in 1970). But then he was signed by MGM and was packaged for Canadian promotion in an attempt to become a north-of-the-border Elvis Presley. For this role he took the name Conway Twitty after two towns, Conway, Arkansas, and Twitty, Texas; it served to attract the intended attention. The lead character in the Broadway play *Bye, Bye Birdie* went into the army like Elvis but had a name like Conway's – Conrad Birdie.

Conway's talent on its own assured his prominence the next year. He composed a hit, 'It's Only Make-Believe,' which has become a rockabilly standard. He cut more hits and ultimately was to appear in six movies including *Sex Kittens Go To College*. During his rock period, Conway also wrote songs for others, including 'Walk Me to the Door,' a 1960 hit for Ray Price.

This proved where Conway's musical affections were, and when the country portion of rockabilly became commercially obsolete by the mid-1960s, he returned to country music. In 1965 he cut country songs for Decca and by the next year had his own syndicated country TV program. Immediately after the transformation he was accepted by country fans. His image – duck-tailed haircut, sensual album art, a working-class identification - fit perfectly with his material's blend of honky-tonk lyrics, raw baritone and hard country instrumentation. Among his many hits are 'Next in Line,' 'To See an Angel Cry,' 'I Won-

der What She'll Think About Me Leaving,' 'Hello Darlin',' 'Fifteen Years Ago,' 'You've Never Been This Far Before,' 'She Needs Someone to Hold Her,' 'Lost Her Love (On Our Last Date),' a vocal version of Floyd Cramer's classic instrumental), 'After the Good Is Gone,' Linda on My Mind' and 'Lost in the Feeling.'

In 1971 Conway paired with Loretta Lynn in one of the classic country matchups of all time. Their personalities, images, voices and styles melded perfectly; the pair won many duet awards and continued to perform and record together. They also co-owned a talent agency in Nashville. Among their many duo successes have been: 'After the Fire is Gone,' 'Louisiana Woman, Mississippi Man,' 'As Soon As I Hang Up the Phone,' 'We Only Make Believe,' and 'Can't Love You Enough.'

Conway Twitty's patented growl and soulful whines are the latter-day country equivalents of Elvis Presley's gyrations, at least in audience impact. To these factors he added an almost mysterious silent image on stage – only his sidemen talked and announced between songs – adding a macho image that served him well in country music. Most of his best songs reflect a classic cycle of a man who is weak/sensitive/guilty/contrite, also a sure-fire country format.

In public, Twitty was very accessible to his fans, reciprocating their devotion. He busied himself with many sidelines, including ownership of the Nashville Sounds baseball team and Twitty City theme park.

Twitty has the most number one songs in country music history.

Conway Twitty in the early days.

Perhaps the most significant fact about Twitty's career is that he had more number one records than any artist in *any* style. (Trivia buffs are often astonished to learn that this includes The Beatles, Frank Sinatra and Elvis Presley.)

Country lost 'the best friend a song ever had' in June 1993. Conway became ill during the bus ride home after a performance at Branson's Jim Stafford Theater. He was taken to the nearest hospital (outside Springfield, Missouri) where, in an ironic twist, Loretta Lynn was visiting husband Mooney, then recovering from heart surgery. Twitty underwent surgery to repair a ruptured blood vessel in his abdomen, but died of heart failure several hours later. The sense of loss shared by all country music fans and artists was summed up by Reba McEntire: 'Conway was the type of person everybody felt they were closest friends with. He always had time for you and was never uppity.'

Tyler, T Texas

The colorful and popular Western singer T Texas Tyler was born David Luke Myrick in 1916 near Mena, Arizona. He was raised in Texas, educated in Philadelphia, and broke into the music business by entering the *Major Bowes Amateur Hour* on radio in the 1930s.

In 1942 Tyler became a member of the Shreveport, Louisiana, *Hayride* on KWKH, and later moved to California, where he cut hit records like 'Bumming Around,' 'Courting in the Rain,' 'Remember Me' and 'Makes No Difference Now.' He wrote the classic recitation 'Deck of Cards' that has become a standard country/gospel number and a hit for many artists through the years, including Tex Ritter, Tex Williams and Wink Martindale.

In the late 1940s, when the genre was in decline, Tyler became a singing cowboy in Hollywood Westerns, starring in movies like Columbia's *Horseman of the Sierras*; later he appeared on television as an actor. T Texas Tyler became a born-again Christian in his later years and resolved to write and perform only gospel music, with which he also enjoyed a fairly considerable following. T Texas Tyler died on January 28, 1972.

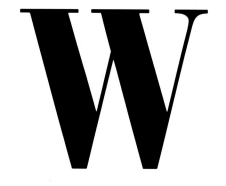

Wagoner, Porter

Called 'The Kid from West Plains' at the beginning of his career, Porter Wagoner has recently been referred to as 'The Last of the Hillbillies.' Indeed his style and repertoire represent a rich country tradition. He was born in West Plains, Missouri, in 1930 and began his career as an outgrowth of playing the guitar during odd moments during his butcher-shop job. He wound up on a radio show singing his songs and plugging the butcher shop.

Porter moved to KWTO in Springfield in 1951 for radio work, and when the station's television affiliate debuted Red Foley's *Ozark Jubilee*, Wagoner became an early regular. The same year he signed a record contract with RCA. It was five years, however, before he had a hit, when 'Satisfied Mind' established his credentials as a fan favorite and a talent of major proportions. He followed with 'What would You Do If Jesus Came to Your House,' and he joined the Grand Ole Opry in 1957.

In 1960 Porter inaugurated a syndicated television show. It featured Norma Jean (Beasler), the Wagonmasters, comedian Speck Rhodes, Buck Trent and Mack MaGaha. The program became one of the most popular shows in the history of television syndication, especially after Dolly Parton succeeded Norma Jean in 1967.

Porter's hit records continued, and through the years have included 'Your Old Love Letters,' 'Cold, Dark Waters Below,' 'Y'All Come,' 'Cold, Hard Facts of Life,' 'Green, Green Grass Of Home' (it was Porter who introduced this country standard), 'Skid Row Joe,' 'Carroll County Accident' and 'Big Wind.' He sang many duets with Norma Jean, Skeeter Davis, and Dolly Parton, as well as

award-winning gospel albums with the Blackwood Brothers. The duets with Parton were remarkable productions of superb material and performances. Their hits included: 'Tomorrow Is Forever,' 'Just Someone I Used to Know,' 'Run That By Me One More Time,' 'Daddy Was an Old-Time Preacher Man,' 'Burning the Midnight Oil,' and 'Please Don't Stop Loving Me.' Their harmonies were some of the most unique in country music, marked by Porter singing harmony to Dolly's lead, an unusual mode; his smooth baritone with her brittle soprano, and his reserved singing with her piercing vocals, did not clash but rather combined in a complementary way.

In 1974 the pair split, first keeping a professional association, but then effecting a total, litigation-wrought, and evidently ugly separation (neither party has expounded on details). Porter continued as a single, but has since been dropped from the RCA catalog, depriving country fans of a body of work that is excellent and rich in tradition and interpretation. He then hosted a popular daily show on the Nashville Network, and his backup included an all-girl country band, The Right Combination. His albums have been produced by the innovative maverick Snuff Garrett.

Porter's 'hillbilly' image no doubt was advanced by his uptown-Saturday-night dress of sequined suits and a bleached pompadour he once sported, but also the country boy in Porter never compromised with styles or material, and in so doing he cut a wide country path that was individualistic and memorable. He sang his share of mainstream country songs, but was at his best with heartache, tragedy and story songs that became some of his trademarks. 'Green, Green Grass of Home' was of course the most commercial of these, but 'Carroll County Accident,' for instance, is squarely in the tradition of the classic 'Wreck on the Highway,' and is part of the long, fine tradition going back to English saga songs through Victorian sentimental ballads. In so choosing his material Porter was both an inheritor and a benefactor of a significant type of country song. Since Roy Acuff died, Porter has become the Grand Old Man of the Grand Old Opry. He is a frequent host on *Opry Backstage*.

Wakely, Jimmy

Jimmy Wakely, a singing cowboy who was once voted the most popular movie cowboy after Gene Autry, Roy Rogers and Charles Starrett, was born James Clarence Wakely in Mineola, Arkansas, in 1914, and raised in a log cabin near Battiest, Oklahoma. In 1937 Wakely formed the Jimmy Wakely Trio with Johnny Bond and Scotty Harrell. Gene Autry, guesting on the local radio ranch, heard the Trio and invited them to Hollywood to join his *Melody Ranch* radio show. In 1940 the Trio joined Autry as an ensemble and part of his larger tour package.

Wakely later left Autry to form his own band, which included Spade Cooley, Merle Travis, Tex Williams, Cliffie Stone and Wesley Tuttle, all of whom went on to great success in country music. In 1942 Wakely dissolved his band in order to concentrate on his movie career. He was getting bit parts in cowboy films, and by 1945 was starring in singing West-

erns as the Melody Kid; in all, Wakely appeared in more than 70 movies, starring in more than 30. He left the screen in 1949, when the singing-cowboy genre was fading.

Between 1953 and '58 Wakely hosted a CBS radio network program of Western Swing, pop and jazz, the transcriptions of which have preserved some fine Western Swing performances. In 1961 Wakely and Tex Ritter co-hosted a country music television program.

Among Wakely's many hits are 'Slippin' 'Round' (one of several duets he sang with pop star Margaret Whiting), 'Too Late,' 'One Has My Name, The Other Has My Heart,' 'Wedding Bells,' 'I Love You So Much It Hurts' and 'Let's Go to Church Next Sunday Morning.' Jimmy Wakely specialized in honky-tonk songs, but sang with a crooner's voice – often called a country Bing Crosby – which obviously contributed to his widespread appeal on records, as well as on the screen and on radio.

Walker, Jerry Jeff

Jerry Jeff Walker was not born in the rural South, like most New Country musicians, and didn't cut his musical teeth on country, honky-tonk, bluegrass, or Western Swing. He began life in 1942 as Ronald Clyde Crosby in Oneonta, New York, and found inspiration in the music of such folk singers as Pete Seeger and Woody Guthrie. In his teens he built a repertoire of traditional folk ballads and started singing at school events and in coffeehouses. When he graduated from high school, he became a traveling minstrel, singing in clubs and on street corners for change, mostly in the West and Southwest. In the early 1960s he began adding his own material to his performance list, and his act crystallized enough for him to schedule engagements in advance. In 1966 he took the downhome-sounding name of Jerry Jeff Walker.

By now singing a blend of folk and

Jimmy Wakely (far right).

4804-45

rock, Jerry Jeff organized a five-piece band called the Lost Sea Dreamers in 1966. He brought it to New York City to look for recording opportunities and, when the group found a place at the Electric Circus in Manhattan, changed its name to Circus Maximus. Its first album, issued by Vanguard in 1967, was *Circus Maximus*. It did fairly well and so did the group, which developed a sizable following among New York rock fans. When artistic differences broke the group up in 1968, Walker went on his own again.

That year he recorded 'Mr Bojangles,' a song about an old street dancer he had met in 1965 in a New Orleans jail. The song has become a classic, sung by performers of every stripe and selling more than a million copies for several artists, including Harry Nilsson and the Nitty Gritty Dirt Band, though not for Walker himself.

During the early 1970s Walker performed and recorded extensively, in New York, at the Newport Folk Festival, and in the West, before finding his way to Austin, the Texas city that complements Nashville as a center for original country music. Walker found it a favorable site for his creative gifts. An unusually sophisticated and versatile composer/singer/guitarist, he brought to the Austin scene a more than average depth and breadth of musical experience, spanning country, rock, and folk, which energized the Texas traditionalists. From 1972 to 1982 he recorded many successful albums for MCA and Elektra/Asylum. Restless and innovative, he and his Lost Gonzo Band or the Bandito Band have explored a wide range of styles, raucous and gentle, and reached an enthusiastic audience with such hits as 'Viva Terlingua,' 'A Man Must Carry On,' 'Too Old to Change,' and 'Cowjazz.' His recording of Gary P. Nunn's 'London Homesick Blues' became the theme song for the syndicated TV concert series 'Austin City Limits,' the national voice of that musical city and a frequent concert venue for Jerry Jeff. He also hosted the Nashville Network show *The Texas Connection*.

Jerry Jeff and his wife Susan started their own record label in 1986 to present his music and that of people he finds promising, such as Chris Wall. Tried & True Music,

whose inventive releases are sometimes rather more experimental than tried but seldom fail to be true, has produced songs like 'Pickup Truck Song,' 'I Feel Like Hank Williams Tonight,' 'Time To Stay Home,' and 'Night Rider's Lament.' His 1992 album *Hill Country Rain* was a carefully controlled studio production, but most successful recordings are made at concerts or at sessions in Jerry Jeff's den, preserving the wild freedom and spontaneity that are the hallmarks of a Walker performance.

Wariner, Steve

A singer who hit the charts singing a ubiquitous form of country pop but who went on to pioneer new types of expression, Steve Wariner was born on Christmas Day of 1954 in Noblesville, Indiana. He began his career in country music as a band member in the Bob Luman and Dottie West shows, and his idol was Chet Atkins, under whom he later recorded at RCA.

Like Atkins, Wariner is an accomplished guitar player, but it was as a vocalist that he gained a foothold in Nashville. He has a mellow country voice reminiscent of Glen Campbell's; in fact, the two sang a duet on 1987's 'The Hand That Rocks the Cradle,' which revived Campbell's career and advanced Wariner's. Among his growing string of top hits are 'All Roads Lead to You,' 'Life's Highway,' 'Starting Over,' 'Some Fools Never Learn,' 'You Can Dream of Me,' 'The Weekend,' and 'Smalltown Girl.'

Perhaps Wariner's main claim to prominence in the late 1980s, however, is what rock critic Ken Tucker has recognized as his stature in the tradition of 'singer-songwriter,' so prevalent in soft-rock music of the late 1960s and early 1970s. Wariner has written many of his own songs, and the lyrical balladeer is best with gentle story-songs and odes to relationships. Even Jimmy Webb – one of the symbols of that movement of the recent past whose adherents have moved into country music – has written songs for Wariner.

Steve Wariner.

Watson, Gene

Born in Palestine, Texas, in 1943, Gene Watson was raised by a family that mixed equal doses of religion and music. He first sang professionally at age 13, and cut a record that was released locally when he was 18. For a time Gene followed a regimen of auto-body work during the day and local club singing at night.

Eventually he gained enough repute to tour with the Wilburn Brothers and appear at the Dynasty Club in Houston. He continued to record for local labels, and in 1975, one of his records so impressed Capitol Records, that they arranged to distribute it nationally: 'Love in a Hot Afternoon,' which immediately made Gene Watson a star. It was a song full of images and evocation, an almost dreamlike account of a steamy affair. Watson's voice, nicely showcased in 'Hot Afternoon,' is a higher and smoother version of the Frizzell/Haggard type of singing.

His other hits included: 'Where Love Begins,' 'You Could Know As Much About a Stranger,' 'Paper Rosie,' 'The Old Man and His Horn,' 'Pick the Wildwood Flower,' 'No One Will Ever Know,' 'Sometimes I Get Lucky and Forget,' 'Fourteen-Carat Mind,' 'Old Loves Never Die' and 'Speak Softly.' His band is named the Farewell Party Band after another hit, and the ensemble performs a handsome, modern honky-tonk sound featuring twin fiddles, steel and piano.

In all, Gene Watson is one of the freshest – and most refreshing – of a small group of traditional voices keeping the flames of love ballads, story songs and honky-tonk alive in country.

Wells, Kitty

'The Queen of Country Music' still reigns after more than 40 years of holding that title. Through the years many have eclipsed her sales and renown, but it was Kitty Wells who changed the profile of the country music business, and for that reason if no other, she will always be remembered as a ground-breaker. Patsy Montana had a million-selling record before Kitty Wells's hits, but it can truly be said that only after Kitty came the deluge of female singers and widespread acceptance.

She was born Muriel Deason in Nashville in 1919. She grew up singing in church, and played the guitar at age 14; soon she was playing dances and local radio dates. In 1938 she married Johnny Wright, and soon thereafter established the Johnny and Jack duo with Jack Anglin. She toured with the group, including the backup Tennessee Boys, and occasionally sang solos on stage, usually gospel numbers. Her husband gave her the stage name of Kitty Wells, from the old Carter Family song 'Sweet Kitty Wells.'

The group secured a spot on the *Mid-Day Merry-Go-Round* in Knoxville and became early stars of the new *Louisiana Hayride* in Shreveport. Kitty recorded some sides for RCA in the late 1940s, but it was a recording for Decca in 1952 that changed her career and opened country music to

Jerry Jeff Walker.

female soloists – 'It Wasn't God Who Made Honky Tonk Angels,' an 'answer song' to Hank Thompson's 'Wild Side of Life.' The single became the first number one by a female country singer since chart-posting was instituted, and led to an immediate offer of membership on the Grand Ole Opry, an association that continued for 15 years.

Kitty has recorded duets with Red Foley, Roy Drusky, Roy Acuff, Webb Pierce and, of course, Johnny Wright. Her hits have included 'One by One' (a duet with Red Foley that remained at the top of the record lists for 26 weeks), 'Dust on the Bible,' 'I'm Paying for that Back Street Affair,' 'Cheatin's a Sin,' 'Searching,' 'Making Believe,' 'Heartbreak USA' and 'Unloved, Unwanted.' In the

1970s, foreshadowing the country-rock crossover movement, she recorded a rather bizarre effort of 'Forever Young.'

Wells's country voice is in the Southeast tradition – brittle, un-adorned, nasal, plaintive and honest. The listener is compelled to wonder why she sings except to pour her heart out; Kitty Wells during her career sang of heartbreak, drinking, cheating and loneliness, but main-tained her sisterly (or at least house-wifey) image, alternately a country ideal and prototype. Kitty Wells was elected to the Country Music Hall of Fame in 1976.

White, Lari

Another of the fine young country singers who writes virtually all her own material, Lari White grew up in west central Florida singing with her parents and a younger brother and sister as The White Family Singers.

From the time Lari was four she performed in churches, community centers and at festivals, traveling with her family in a station-wagon. The traveling ceased when she hit her 'rebellious rock 'n' roll teens,' as she put it. But the music continued.

Lari sang in a band and performed at talent shows during high school and won a full academic scholarship to the University of Miami, where she majored in music engineering and minored in voice.

At night she sang in top-40, jazz and big-band clubs and by day she performed jingles and background vocals. She sang backup on many of the Latin projects recorded in Florida, ranging from salsa sessions to a Julio Iglesias record to a Toyota commercial.

She began writing her own songs, and her career made a quantum leap when she competed in and won the Nashville Network's You Can Be a Star program. An RCA contract fol-lowed. Her CD, *Wishes*, was a smash hit, produced by one of Nashville's solid, Midas-touch studio hands, Garth Fundis.

Whites, The

The Whites are down-home refresh-ment. Their music and their stage presence is refreshing, and so is their

Kitty Wells.

success – an affirmation that tradi-tional harmonies and unamplified music still have audiences in country music.

Buck White, mandolin, piano and vocals, was born in Oklahoma and raised in Texas. As a teen he played barn dances, and while in high school in Abilene, he formed a group that performed as local favorites on radio. Eventually Buck played piano in the Tommy Duncan Swing Band after the latter split from Bob Wills. In 1962 Buck formed the Down Home Folks with his wife Pat and their daughters Sharon and Cheryl. The group was notable in several re-spects. It was a bluegrass ensemble, not out of Buck's primary back-ground; it featured female singers, a rarity in bluegrass, and it pioneered the progressive bluegrass modes of incorporating swing and jazz ele-ments.

In 1973 Pat dropped out (another daughter, Rosanna, has since joined) and the group, now called Buck White and the Down Home Folks, began touring in earnest. In 1975 they met Emmylou Harris, begin-ning a relationship whose sharing of

musical styles led to Sharon Hicks (she had married the band's talented sideman Jack Hicks) and Cheryl singing harmony on Emmylou's landmark album *Blue Kentucky Girl*. The Whites frequently opened road shows for Emmylou thereafter. An acquaintance was renewed with Ricky Skaggs, who fronted Emmy-lou's award-winning Hot Band (the Whites had played with Skaggs on albums and worked with him going back to his apprenticeship with Ralph Stanley); Sharon, who had divorced Hicks, married Skaggs in 1981.

The hit records of the Whites have included: 'More Pretty Girls Than One,' 'Kentucky Waltz,' 'Poor Folks' Pleasure,' 'You Put the Blue in Me,' 'Give Me Back That Old Familiar Feeling' and 'Hangin' Around.' In 1984 the Whites became members of the Grand Ole Opry.

Buck White's superb musicianship – he has hosted world mandolin championships in Kerrville, Texas – is complemented by the sophisti-cated harmonies of his daughters. As

The Whites.

often as not, one of the girls sings lead and he will sing harmony or just pick or play piano. The Whites have a broad background and eclectic taste; they are likely to perform swing, bluegrass or uptown country music, but always in a modified mountain string-band package.

Whitman, Slim

Slim Whitman has become a legend, an American original. In spite of himself and his modest ways, he has grown larger than life and in a sense is as much a symbol as he is a singer.

To those who will never like country music, he is the embodiment of country cliches like sequined outfits and unorthodox vocal stylings. To hardcore country traditionalists, he represents an individual who sings to please himself, the fans he respects and the traditions he reveres. And to modish country radio program directors, he is anathema. He can sell two million albums in six months via television commercials, yet they steadfastly refuse to playlist his oldtime, sentimental and yodeling country records.

The talented, reserved eye of this hurricane was born Ottis Dewey Whitman Jr in Tampa, Florida, in 1924. Like many other future country singers, Slim aspired to a career in baseball, but forsook the big-league offers to take a manual labor job in order to marry. Later he joined the Navy, where he learned to play the guitar and entertain. After discharge, in 1946, he juggled a semipro ball contract and local performances in Florida country music clubs.

In 1949, at the suggestion of Colonel Tom Parker (manager of Eddy Arnold and, later, Hank Snow and Elvis Presley), Whitman recorded for RCA; a single, 'Casting My Lasso to the Sky,' was a hit, and Slim was offered a staff position on the *Louisiana Hayride*. In 1952 he scored perhaps his biggest hit with 'Indian Love Call,' and among his other major successes – which followed in rapid order – were 'Bandera Waltz,' 'Secret Love,' 'Rose Marie,' 'Cattle Call,' 'Beautiful Dreamer,' 'I Remember You' and 'That Silver-Haired Daddy of Mine.' The sources of his hits were taken in equal part from cowboy ballads, traditional country music, sentimental ballads going back to Stephen Foster, and

light-opera and Tin Pan Alley show tunes.

In 1955 Whitman was a member of the Grand Ole Opry, but heavy touring commitments caused him to sacrifice the relationship. Slim Whitman has toured extensively overseas too, including England, where he became a star of major proportions. He was the first hillbilly act to play the London Palladium, and has achieved record-breaking tours and hits, including a recording that was number one immediately upon its release. One record, 'Rose Marie,' maintained a number-one position on British charts (11 weeks) longer than anyone else, including The Beatles.

All of which makes the absence of Slim Whitman on the airwaves of American country radio confounding. There is a large cult around him that has developed through the years – 'Whitmania,' it has been dubbed – and the promotional albums, many produced by Pete Drake, have had phenomenal sales; one estimate claims 50 million albums sold worldwide since 1980.

There is no doubt that Whitman's dress, his pencil-thin moustache and his patented falsetto break that seems to have a mind of its own, contribute to a reluctant reception. But just as off-putting must be his repertoire of old-time sentimental songs and his refusal to record cheating, drinking, honky-tonk or even novelty songs.

Slim Whitman's voice is as sweet as his material. Squarely in tradition of the great yodelers of yesteryear – and probably the last great practitioner of that dying craft – he is of a select group that includes Jimmie Rodgers, Elton Britt, Montana Slim, Patsy Montana and Kenny Roberts. It comes not only in virtuoso displays of clear, pyrotechnic Swiss yodels, but in falsetto breaks that occur in the middle of phrases, words and even syllables.

Wilburn Brothers, The

Virgil Doyle and Thurman Theodore (better known as Doyle and Teddy) Wilburn were born in Thayer, Missouri, in 1930 and 1931, respectively, and raised on a farm in Hardy, Arkansas. Music was a large part of

the Wilburn life, and the boys joined a gospel and old-time family ensemble that rose from singing on street corners to the Grand Ole Opry. When they performed together, Doyle and Teddy formed one of the last of the tradition-based brother harmony acts, and they made their debut in 1938. Two years later they guested on the *Opry* with Roy Acuff, and the family – featuring the 'Singing Wilburn Children' – and were briefly regular staff members. Child-labor regulations, however, terminated the arrangement.

After the Korean War, Doyle and Teddy regrouped and were once again *Opry* regulars; they also toured in package shows with Faron Young and Webb Pierce, and in the mid-1950s started cutting hit records. Among their hits were: 'Go Away With Me,' 'Which One is to Blame?' 'A Woman's Institution,' 'Trouble's Back in Town,' 'Hurt Her One For Me' and 'Roll Muddy River.' The Wilburn Brothers generally maintained the sound of traditional harmonies, but in recordings, more than on stage, the duo veered toward pop flavorings.

The Wilburns were long active as Nashville businessmen, too, managing a successful music publishing business and a talent agency that handled Loretta Lynn (whose career they assisted in her early years) and many other superstars. For years they hosted one of the pioneer syndicated country music television programs. Doyle died on October 16, 1982, but Teddy remained active as a *Grand Ole Opry* regular.

Williams, Don

Don Williams is his own kind of outlaw. In a time when the profile of a typical country singer includes pop-oriented arrangements and rock-derived beats, he has returned to palatable acoustical instruments and gentle love lyrics.

He was born near Floydada, Texas, in 1939, and had his first professional musical work after a hitch in the Army, forming a duo called the Strangers Two. Between 1964 and 1974 he led the folk/soft-rock ensemble The Pozo Seco Singers. He retired to Texas to manage a furniture business thereafter, reportedly

Don Williams – the Gentle Giant.

Don often sings gentle love lyrics.

disenchanted with the hard turn popular musical sounds were taking, but by 1973 he was in Nashville recording country music. He was in very capable hands: those of Jack Clement, legendary studio wizard; and Allen Reynolds, composer and producer, already pioneering a softer country sound with Crystal Gayle. Williams's natural inclinations were of the same kind. His style is simple, unpretentious and totally reassuring – a deep, relaxed baritone. His choice of repertoire was similarly gentle, comfortable, sincere. And it was almost immediately popular.

His first major country record was 'The Shelter of Your Eyes,' and its loping, shuffle-beat and dobro sound set the Williams style from the start. His other major records include 'We Should Be Together,' 'Come Early Morning,' 'I Wouldn't Want to Live If You Didn't Love Me,' 'Amanda,' 'She's in Love with a Rodeo Man,' 'I Recall a Gypsy Woman,' 'The Ties That Bind,' 'Love Me Tonight,' 'Tulsa Time,' 'Some Broken Hearts Never Mend' and 'Till the Rivers All Run Dry.' His patented backup includes an acoustic guitar, dobro, a walking-beat on soft or brushed drums and, sometimes, electric keyboards. Combined with his laid-back, deep vocals, the country listener is comfortable even when pop or rock elements are introduced.

Known as The Gentle Giant, Williams played in the Burt Reynolds movie *W W And The Dixie Dance Kings*. He's been wildly popular in England for many years and toured that country extensively. At the close of the 1980s Williams declared he was retiring from the road, and shortly thereafter said the same of recording. While he's been absent from the radio charts since then, he once again maintains a road band and plays 40 to 50 dates a year. The wholesome material he chose to record was known to mirror his personal modesty and religious beliefs.

Williams, Hank

Hank Williams has become a symbol, and his career a virtual icon in country music. He lived a lifetime in a few short years; he was touched by genius and was a man of the common people; he dreamed of pleasures and love, but sang of bitterness and sorrow. Hank lived a virtual Greek tragedy, because his too-early death, unlike that of Jimmie Rodgers, was all but self-inflicted. And his music is the truest, most honest, gut-wrenching, familiar, lonely, friendly, grief-filled, religious, carnal and straight-out plaintive music produced by any singer/ songwriter before or since in America.

He was born Hiram King Williams in Georgiana, Alabama, in 1923. Hank sang in his church choir at six, and learned the guitar the following year. He soon won $15 in a Montgomery talent contest, singing his own 'WPA Blues.' And at 13 he

Hank Williams – a country music icon.

formed a band, the Drifting Cowboys, with whom he was to play on local radio sporadically for 10 years.

When Hank was 17 he traveled to Texas to become a cowboy, but once drank too much and let a bronc throw him; the resultant back injury plagued him all his life. In 1944 he married his girlfriend Audrey at a gas station. He had met the tempestuous girl the year before at a medicine show, and many of Hank's later songs were thinly veiled chronicles of their love/hate relationship. Audrey drove Hank with a consuming ambition, for herself as well as for him, and she was the cause of both heartache songs and his inspiration to continue in country music.

In 1946 Hank signed with Sterling Records, and was introduced to Molly O'Day, who became the first artist to record Hank Williams songs. She encouraged his gospel writing – at which he was a master of lyrics and melody – and was a mentor. The legendary recording executive Fred Rose also took Hank under his wing, becoming his manager, and reportedly polishing many of his compositions. In 1946 Rose arranged a contract with the new MGM label for Hank, and the first release, 'Move It On Over,' was a moderate success.

Hank was signed to the *Louisiana Hayride*, but when he performed 'Lovesick Blues' on the *Grand Ole Opry* in 1949 – resulting in six demand encores – he became a major country star. In spite of reservations about his drinking problems, the Opry invited him to join the cast in Nashville, and for the next several years Hank Williams dominated both music charts and country music consciousness. Stars in all fields rushed to record his songs, and country singers adapted their vocal stylings to sound more like Hank.

Among his songs are 'My Bucket's Got a Hole In It,' 'Wedding Bells,' 'Long Gone Lonesome Blues,' 'Moaning the Blues,' 'Why Don't You Love Me?,' 'I Can't Help It If I'm Still in Love With You,' 'Cold, Cold, Heart,' 'Kaw-Liga,' 'Jambalaya,' 'Your Cheatin' Heart,' 'Hey, Good Lookin',' 'Honky Tonkin',' 'Settin' the Woods on Fire,' 'Take These Chains From My Heart,' 'House of Gold' and the gospel standard, 'I Saw the Light.'

For all the success, Hank's personal life was in a shambles. His drinking and pill-taking resulted in many missed dates. The Opry suspended him and Audrey divorced him (he married a teenager, Billie Jean Jones, in several public ceremonies soon thereafter). Finally, on New Year's Day of 1953, in the back seat of his Cadillac en route between Oak Hill, West Virginia, and a performing date in Canton, Ohio, the 29-year-old Hank Williams died. Ironically, at the time his exhausted, tortured life came to an end, his charted record was 'I'll Never Get Out of this World Alive.'

A funeral service was held in Montgomery, attended by 20,000 mourners. Ernest Tubb sang 'Close to the Lord,' Red Foley sang 'Peace in the Valley' and Roy Acuff sang 'I Saw the Light.'

Hank's singing was as mournful as his lyrics and, like Jimmie Rodgers, he employed a yodel as a blues device. In fact Hank choked and whined through his heartache songs, emoting almost more than singing. To listeners, the records of Hank Williams almost became vicarious glimpses into his tortured life and restless soul. Between his hope-filled gospel songs and the rambling, despair songs were the blues – and once again, it is only Jimmie Rodgers among country artists who so closely identified himself with the blues in lyric and theme.

Hank's music was derived from the white gospel sound, never more complex than country music's basic three-chord structure. Those who knew him say Hank embodied mood swings between offensive egomania and poetic sensitivity; he died at 29 but had lived a life so filled with heartache, physical pain, depression, disappointment and resentment that he might as well have been an old man riding in that Cadillac.

In a sense everyone else in country music since has been an imitator. Many indeed imitated his style, for years afterwards, but no one quite sounded like him or wrote songs like him. And in his life – recalling the self-destructiveness of so many rock singers, the honky-tonk lifestyles of country singers, and the hope echoed by gospel singers – no one quite lived like Hank Williams, either.

Williams, Hank Jr

On one level, Hank Williams Jr – born Randall Hank Williams and sometimes calling himself Bocephus,

Hank Williams, Jr, or Bocephus, a nickname his father gave him.

a nickname bestowed by his father – had it made in the country music business. He had the name of a legend, not to mention the perpetual income from his father, Hank Williams's royalties; he was an instant headliner, and was assured the good will of everyone he met. On another level, he was also assured that some people would never want him to be more than his father's son.

Born in Shreveport, Louisiana, in 1949, he had practically no time to grow up. At the age of eight he sang on the *Grand Ole Opry*, and by 16 he had a number one hit and was touring the country playing one-night stands. The driving force was his mother, Audrey, whose persistence, by most accounts, both motivated Hank senior's creativity and success as well as his despair and self-destructiveness; somewhat appropriately, her son's first hit was 'Standing in the Shadows (of a Very Famous Man).' The fine song was heard as a tribute to a legend, but is also a thinly veiled plea to be allowed out of another man's costume.

With members of his father's band, The Drifting Cowboys, Hank Jr rolled up an impressive array of hits after his 1965 success: 'It's All Over But the Cryin',' 'All For the Love of Sunshine,' 'Cajun Baby,' the haunting 'Eleven Roses' and a superb blues rocker, 'Rainin' in My Heart.' Many of the songs were written by Hank Jr, and the hits were supplemented by many albums centering around his father – his version of early songs, a narrated tribute, even two control-room-rigged duet albums with Hank Sr, who died when Bocephus was three.

The struggles with his own identity were hard enough on a young performer, but Hank Jr by his early 20s was falling prey to an occupational hazard – a self-destructive cycle of drinking and pill-taking. He had inherited his father's music, but also his weakness for booze and pills. More, he inherited an inner torment. He attempted suicide, came to grips with his name and the feeling that he was missing his father's 'soul' in his own work, and moved out of Nashville, all around 1974.

He moved to Cullman, Alabama, and took as manager his longtime friend James R Smith, but, more important, began feeding himself with new musical influences, particularly

Southern Rock. It was a new sound, and had a new audience, but Hank Jr did more than play mere redneck rock 'n' roll or hardcore rockabilly as others did; he infused it with that Williams soul that had been so elusive. *Hank Williams Jr and Friends*, the first album after this transition, was a creative masterpiece.

The album was barely released, however, when a bizarre accident almost took the life of Bocephus. Mountain climbing in the Montana Rockies, he got caught in an avalanche that sent him falling 500 feet. There was a seven-hour operation, followed by months of rehabilitation, against all odds, before he was performing full-time again.

His albums after the accident were big sellers and creative gems: 'Whis-

Hank Jr is now out of Dad's shadow.

key Bent and Hell Bound,' 'Women I've Never Had,' 'Old Habits,' 'Family Tradition' (about the on-the-edge Williams lifestyle). 'All My Rowdy Friends,' 'A Country Boy Can Survive' and 'Leave Them Boys Alone.' The last is sung with Waylon Jennings and Ernest Tubb, and is an angry assertion of self-determination and musical independence. Affirming his own independence – not his rejection of Hank Sr, – he reverently sings about his father, 'He's still the most-wanted outlaw in the land.'

A very busy life continues from Hank Jr's Alabama base. He wrote an autobiography (*Living Proof*) and oversaw a TV movie based on his life. He still plays many performance

dates, and is arguably a wilder man than Jerry Lee Lewis on stage. With acting in his past (he starred in the movie *A Time to Sing* with Ed Begley and Shelley Fabares) and hosting a TV series (*Sun Country*), the new Bocephus easily fit into a string of television appearances and a special, focusing on him. He has, in other words, hit a stride that has brought him creative satisfaction, a solid performance and recording schedule and widespread acceptance.

The acceptance of fans and fellow performers was seldom mirrored by the Nashville establishment; however, for years Hank, Jr, never received any major awards. (Hank, Sr, was never fully accepted by the establishment either, so another family tradition is noted.) But in 1985

Left: Hank, Jr has his own style.
Below: Tex Williams.

Hank, Jr, did receive an award from the Country Music Association for Video of the Year. He informed the audience wryly: 'You know, I do audios, too.' Within two years he won the CMA's Entertainer of the Year award, and the Academy of Country Music gave him the same honor in 1986 and 1987.

Though he has struggled with substance abuse and image problems in recent years, Hank's fan base remains loyal. A much-publicized failure to appear at a concert and another date ruined by a troubled intoxicated stage demeanor left him at odds with the press for a time, but true to his legend, Bocephus turned even those events into a mystique. With his personal life back on track, he is as popular as ever, especially during football season, when his 'Are You Ready For Some Football' intro to ABC's *Monday Night Football*

is a weekly singalong for millions of gridiron fans.

Hank Williams Jr's two stylistic careers as a songwriter have proved one thing, and his lifelong performing ability (during concerts he plays eight instruments) confirms it. He has an awesome talent, and is one of country music's major figures.

Everyone always knew Bocephus had inherited that inner torment and other pieces of Hank Sr's baggage. But it has become clear that he also inherited a singular genius for songwriting and performing as well.

Williams, Tex

Born Sol Williams in Ramsey, Illinois, in 1917, Tex Williams suffered from polio as a child and endured a limp. When only 13 he played the first of several radio engagements, and at age 15 joined the Reno Wranglers in Washington State. Two years later he moved to Hollywood, where he ultimately appeared in movies with Tex Ritter and Jimmy Wakely. He was to appear in Westerns into the 1950s.

He was a member of Jimmy Wakely's band until Wakely became a featured movie player in 1942; another band member, Spade Cooley, hired Williams as a bass player and vocalist in his own new ensemble. 'Shame, Shame On You' was a big hit record from their association. As Cooley moved on to more pop-oriented big-band aggregations, in 1946 Williams founded his own Western Swing group with many of Cooley's personnel; the following year Tex Williams and his Western Caravan scored big with the novelty hit 'Smoke! Smoke! Smoke! (That Cigarette),' which was the first million-seller for the Capitol label. They had another hit with 'The Rose of Alamo' and made many television appearances in California on that new medium.

The Western Caravan was a band of astonishing vitality, sparked by superb musicians including Joaquin Murphy (steel guitar), Cactus Soldi (fiddle), Pedro DePaul (accordion) and Smokey Rogers (electric guitar). At times it included a harp, vibraphone and brass, and was among the jazziest of the Western Swing dance bands. Williams recorded with pop and jazz singers, and owned his own dance hall and night club, Tex

Williams Village, into the 1960s. His own vocal style included a mock-gruff voice, and he tended toward talking his lyrics, especially on the novelty songs he preferred.

Among Tex Williams's hits through the years were: 'Deck of Cards,' 'Bluebird on Your Window-sill,' 'The California Polka' and 'The Night Miss Nancy Ann's Hotel for Single Girls Burned Down.' Always occupied in activities that made California a country music center during and after the 1940s, Tex Williams was the first president of the Academy of Country and Western Music, now the Academy of Country Music. In 1971 he was the recipient of the organization's Pioneer Award.

Wills, Bob

James Robert Wills was born near Kosse, Texas, in 1905. His father was a fiddle player of local repute and young Jim Rob learned the mandolin and fiddle to accompany his father at square dances. On one occasion he received his performing baptism of fire when his father tarried too long fortifying himself; Jim Rob took the stage, playing his own fiddle on the same few songs he knew – and had the whole barn dancing.

After working as a farmer, preacher, barber and smelter, Bob Wills, as he now called himself, got a job as a blackface comedian in a medicine show in 1929. He made the acquaintance of guitarist Herman Arnspiger and the two formed the Bob Wills Fiddle Band, playing local house parties and dances. In 1930 Milton Brown joined the group and they became the Aladdin Laddies, after their sponsor (Aladdin Lamps) on local radio. Playing an amalgam of country, Western, jazz and fiddle breakdowns to a dance rhythm, the group attracted wide attention and soon gained an even more important sponsor.

W Lee O'Daniel of the Burrus Mills Flour Company offered to engage the expanding ensemble on a network of stations throughout the Southwest. The group became the Light Crust Doughboys, and while 'Pappy' O'Daniel signed on as front man with the ensemble, Wills was also recruited as a truck driver and sack-loader for the Mills between dates.

Milton Brown left in February of

Bob Wills – a master fiddler.

1932 after O'Daniel forbade the band to play dances. Wills auditioned nearly 70 vocalists before hiring Tommy Duncan as a replacement. But in August of 1933 Wills was fired (reportedly because of his drinking problem), and most of the important band members eventually quit to follow him.

Wills formed a new ensemble, Bob Wills and His Playboys, and got a regular spot on WACO in Waco, Texas. But O'Daniel's legal harassment lost them their contract, and after several similar incidents Bob Wills and His Texas Playboys settled at KVOO in Tulsa. For the next 24 years bands of Wills or his brother had a regular berth on the station, flagship for a network that was hungry for the Playboys' brand of music, then called country jazz but ultimately to be known as Western Swing. Wills became so popular that,

in 1935, he bought a flour mill himself and marketed Playboy Flour in competition with his former boss.

The Playboys ranged in number from 13 in the 1930s to 22 members at one point in the '40s. Wills always rejected a 'country' label, and the composition of the group tended to reinforce his distinction. There were drums and electrified instruments early on, as well as horns and reeds. Solo runs were squarely in the jazz mode, and in truth the Texas Playboys were a Big Band in the Swing era. However, the common origins of fiddle breakdowns and yodeling, the touchstone of Jimmie Rodgers's influence and many other elements of cross-pollination, make Wills's point academic. What made Western Swing a variant of country music was the dance-band function; a driving, infectious beat; an emphasis on improvisation (although here there is an affinity with bluegrass) and jazz chord progressions.

Wills's brand of music swept across wide portions of the Midwest, Southwest and West Coast, and began a musical revolution; scores of Western Swing bands sprang up. Milton Brown and his Musical Brownies may have technically preceded Wills (after the Doughboys) by a year, but Bob Wills was the figure everyone recognized as the King of Western Swing. His personality – he possessed a great sense of humor, would toss off humorous asides during soloists' vocals and banter with the audience – was as magnetic as his talent. Wills was a fine fiddler and attracted the best musicians in the field to his band.

Among the Playboys through the years were Tommy Duncan, vocals; brothers Johnnie Lee Wills, banjo, and Billy Jack Wills, drums; Leon McAuliffe, steel guitar; Eldon Shamblin, guitar; Al Stricklin, piano; Tiny Moore, mandolin; Johnny Gimble, mandolin and fiddle; Joe Ferguson, bass, sax and vocals; Joe Holly, fiddle; Smokey Dacus, drums and Leon Rausch, vocals.

Besides a massive radio audience and huge record sales, the Playboys would frequently draw large crowds at personal appearances. World War II disrupted the ensemble, but most members returned thereafter. The Playboys toured constantly, even during the decline of big-band sounds, but after heart attacks in 1962 and 1964 Wills quit the road. The Playboys continued to record, however, and the 1960s were as prolific a decade as any of their existence.

Among the many classic songs identified with the Playboys were: 'San Antonio Rose,' 'New San Antonio Rose' (the vocal version), 'Time Changes Everything,' 'Lone Star Rag,' 'Maiden's Prayer,' 'Steel Guitar Rag,' 'Take Me Back to Tulsa,' 'Cotton Eyed Joe,' 'Right or Wrong,' 'Cherokee Maiden,' 'My Window Faces the South,' 'Cotton Patch Blues,' 'Bubbles in My Beer,' 'Milk Cow Boogie,' 'Yearning,' 'Big Balls in Cowtown,' 'Beaumont Rag,' 'Whose Heart Are You Breaking Now,' 'Roly Poly,' 'My Confessions,' 'Home in San Antone,' 'Brain Cloudy Blues' and 'Faded Love.' Wills's inevitable 'guying' of Duncan during vocals,

his approving 'Aaaahs!' during solos and phrases like 'Take it away, Leon!' and "Willie, Willie'" were reminiscent of both Gid Tanner and Fats Waller; appropriately, Western Swing drew from both of their modes.

Wills, who also starred in 26 Western movies, was inducted into the Country Music Hall of Fame in 1968. The next year he received a special citation from his beloved state of Texas, and suffered a debilitating stroke the following day. He partially recovered by 1973, at which time he oversaw a reunion of the Playboys – with some new talent, like Merle Haggard – for a landmark recording session. United Artists released the outstanding double album, *Bob Wills and the Texas Playboys For the Last Time*. And it proved to be the last time they all were together, for after the first day's session Wills suffered another stroke that left him in a coma until his death on May 13, 1975.

Since then the reorganized Playboys have kept in touch; they occasionally perform and record under the direction of Leon McAuliffe. Johnny Gimble has assembled other old-timers (including veterans of the Brownies, Adolph Hofner's Lone Star Boys, and other groups) as the Texas Swing Pioneers. Merle Haggard sparked a resurgence of Western Swing with his tribute album *The*

Best Damn Fiddle Player in the World, which he dedicated to Bob Wills in 1970, and Asleep at the Wheel recorded yet another tribute-jam album in 1994.

Wiseman, Mac

Malcolm B Wiseman was born near Waynesboro, Virginia, in the Shenandoah Valley whose music he reveres and lovingly perpetuates, in 1925. A fascinating symbol of old-time traditions, Mac Wiseman was classically trained and is well equipped to experiment in uptown-country and even Western Swing as he has. But he invariably returns to the mountain/old-time/bluegrass traditions of his youth.

Mac began playing the guitar seriously at 12, and early admired the singing and playing of Bradley Kincaid who, in addition to being a consummate performer, was also a dedicated student and collector of old-time country and folk songs. Mac attended the Shenandoah Conservatory of Music in Dayton, Virginia, and after graduation took a job as radio announcer in nearby Harrisburg; at night he frequently performed locally, putting together a backup country band called the Country Boys.

Mac Wiseman (second from right), nicknamed 'The Voice With a Heart'.

In 1946 he took a job as bass player for the legendary Molly O'Day, bowing and cutting his first recording, when some of Hank Williams' earliest compositions were recorded. Molly O'Day served as a kind of musical and performing mentor for Williams for three years in the late 1940s.

There was another ripple in the country music waters at the same time, and Mac Wiseman was also in the middle of that. Bluegrass music had finally been synthesized, and in his region of America. Mac played guitar and sang harmony with Bill Monroe and His Bluegrass Boys, and also was instrumental in the establishment of Flatt and Scruggs and the Foggy Mountain Boys. Mac, who had played with Flatt and Scruggs, was hosting the *Farm and Fun Time Show* on Bristol, Virginia, radio, when Cedric Rainwater, who had quit Monroe about the same time as Flatt and Scruggs, suggested the formation of a new bluegrass group. Wiseman was recruited as the rhythm guitar player and harmony vocalist for the very first incarnation of the legendary Foggy Mountain Boys, and served as business manager for the group in its early days.

In 1951 Mac went solo, and signed with Dot Records, where he recorded some truly classic bluegrass and old-time songs. From 1957 to 1961 he moved to the business side, and handled A & R affairs for the label. In the 1960s he recorded for RCA, experimenting with string backgrounds, mainstream country music, and even an album with an all-steel guitar backup. He cut a notable novelty hit, 'Johnny's Cash and Charlie's Pride,' at this time.

Also for the label he teamed up once again with Lester Flatt after the latter split with Earl Scruggs in 1969. The pair recorded three classic albums – *Lester 'n' Mac*; *Over the Hills to the Poorhouse*; and *On the Southbound* – that contained superb recordings of modern bluegrass/old-time music. Flatt and Wiseman were each masters of tradition, and included many of their long-time standards, but also recorded newer songs with a backup of fiddles, dobro, banjo, mandolin, piano and drums. For while Flatt and Wiseman formed one of the most popular touring acts out of Nashville.

Mac continued to tour to bluegrass festivals, fiddlers conventions and country fairs (among the graduates of his occasional touring band The Country Boys has been banjoist J D Crowe). In his career he has also been a member of practically every major radio show in the field; the WSM *Grand Ole Opry* with Bill Monroe; the WRVA *Old Dominion Barn Dance* with Flatt and Scruggs; Atlanta's *WSB Barn Dance*; *The Louisiana Hayride* and the WWVA *Wheeling Jamboree*. For years the Saturday night *Jamboree* was followed by the *Mac Wiseman Record Shop Show* hosted by Gus Thomas, beaming information about country and bluegrass music to the country-starved Northeast.

Among Mac Wiseman's own hits are his theme song, 'Tis Sweet to Be Remembered,' and many others identified with him: 'Jimmy Brown the Newsboy' (which spent 33 weeks on the charts), 'Shackles and Chains,' 'Tragic Romance,' 'I'll Be All Smiles Tonight,' 'Are the Bluebirds Singing for Me,' 'Love Letters in the Sand,' 'Put My Little Shoes Away,' 'I Wonder How the Old Folks Are At Home,' 'Little White Church,' 'I Still Write Your Name in the Sand,' 'Going Like Wildfire,' 'I Saw Your Face in the Moon,' 'I'm a Stranger Here' and 'Just a Strand From a Yellow Curl.'

In the 1980s Mac had a very active recording schedule, with Starday and, especially, CMH Records, where he cut albums of his favorites and *The Essential Bluegrass Album*, a double-record set of excellent material with the Osborne Brothers. Johnny Gimble also produced a double album of Mac singing Western Swing classics, wherein he sounds as smooth and jazzy as Tommy Duncan. He has also cut a double record set with Chubby Wise.

Mac's guitar is played in the traditions of Riley Puckett, Maybelle Carter and Lester Flatt – bass melody picking and brushed chords punctuated by 'runs.' Nicknamed 'The Voice With a Heart,' Mac's most distinguishing feature, however, is his airy, soulful tenor. His precise phrasing may betray his professional training, but his choice of material – keeping the old songs alive and vital to modern ears – shows that his heart is still in the hills.

In recent years Mac Wiseman's recording schedule – mostly, the flurry of projects with CMH Records – has slowed down. He has performed locally around Nashville, and when he does road shows his fashion is to book himself solo and confer with a local pickup band about his numbers; he doesn't travel with charts, and the musicians either know his material or follow the chord progression via Mac's strong vocal leads. They are invariably folksy and entertaining shows.

Beyond his great talent, Mac Wiseman is a walking encyclopedia of country music influences, experiences, and anecdotes. He has been involved in many important areas of country music since the 1940s, and it is an injustice that he has not yet been named to the Country Music Hall of Fame.

Wright, Michelle

As a country music ambassador from the North, Michelle Wright brings a fresh perspective to New Country but proves that certain fundamental principles transcend national boundaries. Born in Ontario, Canada, Michelle was raised in the small farming towns of Chatham and Merlin. She was inspired by parents who were both fans and local performers of country music, and was drawn

Canadian country star Michelle Wright.

into the tradition at an early age. She recorded her first album the year she graduated from high school, in 1988.

Michelle had achieved a considerable reputation at home and had received many awards from the Canadian Country Music Association (including Female Vocalist of the Year) when songwriter Rick Giles saw her act in Ontario and invited her to Nashville. Though still unknown in the United States, she was quickly signed up by the recently formed Arista Records.

Michelle Wright, her first album with Arista, met with a good response in 1991 when it was issued and contained the popular single 'New Kind of Love.' Hits from her second album, *Now and Then*, included the title song, 'Take It Like a Man,' and 'One Time Around.' A singer of great authority and emotional depth, Michelle has experienced much of what she sings about. Her experiences growing up in a broken home and recovering from alcoholism give authenticity to the human problems described in her lyrics.

A welcome guest from Canada, Michelle Wright lends an original and exciting voice to American country music. She has appeared with the Marlboro Music Military Tour to U.S. bases and has toured with Randy Travis, Alabama, and the Nitty Gritty Dirt Band.

Wynette, Tammy

Virginia Wynette Pugh was born in 1942 in Itawamba County, Mississippi, near the Alabama border. Tammy Wynette's father died shortly after her birth. Her mother sought employment in defense plants, and Tammy was raised by grandparents. She chopped cotton during an impoverished childhood, and followed the traditional pattern of country singers and writers in finding relief in music and playing locally in churches and on radio.

At 17 Tammy married but did not emerge from rural poverty. She attended beauticians' school in Tupelo, Mississippi, and later in Birmingham, Alabama. Divorced, and with three children, she juggled being a housekeeper, mother, hairdresser and a singer on an early-morning television program, *The Country Boy Eddie Show*. As a singer

Tammy Wynette and George Jones.

she attracted some attention and made some appearances with Porter Wagoner.

She determined to make a career in Nashville, and moved there with a do-or-die resolve. After being rejected by several record companies, she became a protege of Billy Sherrill of Epic Records (who suggested her stage name), and in 1966 recorded 'Apartment #9' for Epic; it was an immediate hit. Tammy's voice is a hoarse, airy alto that seems perpetually choked with emotion. Her most successful lyrics have been similarly packed with emotion, heartache and torch-bearing; the formula for the Wynette song was established early on, and has proved to be a classic combination in country music.

Her others hits have included 'You're Good Girl's Gonna Go Bad,' 'I Don't Wanna Play House,' 'D-I-V-O-R-C-E,' 'Stand By Your Man,' 'Singing My Song,' 'I'll See Him Through,' 'Run, Woman, Run,' 'The Wonders You Perform,' 'We Sure Can Love Each Other,' 'Till I Get It Right,' 'Kids Say the Darndest Things,' 'Another Lonely Song,' 'Woman to Woman,' 'I Still Believe in Fairy Tales,' 'They Call It Making Love,' 'Cowboys Don't Shoot Straight (Like They Used To)' and 'Still in the Ring.' She recorded successful duets with David Houston, including 'My Elusive Dreams.'

As a duet singer with George Jones, whom Tammy married in early 1969, she recorded some of country's classic sides. Both of their vocal styles, similarly choked and emotion-laden, sing of affairs equally troubled and blissful. Their own life together was also ill-starred, and the artists sang from their hearts of lovers' joys and sorrows. Among their soulful records together are 'Take Me,' 'We're Gonna Hold On,' 'Golden Ring,' 'Southern California' and 'Old-Fashioned Singing.' Tammy and George divorced in 1975, although they still sing together on occasion. Tammy, after publicized affairs with Burt Reynolds and others, married George Richey, a country-music producer, writer and arranger.

Tammy Wynette won the Country Music Association's Female Vocalist of the Year awards in 1968, '69 and '70, and wrote an autobiography, *Stand By Your Man*, which was made into a TV movie.

Elevated to the status of folk icon by her long, productive career and a measure of acceptance by young fans of certain alternative pop and rock groups (a following that even she is at a loss to explain), Tammy is perhaps at the peak of her popularity today. Duets with emerging megastar Wynonna Judd and her former husband/partner George Jones fuel a busy schedule of live appearances. In December 1993, complaining of abdominal pains, she was taken to a Nashville hospital, where a serious liver ailment was diagnosed. (The singer has been plagued for most of her life with intestinal disorders, and has undergone close to 20 operations.) Though the illness was nearly fatal, she was back on stage less than three weeks later.

Wynonna

The Judds – Naomi (christened Diana) and her daughter Wynonna (born Christina) – were among the most successful mother-and-daughter duets in country music history, and when Wy became a solo performer after nearly eight years of partnership with her mother, her success was by no means certain. They had come out of Kentucky, looked for a career in Hollywood (where Wynonna's sister Ashley had found a regular slot on the TV series *Sisters*), and returned to Kentucky. They went on to Nashville, where Naomi worked as a nurse and a model while they tried to break into the music scene. At last someone at RCA heard one of their demo tapes and gave the pair a contract in 1983.

It was a good move for both the singers and the studio. The pair were a hit from the start; every one of their albums has reached the million dollar sales mark that certifies it gold, and several have sold a million units, earning the status of platinum. They had numerous singles on the country music charts, including such hits as 'Had a Dream,' 'Mama He's Crazy,' 'Change of Heart,' 'Guardian Angels,' 'Love Can Build a Bridge,' and the 1986 number one hit 'Grandpa (Tell Me About the Good Old Days),' with words and music by Jamie O'Hara. Among the awards they or their records won were the Horizon Award in 1984 and Vocal Duet awards every year from 1985 to 1991 from the Country Music Association, Vocal Duo awards every year from 1984 to 1991 from the Academy of Country Music, and Grammies for Country Song of the Year.

When Naomi retired in 1992, citing health concerns, Wynonna continued performing, dropping the family name to assert her independence. For her daughter's first solo album Naomi interrupted her retirement to sing harmony on 'When I Reach the Place I'm Goin'' and to collaborate with Mike Reid on the composition of 'My Strongest Weakness.'

Wynonna's husky, assertive voice, recalling the rock groups she enjoyed while she was growing up in California, is consistent with the driving beat she seems to prefer. Her first album, *Wynonna*, featuring the hit singles 'She Is His Only Need' and 'No One Else on Earth,' assured her a solo career as successful as the one she shared with her mother. In 1994 Wynonna toured with Clint Black on the 'Black and Wy Tour.'

Tammy Wynette sings solo.

Yearwood, Trisha

When Georgia-born Trisha Yearwood was an ambitious unknown, she and her fellow aspirant Garth Brooks agreed that whichever of

them made it first would help the other. A few years later Garth broke through into stardom and was as good as his word; he made Trisha the opening act for his touring show. The striking blonde had some special qualifications for a job in the industry: she had studied music business at Nashville's Belmont University and had worked as a receptionist and in the publicity department of record companies. But nothing on her resumé would have won her a job as a singer; for that she needed – and she does possess – a great voice.

Trisha's flexible and expressive voice had found another performance venue beside the stage or the airwaves: the recently evolved job of demo singer. Garth Fundis, a well-known producer, was so impressed when he heard her perform another hopeful's song that he recommended her to MCA Records and advised her when they signed her up. Her self-titled debut album had the support of some of the best musicians in the field: Garth Brooks wrote two of the songs and was joined by Vince Gill on harmony; rock star Al Kooper played organ. The album was a resounding success, and its first cut, 'She's In Love With the Boy,' became number one in the charts.

Trisha won nominations from the CMA for both the Horizon Award and Best Female Vocalist of the Year in 1992, and Don Henley unexpectedly joined in her rendition of 'Walk Away Joe,' to everyone's delight, at the televised ceremony.

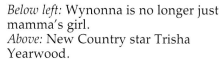

Below left: Wynonna is no longer just mamma's girl.
Above: New Country star Trisha Yearwood.

A powerfully independent spirit, Trisha selects material that expresses her forceful personality and her rejection of gender stereotypes. When she left the management of Garth Brooks to join Randy Travis's tour in 1992, people thought there had been a breach between the old friends. In fact, it was a typical expression of Trisha's determination to be her own woman. Recent recordings include the singles 'XXX's and OOO's' and 'Like We Never Had a Broken Heart,' and the CD *Thinkin' About You*.

Yoakam, Dwight

An original who stands defiantly outside the mainstream of the establishment, Dwight Yoakam nevertheless represents a radical restoration of traditional country music values that mark him as a new, but rebellious, traditionalist. He was born in Pikesville, Kentucky, but he didn't grow up in the rural South; he was raised, rather, by the owner of a gas

station in Columbus, Ohio, and his complex musical style evolved out of his childhood exposure to honky-tonk and the music of Hank Williams and Bill Monroe. In the late 1960s and early 1970s he was singing bluegrass in the style of Ralph Stanley, and the first band he formed played hillbilly music with a drivin' rock'n'roll beat.

His first attempt at finding acceptance for his rockabilly sound in Nashville was not a great success. Traditional country was not the fashion in the cradle of country music in the mid-1970s, and after trying his luck for a time Dwight left for Los Angeles to reconsider his approach to the market. Without retreating from his belief in the natural affinity of late honky-tonk music and early rock'n'roll, he decided that his route to success lay rather through the rock scene than through the inhospitable world of country. He gave up on Nashville for the moment and took his driving rockabilly beat to West Coast clubs attuned to rock.

He had gone to the right place at the right time with the right sound. Los Angeles, with its concern for cultural roots, was uniquely receptive to the authenticity of his music. Yoakam not only found the approval he had sought in Nashville but also attained the following of a cult hero.

He contributed a song to the first of the *Town South of Bakersfield* albums and caught the ear of producer Pat Anderson. The two

Dwight Yoakam – a new style of hillbilly.

recorded a mini-album named *Cadillacs, Guitars, Etc., Etc.* which broke through Nashville's resistance at last. Warner Bros./Reprise expanded the mini-album and released it with the same title. It met with a sensational response and has reached the status of platinum, having sold over a million copies. Its first hit single was a revival of Johnny Horton's classic rockabilly number 'Honky Tonk Man,' and Dwight's later albums have followed the same formula in resurrecting hits of such earlier stars as Stonewall Jackson and Lefty Frizzell and injecting them with some of his new, hard-edged, electric intensity, both restoring and reanimating the traditions of the past. He revived Gram Parson's beloved 'Sin City,' performing it as a duet with k. d. Lang, and he brought Buck Owens into the studio and onto the concert stage. A long-time fan of Owens, Yoakam walked into his hero's office in Bakersfield one day and the two became friends. They recorded such duets as 'The Streets of Bakersfield' together, and Dwight propelled Owens into a concert tour and a two-album comeback on the Capitol label.

Dwight followed *Cadillacs* with a succession of innovative and highly successful albums that reflected many of the styles of his youth and gave them new vitality and energy. His dynamic *Hillbilly Deluxe* fused the rockabilly and the electrified 'Bakersfield' sounds. *Beunas Noches From a Lonely Room* introduced a new note of reflection and introspection into his delivery without abandoning the old styles with which he had become identified. With *If There Was a Way* he reverted to his original style, with its fun and bounce. The album included a duet with Patty Loveless, 'Send a Message to My Heart,' and a collaboration with Roger Miller. A veritable archive of classic material, Dwight Yoakam does not project a curatorial image. His signature wardrobe consists of torn jeans and a western hat, and he affects a continuous confrontational scowl in his public appearances, all very much in keeping with his brash performance style and in-your-face vocal delivery. He hasn't made his peace with Nashville, nor they with him, although he is said to visit it often. But if the Country Music Association of that city has persisted in

snubbing him, he has been amply recognized by his own world – the box office, the record shops, and the West Coast-based Academy of Country Music, which named him Top New Male Vocalist in 1986 and presented him and Buck Owens with its Vocal Collaboration Award in 1989.

Young, Faron

Faron Young, The Singing Sheriff, was born in Shreveport, Louisiana, in 1932 and was raised on a small farm. As a youth he taught himself the guitar and by his teens had formed a country band that played local dances.

In the early 1950s Faron signed with the *Louisiana Hayride* and with Capitol Records. He toured with the Webb Pierce show, and had initial solo hits with 'Tattle-Tale Tears' and 'Have I Waited Too Long.' In 1953 he joined the Grand Ole Opry after which time national hits came fast and steadily. Through the years his big sellers, some of which have crossed over into pop and international markets, have included 'Goin' Steady,' 'If You Ain't Lovin',' 'Live Fast, Love Hard, and Die Young,' 'Sweet Dreams,' 'Alone With You,' 'Country Girl,' 'Hello Walls,' 'Three Days,' 'She Went a Little Farther,' 'Your Time's Comin',' 'Wine Me Up,' 'Occasional Wife,' 'If I Ever Fall in Love with a Honky-Tonk Girl,' 'Step Aside,' 'Four in the Morning' and 'Here I Am in Dallas.'

Faron Young's singing style is one of the most pleasing in country music. He is a country crooner – never forsaking his base – smoothly caressing notes and suavely gliding through lyrics. His polished vocals are a neat counterpart of the basic, honky-tonk, twin-fiddle country backup that is his trademark. His albums, especially during a long association with Mercury, are masterpieces of repertoire and interpretation. Faron's personality, while plainly free and engaging on record, is best beheld in his stage act, which is spirited and uninhibited.

A prominent Nashville businessman, Faron founded the influential trade paper *Music City News*; he has also acted in many motion pictures. He recently collaborated with Ray Price on the critically acclaimed CD *Memories That Last*.